Subchaser

SUBCHASER

Edward P. Stafford

NAVAL INSTITUTE PRESS
Annapolis, Maryland

Some names have been changed to protect the privacy of individuals.

Library of Congress Cataloging-in-Publication Data

Stafford, Edward Peary.
Subchaser / Edward P. Stafford.
p.   cm.
Bibliography: p.
Includes index.
ISBN 0-87021-692-9
1. Stafford, Edward Peary.   2. World War, 1939–1945—Naval operations, American.   3. World War, 1939–1945—Naval operations—Submarine. 4. World War, 1939–1945—Campaigns—Mediterranean Area.   5. World War, 1939–1945—Personal narratives, American.   6. Sailors—United States—Biography.   7. United States. Navy—Biography.
I. Title.   88-3521
D773.S78 1988   CIP

Designed by Moira M. Megargee

Printed in the United States of America

For all the men who manned the little ships, the SCs, YMSs, and PCs, and in them sailed the hostile seas with skill and courage in their country's cause, but especially for those, as in SCs 694 and 696, YMS 30, and PC 496, who did not return to those they loved.

CONTENTS

ACKNOWLEDGMENTS

For all the official sources on which the book is based, war diaries, action reports, and facts and figures not included in my personal journal because unavailable or unknown at the time, I am indebted once again (for the fourth time since 1958) to Dr. Dean C. Allard, Senior Historian and Head, Operational Archives, U.S. Naval Historical Center, Washington, D.C., and to his capable and courteous staff.

Roy J. Washer, Charles D. Casey, Harold Braverman, and Anthony Curato of the 692; Benjamin W. Partridge of the 978; and Prentice C. Horne of the 535 have helped significantly with their memories of the people and events of 1943.

I am grateful to my late mother, Marie Peary Stafford, who in a true labor of love personally typed and had bound in legible and preservable form the four ledger books filled with my impossible longhand that composed the original journal, and to my dear wife, Charlene, who performed the same typing chore for the first half of the manuscript, written before I saw the light and went to a word processor. The general quality of the book has been significantly improved by the highly professional editing and perceptive clarifying questions of Marilyn Wilderson of the Naval Institute Press, and she has my sincerest thanks.

Subchaser

PROLOGUE

Late 1942 and early 1943 were desperate times for Allied seamen in the Atlantic. On any given day more than one hundred U-boats, operating in wolf packs of six to ten, infested the arteries of supply between the Old World and the New. In November they sank 106 ships, in December 46, in January 27, in February 46, and in March 82. In January a convoy with a four-warship escort sailed from Trinidad with nine tankers and arrived at Gibraltar with two. In February an eastbound convoy, even though escorted by two U.S. Coast Guard cutters, a Polish destroyer, and five British and Canadian corvettes, lost seven merchantmen with heavy casualties. In March a westbound convoy with the same escorts plus a United States destroyer lost seven more. In the same month two other convoys lost nine and eleven ships respectively.

Even the weather seemed to be an enemy, with mountainous breaking seas, high winds, bitter cold, snow squalls, and icy rain. From November through March, ninety-two ships were lost to the elements alone, at no cost or risk to the German submariners, who had all they could do to keep the sea themselves. In the savage weather rescue was

1

difficult or impossible, and hundreds of seamen abandoned their burning, sinking ships only to be drowned or frozen before the eyes of their helpless countrymen.

To counter the terrible losses at sea, shipyards, boat yards, and even yacht yards on both sides of the Atlantic in those dark days worked three shifts, seven days a week, turning out both merchantmen to carry the vital cargoes that meant victory or defeat and the armed escorts to guard their passage. But the ships were useless without the crews to man them, and up and down the coasts the training centers were full of earnest young men studying and practicing with an intensity born of the knowledge that learning now could, in only a few weeks, mean not only success against the enemy but personal survival as well.

This is the story of one small ship and her crew of thirty men, a tiny sample, if you like, of the hundreds of ships and thousands of men preparing to take the sea against the killer submarines in those crucial days.

In an era of mass-produced steel hulls, this little ship (110 feet long, with an 18-foot beam and displacing 106 tons) was carefully and lovingly built of seasoned juniper by Yankee shipwrights and craftsmen a few miles north of Boston and south of Gloucester at the Calderwood Yacht Yard, in Manchester, Massachusetts. Her design was tried and true: scores of similar ships had fought the U-boats of the kaiser "to make the world safe for democracy" just one short generation before. Her lines were clean and salty: a sharp, high bow with an unbroken sweep of deck line sloping to the stern; a pilothouse with a flying bridge atop and a single mast, about a third of her length abaft the bow. A stubby 3-inch gun was mounted forward, two heavy machine guns amidships, and twin depth-charge racks at the stern. There were quarters for her twenty-seven-man crew forward and aft, and for her three officers below the pilothouse. The after-crew's quarters doubled as mess hall, with the galley just forward in the same compartment. Below, the three gasoline engines of the previous war had been replaced with twin 500-horsepower diesels, and all the way forward, aft of only the ground tackle, was another improvement over the days of World War I, a double rack of launchers, known as "mousetraps," which could hurl eight fast-sinking, contact-firing projectiles two hundred yards ahead to rupture the pressure hulls of her enemies.

A doughty, sturdy little warship, but one without a name. She was just a subchaser and there were too many to name. But as of 25 November 1942 she was a commissioned warship, the tapered commission pennant streaming at her truck, a United States ship entitled to the prefix "USS," so her name became what was painted in white letters on her gray bow, SC 692—the *USS* SC 692.

At exactly 0817 on the first day of December, the SC 692 left her builder's yard for the first time, for the four-hour voyage to Boston and two weeks of fitting out and taking on ammunition, fuel, stores, and spare parts. Among the other new subchasers undergoing the same process there was one with which she would share many other ports, both near and distant, many voyages, many missions, a handful of major actions, and a score or more of lively skirmishes with the enemy—the SC 978, ably commanded by twenty-seven-year-old Lieutenant (junior grade) Ben Partridge.

On the seventeenth, fitting out completed, the 692 began making her way southward toward Miami, where she was scheduled for a period of intensive training to make her ready for operations at sea.

While the 692 was fitting out in Boston, transiting the Cape Cod Canal, standing down Buzzards Bay, and making port in Long Island, Staten Island, Gravesend Bay, Delaware Bay, Norfolk, and Charleston, a thousand officers and men were training hard, ashore and afloat at her destination, the Submarine Chaser Training Center, universally known as SCTC, on Pier Two in Miami.

Although there were classrooms (hastily partitioned out of a former warehouse, noisy, and poorly ventilated), and books and exams and homework, SCTC was no school. It was precisely what its name denoted, a training center. There were no teachers, only instructors, and they had no interest in educating their student sailors and student officers, only in inculcating as rapidly and thoroughly as possible the information, procedures, techniques, and motivation required to operate a subchaser efficiently and effectively. In the final analysis that meant keeping the sea and locating and destroying the enemy, primarily subsurface but also on the surface, in the air, and even ashore.

A typical week at SCTC went as follows. On Monday, classroom instruction in antisubmarine warfare (ASW) from 0800 to noon. After an hour off for lunch, an hour's medical lecture (on an SC the captain was the doctor), then three more hours of ASW. On Tuesday morning, two more hours of medical instruction and two more of ASW, culminating in an exam. In the afternoon, four hours of seamanship drills aboard a yard patrol (YP) boat. On Wednesday, two hours of communications instruction, an hour of ASW, and a medical exam in the morning, followed by four hours of ASW in the afternoon. On Thursday, docking practice on a YP all morning with two hours of ASW and two of radar instruction after lunch. On Friday, five hours

At the right is the Submarine Chaser Training Center at Pier Two, Miami, in 1943 at the height of its training activity. The dozens of SCs and the larger PCs moored alongside are undergoing shakedown or refresher training. During World War II, SCTC shook down 598 such U.S. ships, plus 79 for Allied nations, and provided refresher training to the crews of another 233 small warships. At left and center is the Dade Drydocking Company, which worked closely with SCTC to maintain the ships in training. The street at the top is Biscayne Boulevard. (National Archives)

of ASW, a radar exam, and two hours of navigation instruction. Saturday was a good day—at sea all day for gunnery drills. On Sunday, depending on what group you were in, you spent the day in either gunnery, communications, or "tentative command."

Another week was given over entirely to gunnery, with one or two hours devoted to mousetraps; depth charges; principles of spotting; ammunition; pyrotechnics and safety precautions; fire control doctrine; 3-inch/50 caliber and 3-inch/23 caliber loading drills; antiaircraft firing; battery control drills; .50-caliber machine gun tracer firing; 20-millimeter machine guns; and rifle, pistol, revolver, and submachine gun instruction—all thoroughly interspersed with one-hour exams.

Despite the welcome warmth of the famous Florida sun, most of us at SCTC still showed the pallor of the northern winter, because for the sixty days of the curriculum we were free only on alternate Sunday afternoons. Trainees had a chance at the sun only on the occasional days at sea for gunnery or tactical practice and during the three-day cruise toward the end of the course.

The three-day cruise was intended to provide officers with an understanding of enlisted functions under way, with the student officers standing actual watches on lookout, the helm, the guns, sonar, depth charges, in the engine room, and as quartermaster. Instructions were specific. Each student officer was to bring aboard: "1 small hand bag, 2 bath towels, 1 set shaving gear, 1 soap, 1 comb, 3 khaki uniforms (wear one) without coat, 1 skivvies, 2 handkerchiefs, 2 sox, 1 toothbrush and powder, 1 notebook and pencil." Meals cost $2.50 (total for the three days), and there was a laundry charge of thirty cents. Officers' quarters and wardroom were out-of-bounds. Mattresses and blankets were furnished in the crew's quarters.

If any further motivation for learning was required beyond the news of losses at sea reported daily in the press and on the radio and the natural desire of red-blooded young men to defend their nation against threats of tyranny from a powerful enemy, it was provided by the commanding officer of SCTC in the form of a prominently displayed lifeboat, riddled by machine gun fire and stained with blood. To each new class of student officers and men, the CO personally delivered a fiery lecture at the site, relating in detail the slaughter of survivors in the boat and dwelling heavily on the callousness and brutality of the enemy his listeners were soon to face. Subtle it was not, but memorable and effective it surely was.

With such a program and the necessary three to four hours of study required each evening, the sixty days went by with astonishing rapidity. And, as it turned out in my case, not everyone completed the full two months.

I had reported to SCTC on 20 November. At 1500 on 8 January I was called out of a navigation class and ordered to report to the operations officer. I found him at one of several desks in a large room on the second floor of the training center building. The masts of some SCs and the larger, steel PCs were close outside the windows. The operations officer was a lieutenant commander. I was a lieutenant (junior grade), a "jaygee". Although only two grades separated us, it was a chasm. I stood before his desk. He remained seated behind it.

There were no preliminaries. "Mr. Stafford," he said, "I need a commanding officer for an SC. Can you take command and get under way for Key West by 1800?"

The abruptness of the question, the offer, the order, momentarily severed the link between my brain and tongue. Command? Of course I wanted command. I was twenty-four years old, the sea was in my blood, and there was a war on. But was I really ready, really qualified? For a year I had been instructing in seamanship, navigation, and gunnery, but that was "book learnin'"; the only time I had been at sea in the navy was one summer as a midshipman on a battleship. I had to be honest.

"Sir," I answered when I finally got my tongue and brain hooked up, "I think I know all I need to know from the books, but I've never applied that knowledge at sea."

I had wasted my breath. The operations officer's voice was cold and impatient, his eyes level and searching. I was being tested.

"Never mind all that bullshit, Stafford," he said, "Yes or no?"

"Yessir" (no hesitation this time), and with those two syllables a door opened and closed; behind it in that instant, the land, home, family, young wife, peace; ahead, the sea, the war, the responsibility of command, the unknown.

"Good!" The operations officer's voice became normal, with perhaps even a hint of friendliness. "We've been watching your work here. You've done well. Don't worry, you can handle it. Now here's the situation. There's a new SC just in from the builder's yard, a good ship with good men aboard. Skipper is a good seaman, a yachtsman, but he and his XO haven't been able to pull their men together into a crew, a team. Drills and exercises here have been unsat. We are relieving all three officers. The new XO and gunnery officer have been aboard only a couple of days. I wish I could give you a few days of shakedown here but they need escorts in Key West pronto. You'll have to whip the crew into shape at sea, between assignments, whenever you can. We'll try to get you back up here and give you a hand in a few weeks. Right now you just about have time to inventory and sign for the registered publications and Title B gear and get your personal effects aboard. Good luck."

That was a lot to swallow, but I was beginning to adjust to this incredible afternoon, and there was something important the ops officer had better know. "Thank you, sir," I said, "but there's one thing you should know. I've never had the conn of an SC, only the YPs during docking drills."

That news didn't upset him in the least. "That right?" he said. "Hey Joe, take Stafford here out in the turning basin on our SC and let him turn her around a couple of times and bring her back alongside."

With Joe, a lieutenant in the SCTC's operations department, I went aboard an SC kept at the school for training; the crew manned their special sea details stations, and Joe backed her away from the dock and into the narrow western end of the harbor. There I took over and, with coaching, went ahead on the starboard engine and astern on the port with full left rudder, adjusting RPM on both engines so that she turned completely around to port without moving either ahead or astern more than a few feet. Then we reversed the procedure, turning this time to starboard. It wasn't hard. In fact it was fun. The SC responded instantly to her rudders and engines and was a pleasure to handle. After perhaps twenty minutes I took her back to the dock, coming in slowly, port side to, at a shallow angle and backing the starboard engine to stop her and swing the stern in so she paralleled the pier.

Then Joe walked me down the long dock to berth H, where my new command was moored. Even in the mild state of shock engendered by the events of that busy afternoon, I knew that my first glimpse of her would be one of the memorable moments of my life. Under the weight of the afternoon sun, the pier smelled of diesel fuel and fresh paint. We passed several other subchasers; then Joe said, "There she is." We approached her from the stern. The gray paint was new on her fantail and on the heavy pipe screw guards on each quarter. Half a dozen depth charges were lined up in each of her stern racks and they too were shiny with fresh black paint. Abaft the pilothouse a dark-haired young sailor was working on the starboard 20-millimeter machine gun, its heavy coiled recoil spring shiny with lubricant. On the fo'c'sle forward of the short-barreled, 3-inch gun, a heavily tattooed sailor and a younger, huskier, darker man with curly black hair were splicing eyes to manila mooring lines. On the port side of the sharp, high bow, all the way forward, was her number—her name— five characters I would never forget, "SC 692."

The feeling I got from my first sight of the SC 692 was of her newness and innocence, nubility—an unexpected feeling toward a warship of whatever size. She was complete, with all the equipment she would need to fulfill her destiny, and beautiful in the way an armed yacht would be beautiful, but so new, so obviously inexperienced and untried! Even the sailors on her decks, with the exception of the tattooed man, had the smooth, fresh faces of youth. A French phrase I had read once in a Hemingway novel sprang to mind: *"Fraîche et rose comme au jour de bataille."*

CHAPTER ONE

KEY WEST

Predictably under the circumstances, the captain of the 692 was reserved and subdued but polite and businesslike in his tiny wardroom. His own bunk to starboard, both upper and lower berths to port, and the table, which folded out from the forward bulkhead, were covered with registered, classified publications and documents. Each had to be personally sighted, its number verified, and its pages inventoried by both of us. Although I was tempted to accept the numbers of pages listed on the covers, he was not. He was going literally by the book. The impression he gave was that he had been burned once and summarily relieved, and his neck was not going to be out again, not even one inch of it.

After two hours of checking and counting, a third of the job was done, and there was still the inventory of portable, accountable, Title B equipment. Obviously it would be impossible to be under way by 1800. I anticipated a blast from operations but when that news was reported, they unexpectedly granted a reprieve of twenty-four hours. It was close to 2300 when the papers changing custody and responsibility were all duly signed, witnessed, and returned to the safe.

As I drove north on Biscayne Boulevard through the palm-lined, jasmine-scented tropical evening, a little war was going on at the seat of my emotions, with pride, excitement, and anticipation arrayed against doubt, loneliness, and anxiety. I was proud to have been selected by those with experience in such selections, which implied their high regard for me, but since my abilities as the CO of a warship were unknown quantities, I was nagged by prickles of doubt about how I would measure up. I was excited at the prospect of command, of voyages to lands and ports unknown to me, in the cause of my country. But I would be separated indefinitely from my beloved young wife of fourteen months, who was expecting our baby in July. Along with the heady anticipation of action with the enemy came the unavoidable anxiety of a realistic awareness of my own mortality. Happy thoughts warred against sad, and the battle surged back and forth through my heart and head with first one and then the other dominant.

Before I had arrived at our apartment on the bay at Thirty-fourth Street, the hard, objective, irrefutable facts themselves imposed if not a peace, a truce. Command of the 692 had been offered to me and I had accepted. Orders had been issued, custody assumed. Events were on the march, the die cast, the course set. Doubt or anxiety could only be destructive and would lessen as I gained experience. Loneliness I would have to subdue and tolerate.

The next morning at 1015 the twenty-seven sailors of the USS SC 692, in immaculate whites, formed three sides of a square abaft the pilothouse and inboard of the tall, zenith-pointing 20-millimeters. The incoming and outgoing COs, in dress khaki, backs to the pilothouse, stood in the open fourth side of the square with the two other ship's officers behind them. The captain read his orders detaching him and sending him on to other duty. I read mine. Like the little change-of-command ceremony itself, the orders were short but definite and decisive.

LTJG EDWARD P. STAFFORD DVG USNR HEREBY DETACHED PROCEED
TO PORT IN WHICH THE SC 692 MAY BE AND UPON ARRIVAL ASSUME
COMMAND OF THAT VESSEL.

When I had read my orders, I saluted the former skipper and spoke the simple, timeworn words by which command at sea has changed since the days of Drake and Nelson, "I relieve you, sir."

As he said a few words of good luck and farewell, I looked around at the men with whom I would share my life, men whose lives and welfare were now my responsibility. I was glad to see a few rating badges. The man with the tattoos who had been working on the fo'c'sle the previous day was a bosun's mate first class and his huskier, hairier helper was a seaman first. There were a first-class motor machinist's mate and a couple of second class, a third-class gunner's mate, a signalman second, a quartermaster third, a yeoman second, an electrician's mate second, a couple of third-class radiomen, a sonarman third, a mess attendant third (the only black face in the crew), and a ship's cook first class. The rest were seamen and firemen, most of whom looked like exceptionally serious high school juniors. Among the nonrated men I recognized the dark-haired sailor, apparently a gunner's mate striker, who had been lubricating the 20-mm guns when I had first seen the ship.

I caught myself wondering how these men and boys compared to the German submariners who were their mortal enemies—at least one U-boat of them was probably within fifty miles at that very moment. And why had this clean-cut, alert-looking crew and this trim and tidy little warship been found "unsat" by the training officers at SCTC, and what could be done to weld them into a sea-going, fighting entity able to face and defeat the redoubtable enemy? First things first, I thought. Let's get the 692 to Key West, evaluating the crew's performance in a night passage offshore, see what operations are scheduled, what facilities and time are available for training, and go from there.

Immediately after the change-of-command quarters, I met for the first time the other officers of the SC 692. One was Lieutenant (junior grade) Charles Shelby Coffey, Jr., from Lookout Mountain, Tennessee, a graduate of George Washington University, who had also completed two years of law school there. Now he was executive officer, communications officer, administrative officer, personnel officer, and engineering officer of the USS SC 692. The other was Ensign Roy Jordan Washer, who held a B.A. in business administration from the University of Richmond. Ensign Washer was now gunnery officer, supply officer, welfare officer, recreation officer, and wardroom mess treasurer of the 692.

Since by decree of the SCTC, in a standard ship's organization book for SCs, the CO was also navigator, ASW officer, medical officer, and morale officer, all the responsibilities necessary for the day-to-day functioning of the ship were now assigned and covered by these three men. All the elements that would shape a new entity were in place. The result would be an individual small U.S. warship, with her own unique character and personality, her own capabilities and limitations, and her own personal and professional reputation among her sisters and her seniors. The plans were drawn and the building materials on site; the process of creation could now begin. But the merit of this finished product would not be judged by critics next year; it could well be tested under fire next week. And here success might mean survival, but poor workmanship was punishable by death.

At 1500 on Saturday, 9 January 1943, having fueled to her full 4,400-gallon capacity, the USS SC 692 stood out the long, straight, narrow channel known as Government Cut, which leads from Miami to the sea. Only a few yards to port the afternoon traffic flowed east and west along MacArthur Causeway between the separate cities of Miami and Miami Beach. Ahead, to seaward, on this short winter day, the sky was already noticeably darker than that over the land astern. From the causeway the little ship must have looked determined and formidable, her guns plainly visible in silhouette, the ensign snapping at her truck, a curl of white water at her bow, and a cluster of officers and men in evidence on her open bridge.

But from ashore, however close, there was no hint of the intensity or variety of emotion contained in and on that little hull. Only six weeks out of the builder's yard, she was sailing on her first operational mission into a sea contested by a hidden but deadly enemy. Having failed in her training exercises, she was, in effect, certified unready. No man aboard could accurately guess, beyond her immediate destination, where she was going, how long she would be there, or exactly what she would be doing. The officers, on whom their lives depended, were strangers to the crew; and the crew, on whom the lives of the officers equally depended, were a similarly unknown quantity.

The 692 came away from the dock cleanly and sweetly, reacting instantly to helm and engines, turned neatly on her heel, and settled steadily on course down the channel's center. She felt good under the feet. The crew was alert and responsive, sensing the moment and determined to show their mettle. The 150 nautical miles to Key West were marked at frequent intervals with lighthouses, and the sea was predicted to be calm. I was on my way to sea for the first time, age twenty-four, standing to sea in wartime on my own bridge, entrusted with this fine warship and her crew by the United States of America. I was doing my best to appear assured and confident, knowing instinctively the absolute necessity of appearances to the other twenty-nine men in that small hull in these critical hours. I even managed what I hoped was a confident wave to my wife and her mother, who followed for a while in our car along the causeway.

Then, quickly, we were down to business. The night's courses were all laid off on the chart: the Miami sea buoy south to a point three miles east of Fowey Rocks; thence on ever more southwesterly and westerly headings to pass the same distance abeam of the lighthouses at Triumph Reef, Pacific Reef, Turtle Reef, Carysfort Reef, The Elbow, Molasses Reef, Alligator Reef, Tennessee Reef, Sombrero

Key, and American Shoal before turning due north into the Main Ship Channel at the Key West sea buoy.

On the chart the passage appeared straightforward and easy in the extreme—the nautical equivalent of a night stroll down a broad and curving avenue with a lamppost on every corner—and for a different ship with a different crew on another night, it would have been exactly that. Arcs drawn with a compass from each lighthouse at a distance equal to its charted range of visibility showed that for 80 percent of the voyage there would be a major aid to navigation in sight; for almost half the trip there would be two, permitting cross bearings and good fixes. Three miles to seaward of the reefs was a comfortable distance yet close enough to avoid the northward current of the Gulf Stream, which a little farther out ran at more than three knots. The sun set out of a clear sky into a calm sea. The wind was just a breath out of the northeast, making dark patches of ripples in the dusk.

It was a night for a pleasure cruise, or a holiday or honeymoon. But aboard the USS SC 692 it did not feel that way at all. The ship was darkened. Radio silence was in effect. Gun crews stood by on the 3-inch forward and one of the 20-millimeters amidships. Another man stood by the depth-charge racks back aft. The sonar probed ahead with its long *piiiiing.* On each side of the bridge, lookouts swept the horizon ceaselessly with binoculars. Below them the helmsman kept the ordered course (175 degrees magnetic) by the big, red-lighted steering compass just forward of the wheel, and to his right another man stood at the engine controls, where other red lights showed the ordered speed (1100 RPM for 12 knots). Abaft the two men and on the starboard side of the pilothouse, the chart was spread out on its table, with parallel rulers, pencils, dividers, and a stopwatch picking up the glint of the shaded red chart light on its gooseneck.

In accordance with the doctrine specified at SCTC and in force throughout the U.S. Navy, the ship was in Condition of Readiness III; that is, one third of the crew was on watch, one third of the armament manned. At eight P.M. (2000) the first section took the watch; the second section would take over at midnight (2400) and the third section at 4 A.M. (0400). Every officer and man aboard except the cook was assigned to a section and thus stood watch for four hours and was off for eight. Under more hazardous conditions, the ship would go to Condition II, with half the crew on watch and half the armament ready. Condition I was general quarters, battle stations, with all hands on watch and all weapons, sensors, and controls fully manned and ready.

I was officer of the deck (OOD) in the first section, with Mr. Coffey and Mr. Washer heading up the second and third. The quartermaster of the watch in the first section was the only rated QM aboard, a young third class from Chicago named Elmer André. In my first night passage in command, it was a comfort to have a rated quartermaster to assist with the navigation.

Since the 692, like all subchasers, was without a gyrocompass, it took three men to take and plot each visual bearing. One man on the flying bridge took the sight through the vanes of a dummy compass called a pelorus, the "north" or zero-degree mark of which was always the ship's head. He called "Mark!" and the relative bearing down the voice tube to the pilothouse, where the helmsman announced the heading on the magnetic compass at that instant. The third man at the chart table recorded the bearing, heading, and time; converted the relative bearing to a magnetic bearing; and corrected that for deviation and variation to obtain the true bearing, which could be plotted on the chart.

Since a fix requires at least two nearly simultaneous bearings (three are better but hard to get at night south of Miami), piloting took considerable time and effort that first night under way. And it received the full concentration of the new CO; I was not about to add my new command to the long list of ships that since the days of Columbus have left their broken hulls on the reefs that guard the Keys.

Not far into that first passage, the first inadequacy in crew training came to light. When only one lighthouse is in sight, and therefore only one line of bearing is obtainable, there is a handy method of fixing a ship's position with almost as much confidence as with a pair of crossed bearings. It is called doubling the angle on the bow, and the most convenient case under that category is called a "bow and beam bearing." All the navigator has to have is a knowledge of his speed over the bottom and the precise times that the light bears broad on the bow (045 degrees relative in this case) and exactly abeam (090 degrees relative). The geometry works out to an isosceles triangle in which the two equal sides are the distance the ship has gone between the times of the two bearings, and the distance from the light to the ship at the time of the second bearing. In other words, the ship's distance from the light when she is abeam of it is equal to the distance run between bearings. Thus, as in the case of the 692 that night, if a ship is making 12 knots and the time between the bow and beam bearings is twenty minutes, she will be four miles (the distance run in one-third of an hour) off the light when it is abeam.

It is such a quick and simple device that I thought I might be able to turn my attention to other things for a while and said to the quartermaster, "André, I'll be up on the flying bridge with Mr. Washer. Go ahead and shoot bow and beam bearings on Pacific Reef and Turtle Reef and let me know how they look."

"Shoot what, sir?"

"Bow and beam bearings, André. You know, just double the angle on the bow."

"I'm sorry, Captain. You'll have to show me."

André, a rated quartermaster, had never heard of this elementary exercise in piloting. But he learned that night. On his own watch, and the next one as well, he took the bearings personally, worked them out, and plotted the ship's position abeam of every light. At the end of the mid watch, it was from André's fix off American Shoal that we plotted our course to the sea buoy off Key West.

Between American Shoal and the sea buoy we had our worst moment of the passage. Mr. Coffey had relieved me as OOD for the morning watch, i.e., the 0400–0800, but since we were beginning our approach to Key West I had stayed on the bridge, enjoying the fresh coffee brewed for the new watch. Coffey and I heard it at the same time, a low-pitched indefinable sound emerging just above the background noise of our own engines, the wash of the waves pushed out from the bow and the whisper in our ears from the breeze of our own passage. But it grew quickly louder, seeming to come from somewhere ahead and to starboard. We both put our glasses up, searching in that direction, but the starboard lookout saw it first. "A ship, Sir," he reported, "broad on the starboard bow. Looks like she's coming this way."

Out there in the dark a knife bow was slashing through the sea toward us, sending curls of white water upward and outward. Now the strange sound was recognizable as steam turbines turning at high speed and forced draft blowers. A blacked-out destroyer loomed out of the dark and roared across our bow at what looked like 25 or 30 knots. She never deviated a degree from her course, nor did she show a light or a signal of any kind. If she had sighted us she gave no sign of it. And perhaps three hundred yards in her wake came an identical ship, and in her wake another. The third was so close we needed full right rudder to stay clear, and the destroyer's gray port side was a steel wall tearing by fifty or a hundred yards away.

In a minute or two the rushing ships were gone and we were crossing their wakes, which ran like a broad, white avenue off to the eastward. We could feel the turbulence left by the six racing props tugging at our keel.

"Jesus!" Coffey breathed. "They were in a hell of a hurry!"

"Yeah," I answered, trying to keep my voice steady, "they must be on a really urgent mission." What we were both thinking but neither said was that they could have cut us cleanly in half and chopped us all into hamburger in their props with only minor inconvenience.

At the Key West sea buoy, a new and critical phase of our maiden voyage began—entrance into an unfamiliar port in the dark of the night. The ship accomplished this in the most ploddingly conservative manner imaginable, by laying off compass courses from channel buoy to channel buoy, illuminating and checking off each buoy by number as we passed it. In this way, with her special sea details stationed and at a cautious one-third speed, the inexperienced little warship, like a tiger cub sniffing for its lair, groped her way three miles due north past the shoals and coral heads of East Triangle, then on a dogleg for a mile to the north northwest. There a signal light began to flash from a high point on the darkened land ahead.

"AA, AA," it blinked. Who are you, what is your call sign? "P692," we flashed back. "Roger, proceed to Craig Docks."

Charlie Coffey and I looked at each other and shrugged. Where the hell was or what were Craig Docks? When a careful inspection of the harbor chart failed to turn up anything by that name, we got back on the light, "Int Craig Docks?"

"North of NOB," was all the help the laconic watch at the Harbor Entrance Control Post (HECP) was able to provide.

At dead slow, the 692 eased northward in the channel, past the dimly seen coral rock walls of Fort Taylor, close aboard to starboard, past the narrow entrance to the enclosed basin of the Naval Operating Base to where Key West Bight opened out to starboard, and there, suddenly, were rows of SCs nested at what had to be Craig Docks. After some minutes of searching with her 12-inch signal light, she found an empty space on the north side of the long pier, eased in, and got over her lines without the benefit of any help from the shore or the other sleeping subchasers. The time was 0545. The bridge and engines were secured, the gangway watch stationed, and all hands immediately turned in.

I had no more than lost consciousness in blessed relief at having met the first challenge of my new command, and after twelve hours on the bridge, when a hand was on my shoulder, shaking me awake. I looked up to see the strange face of a chief petty officer and to hear him say loudly and with no preliminaries or any such routine niceties as "Sir" or "Captain," "I'm from the port director's office. You are to shift berth immediately!"

From somewhere deep inside came an instant flood of angry resentment at both the order and the tone, and I sat bolt upright in the bunk in an unconscious effort to attain at least some dignity in the face of this intrusion. "Chief," I told him, "get the hell out of my cabin and off my ship *now*. I will report to the port director at zero eight hundred for berthing assignment."

It was only later, after the chief had retreated back up the ladder, that I recalled using the pronoun "my" twice and realized how closely I had already identified with the little entity of juniper, steel, and men that was the SC 692. At 0745, en route to the office of the port director, I held a brief training conversation with young soundman Roland Senecal on gangway watch on the advisability of holding visitors, of whatever rank or rate, on the quarterdeck while notifying the CO, or in his absence the OOD, personally, or by phone or messenger, of their presence and business.

It was after 0930 before the SC was in her new berth on the south side of the same pier at Craig Docks. Apparently whatever urgency had existed concerning the change had been inside the head of the officious chief alone.

That sunny day, 10 January 1943, began a new chapter in the life of the new SC, one in which continued training alternated with her first operational assignments, which in themselves served as a kind of advanced training.

At the port director's office and later at headquarters at NOB, the questions that had occupied the minds of the officers and crew as she departed Miami were answered, at least for the present and the immediate future. The many nests of subchasers at Key West were organized into task units of three to six, usually including a wooden "yard" minesweeper (YMS), or a converted yacht (PY), whose mission it was to escort convoys of freighters to and from various ports in the Caribbean and the Gulf of Mexico. For the present all of those task units were fully formed, and the 692, arriving late because of the delay in Miami to change command, was an extra ship. As such she would be assigned to fill in when she was needed and to escort individual ships should that be required. In the meantime she would do a lot of training, in accordance with the strong recommendations received from SCTC.

All of the above was welcome news. Obviously, the ship could use the training, and her men welcomed it if only as survival insurance. The prospect of actual operations, of proving her worth and making a start at a return on the nation's investment in matériel and personnel, was exciting. That was what most of her men had joined the navy to do. Key West itself, with its palms and beaches and balmy trades and emerald waters, was not the toughest place in the world to do duty. And, best of all, it was a U.S. port where a man's family could join him and where there was every prospect of remaining for a period of at least a month or two. The possibility of permanent departure and separation, which had existed only yesterday, had now evolved into the prospect of operating out of a pleasant port with frequent returns to a temporary home ashore.

But there was a job for the 692 right away. After only one day at Craig Docks, she was under way at 1630 on the eleventh with the SC 682 and YMS 36 and two hours later rendezvoused off the sea buoy with the HMS *Phoebe,* a Royal Navy light cruiser with boiler plate welded over a huge torpedo hole in her port side just forward of the bridge. She was an impressive ship, more than 500 feet and 5,000 tons, with three twin 5-inch mounts forward and two aft, bristling with 40- and 20-millimeter antiaircraft guns, and with two triple torpedo mounts. The cruiser could make only twelve and a half knots with that hole in her side, and for two days the two subchasers and the minesweeper patrolled ahead and on both her bows at thirteen, sonar probing the clear blue waters of the Gulf Stream for any U-boat that might be tempted to finish the job, while she made her way toward the navy yard at New York for permanent repairs. As though to underline the value of our charge, at least one aircraft from the Naval Air Station at Banana River circled overhead and made protective sweeps around the horizon from noon until dark each day.

Off the mouth of the Saint Johns, the *Phoebe* signaled a cheery "Thank you very much" and headed up the river to Jacksonville. The three escorts were released, and early on the morning of the fourteenth the 692 tied up port side to the 698, back at Pier Two, Miami.

It was there the next day, during two hours of underway drills, that one of the factors that had resulted in the 692's "unsat" designation was discovered and corrected. The problem had been major—she had been unable to hit anything with her 3-inch/23 main battery, the rounds consistently falling well over and beyond the target. The solution was as simple as the problem had been serious. The short-barreled 3-inch gun was pointed and trained by one man whose shoulder fit into a padded, vertical, shallow arc. To elevate the gun, he lowered that shoulder; to depress the gun, he raised it. But the man assigned to that important job was short, so short that even on tiptoe he could not depress his sights below the horizon, but for reasons presumably of vanity and saving face, he had not admitted the inadequacy of his stature. A taller man took over the gun and the normal proportion of hits and near misses to be expected from this not very accurate weapon resulted at once.

The run back to Key West the next night held none of the tension or anxiety of the maiden voyage. The tiger cub was rapidly maturing and forged up the dark Main Ship Channel to her berth at Craig Docks as though it had been her home base for a season instead of a week.

The next two months, in retrospect and in view of those that followed, as nearly as any naval operations in wartime can aspire to that term, were idyllic. The crews of the SCs were still infused with the unspoken conviction of personal immortality natural to their youth. They had an important job to do, with just enough risk to lend glamour and excitement. They sailed out of a pleasant and picturesque little port over mostly gentle tropical seas to other pleasant harbors of which most of them had only read, harbors with intriguing names like Trinidad, Guantánamo, Coco Solo, and San Juan, and returned like the warriors and adventurers they were, to heroes' welcomes and a few delightful days ashore on the beaches and tennis courts and in the hotels and bars of Key West.

The danger, however, was always out there. Although the U-boats were now concentrating on the lifeline across the North Atlantic and beginning to go on the defensive, an occasional ship was lost, and sometimes in the silence of the night the SC sailors on convoy duty could hear the hiss and bubble of blowing ballast tanks and the clank of hatches closing. But no SC was lost in those days and the conviction of immortality seemed confirmed.

For the SC 692, January and February were a kind of extended shakedown, a period of serious advanced training in the skills of navigation, seamanship, and gunnery she would need to function and survive when the enemy was closer and the lead began to fly.

There were long days offshore in pursuit of "tame" World War I R-class submarines under the expert auspices of the Fleet Sonar School, speed runs between the sea buoy and Sand Key to test and calibrate the engines, hours spent steaming on various courses to compensate the magnetic compass, a couple of days out of water on the marine railway for shaft and bottom work, a day or two alongside the dock at NOB for "industrial availability," while a score or so of minor discrepancies were attended to and minor alterations and improvements made.

In early February the 692 was assigned a mission to the port of Nuevitas on the north coast of Cuba as escort for a single Liberty ship, a placid cruise out ahead of the big ship through waters so clear that at the narrow entry to the port I was horribly certain we would ground at any second. I backed down hard, only to find when the lead was cast that there were six fathoms under the keel.

Every assignment brought something to be learned, further maturing the little ship and her capabilities. On the run to Nuevitas, there were two such lessons, in addition to the illusion of proximity to the bottom created by the clear tropic seas. As we were taking station ahead of the Liberty at the beginning of the passage, and she was working up to cruising speed, I gave the order to the helm from the conning station on the bridge, "Left standard rudder," to keep the SC clear of the big ship's bows. Somehow the helmsman misunderstood the order and put the rudder thirty degrees to starboard instead of to port. Before the turn could be reversed we had crossed directly ahead of our huge charge. Her stem towered threateningly several stories above the stern, the air was rent with the repeated blasts of the danger signal from her whistle, and only the instant application of flank speed kept the small ship from being ground under by the big one. From that moment an immediate and shouted repetition of each rudder order was standard practice in the SC 692.

The second lesson was the result solely of an error by the SC's captain and navigator, who unforgivably forgot to consider the effect of the three and a half knots of northerly current in the Gulf Stream when crossing the Straits of Florida. We thus made our landfall not on Sand Key but on American Shoal and were two hours over our official estimated time of arrival (ETA) at Craig Docks.

Such lessons, although well learned and not to be forgotten, and the hours of training offshore, were softened and leavened by the time ashore when they were finished. The wives of the 692's three officers shared with their husbands spacious ocean-front rooms at the gracious Casa Marina hotel, with its long, red tile roof clearly visible from most of the operating areas to seaward, and each return from an escort mission was an occasion. It was, for a while, a storybook war, fought in perfect weather on romantic seas by intrepid young seafarers who returned frequently to the arms of their beautiful young wives to gain further inspiration for still more adventures—a war, best of all, with no casualties.

At sea it was a war in which half a dozen iridescent flying fish would be found on an SC's deck each dawn, and turtle steaks could be had for all hands by dropping a concussion grenade into the sea beside one of the dozing monsters and hoisting him aboard; a war in which a lively and healthy competition in shiphandling infected the young skippers, with the sailor who could bring his ship alongside or take her to sea with the fewest bells (orders to the engines) the winner.

For a day or so, before a general consensus branded the practice unethical and illegal, the 692 held the championship by making an approach and landing with *no* bells, to the astonishment of a nest full of critical onlookers. The feat was accomplished by stationing a man inconspicuously at the engine room hatch with a clear view of the bridge. If the conning officer scratched his head with his right hand, the command "Starboard back one third" was softly relayed to the en-

The island of Key West in World War II. The harbor at bottom center is the Naval Operating Base, the one at the extreme left Craig Docks. The Casa Marina hotel is on the shore at the right, about opposite Craig Docks. (National Archives)

gine; with the left hand, the same for the port engine; and if the officer removed his hat, it was the signal for "All stop."

Although basically constructive in sharpening the skills of the officers and improving the morale of the crews, the shiphandling competition on at least one occasion turned seriously destructive. Some of the newer subchasers arriving at the convoy center, usually those with four-digit-number names, were equipped with 1,200-horsepower, radial-diesel engines, which gave them an advantage over their conventionally powered sisters of better than 5 knots, bringing their flank speed to more than 20 knots. An added advantage of the so-called pancake diesels was the maneuverability provided by their variable-pitch propellers. In those ships it was not necessary to stop the engine, shift to reverse, and throttle up again to back down; one had only to go to reverse pitch while retaining the engine's normal RPM unaltered. The trouble was that the variable-pitch control mechanism, still very new, had a few bugs that caused occasional malfunctions.

The skippers of these new and improved SCs were understandably proud of the superior performance of their ships and somewhat given to demonstrating it with more than a little dash and drama. One young officer brought his little ship into the squared-off oval of the NOB basin on a certain morning to tie up starboard side to another SC directly in front of the tall, white headquarters building housing the offices of the rear admiral commanding the Gulf Sea Frontier and the captain in command of the Naval Operating Base. To say that he did so with dash and drama would be to understate the actuality.

The shiny new subchaser came through the narrow entrance at a good 10 or 12 knots, where a third or less of that speed would have been more than normal, turned smartly to port, and bore down on the nest of SCs moored at the closed end of the oval, with the oily harbor water curling at her bow and the bright ensign riffling bravely at the truck. As she approached the stern of the outboard ship, officers and men standing open mouthed in the nest, along the adjacent dock, and in the windows of the headquarters building could see the skipper on his bridge lean down and speak into the voice tube to the pilothouse, presumably to give the only order possible under the circumstances, "All back full!"

But no slackening of the SC's forward rush was evident. The skipper spoke again into the tube, and this time the order was clearly heard afloat and ashore since it was given with considerable emphasis. By now the speeding little ship was abeam of the nest and close enough so that the next order, shouted in a voice that bordered on hysteria, could be executed: "Get over your lines!"

Three or four eyes of four-inch manila line flew across to the outboard ship and were smartly grabbed and thrown over cleats and bitts, and in succession came three or four sharp, cracking reports as the lines were made fast on the moving ship and instantly parted. A ship's-length forward of the SC nest was the northern end of the rectangle, a heavily reinforced wooden dock faced with well-seasoned twelve-by-twelve oak timbers, and into it the errant subchaser plowed at still undiminished speed. There was a splintering crash as the little ship's wooden stem broke and her mast came down. Every man aboard was thrown to the deck. From below decks came the thump and rumble of loose and loosely secured gear moving suddenly forward. Then all was quiet again in the NOB basin as a messenger made his way from the admiral's office to the dockside with a personal note for the subchaser captain.

The voice tube through which the unfortunate young officer had given his futile orders to the engines was a problem to the officers conning the SC 692 as well, although in a far less serious way. The tube was logically located squarely amidships at the forward edge of the bridge, an ideal position for all purposes except for bringing the ship alongside, taking her out, or any evolution requiring the conning officer to have a clear view of either side of the ship or her stern. In such cases he had to look, decide, and move back to the tube to give the necessary maneuver order, a clumsy and time-consuming process that complicated shiphandling at close quarters.

After complaining about this situation on several occasions, I arrived on the bridge one morning to get the ship under way and found the problem solved. Attached to the voice tube was a long, gray, flexible hose with about the same diameter, ending in a hard cylinder for holding in the hand and speaking into. Welded to one of the stanchions on the leading edge of the bridge was a spring clamp, also painted gray, which held the hose and mouthpiece securely when not in use. With this simple but ingenious device, orders could be given to the helm and engines from the necessary point of observation, and efficiency and safety both greatly improved.

The flexible voice tube was the first instance of many to come of the *modus operandi* of Boatswain's Mate First Class Patrick Ignatius Murphy, leading petty officer of the deck force. The device was an ordinary vacuum cleaner hose, like everything Murphy acquired by whatever means, immediately welded or bolted into place and painted gray, instantly becoming to the unknowing an original and integral installation. When questioned as to the source of the new acquisition, Boats's response was always the same—"A guy give me that, Captain."

At thirty-seven, Murphy was by about a decade the oldest man aboard (except for his opposite number in the engineering force, Motor Machinist's Mate First Class Morton) and unchallengeably the most colorful, as Irish as Pat Murphy's pig and literally covered with tattoos. Like about half of the SC's sailors, he was regular navy, but with far more experience, including a couple of tours on the "China station," and thus more knowledge in his field of expertise. But the tattoos were an indication of his character and his career. They covered his body without pattern or order as though, no doubt the case, they had been applied on the spur of the moment under the influence of more than a few drinks.

His chest and back held broad and high representations of full-rigged ships at sea, but there conventional tattoo artistry ended. The outer joints of his knees and elbows were inscribed with spiderwebs with the arachnid itself at the center, and the inner parts of the same joints were decorated with hinges. From the fronts of his two thighs Maggie and Jiggs observed each other, and from chain bracelets around his ankles a pair of snakes wound upward to look each other in the eye from just below the hinges and cobwebs of the knees. On both upper arms were faded hula girls who could be made to dance by a subtle flexing of the biceps. His lower arms held the names and hull numbers of several ships on which Boats had served; at the fleshy triangle between thumb and forefinger were tasteful red, white, and blue stars; a blue letter on the back of each finger and thumb spelled out together a woman's name, and it was reported on good authority that a realistic rendering of large twin propellers decorated his buttocks. As though all this had failed to satisfy, wherever space allowed were faded, and now fortunately illegible, four-line limericks. A very Irish face with alert blue eyes and ears so large and loose they actually flapped in the wind completed Boats's salty, far-from-ordinary appearance.

At the opposite end of the spectrums of both personality and appearance was Murphy's opposite number in the tiny organizational hierarchy of the little ship, Motor Machinist's Mate First Class Harvey Arthur (Ham) Morton, leading petty officer of the engineering force. Morton was quietly but effectively competent both in his knowledge of the engines on which the ship was utterly dependent and their associated generators, air compressor, and auxiliary equipment, and as a trainer and leader of the men in his charge. And, since none of the SC's officers had more than a cursory and theoretical knowledge of the two big, straight-eight diesels that powered their ship, he had more real responsibility than Boats and handled that responsibility with coolness and confidence.

In the first days after I joined the ship, I had called Morton down to the little wardroom, freely admitted my ignorance in his field, and told him there were only two requirements I would insist upon: first, that he would always be able to answer bells, and second, that I would be able to visit the engine room at any time and find it clean and shipshape, with all the machinery in full working order unless I had been advised of a problem in advance. Within those broad parameters he had full authority over engineering spaces and personnel and would be, in effect, the engineering officer. He accepted the challenge and the responsibility and never, at any time or under any circumstances, failed in either.

In any warship of any size there is always an underlying chicken-and-egg argument between the engineers and the gunners: the one saying, without us your guns are no good, and the other responding, your only reason for existence is to get us to where we can put ammo on the target. In the 692 the man under Roy Washer (who was the gunnery officer) responsible for the day-to-day, hands-on maintenance and operation of the ship's weapons was Gunner's Mate Second Class Joseph A. Walter. Joe Walter, known aboard according to long tradition as Guns (along with Boats and Flags and Wheels and Chips for the leading petty officers in other rates), was as good a gunner's mate as they come, although a hell-raiser and carouser ashore. He had seen the old *Lexington* sink from under him in the Coral Sea and knew the seriousness of the war and the importance of "keeping his powder dry." That knowledge and attitude stood him in good stead at captain's mast on the numerous occasions when he returned from liberty late, in bad shape, or both.

A key man in the SC's tight and tiny organization, one who was never seen at mast except to keep the record, was Yeoman Second John Roughan, late of Los Angeles. Sensible, serious, intelligent, and conscientious, Roughan was the kind of sailor every CO would like to have. He organized and maintained the files, kept track of incoming and outgoing official correspondence, typed all required reports, and was generally a one-man ship's office, all in a space about five by five, just forward of the wardroom. And Roughan's expertise was not limited to the duties of his rate; he was by far the best helmsman in the crew, including the rated quartermaster, and manned that critical station at general quarters, special sea details, fueling at sea, and at any other time when alert and accurate steering was essential. It took only a few minutes of conversation with Roughan to realize that his potential extended far beyond the scope of his present status.

The weeks at Key West were as much a time for getting acquainted with ships as with men. It was a time for getting used to a bunk into which, despite all attempts at remedy, water dripped on every starboard roll in rain or heavy weather. For making peace with an officers' shower that had only one tap (cold), in which there was only one precise location where a tall man could stand erect, his head framed by the interstices of the plumbing.

Because each of the little warships quickly developed its own distinctive personality out of such divers factors as the competence and character of its captain and exec; its physical appearance (neat and shipshape, paintwork fresh and clean, brightwork bright, lines well kept and coiled, or otherwise); the efficiency of its deck force in the handling of lines; its punctuality in meeting underway times, ETAs, and rendezvous; its scores in the antisub and gunnery practices; the precision with which it kept station and executed the necessary maneuvers involved in the escort of convoys; the proficiency and alertness with which it responded to communications by flashing light, semaphore, and radio. Perhaps because there were no names, the numbers themselves became names associated irrevocably with the personality of the ship on whose bow they were painted.

On the first day of March, the 692 was assigned to one of the "Killer" groups at the Key West convoy center, formally designated Task Unit 91.1.2. She sailed that same noon with a convoy of nine merchantmen and four other SCs on a run down across the Straits, eastward along the mountainous Cuban coast, around Cape Maisí and through the storied Windward Passage to Guantánamo Bay. It was her first convoy, and despite the gentle weather, it too had its lessons. Chief among them was the difficulty of maintaining contact and keeping station at night, especially during course changes when visibility was considerably less than the distance from the assigned station to the nearest ship.

During daylight, station was maintained by sighting on the convoy guide with the pelorus on the bridge and by statimeter readings for range, since none of the SCs operating out of the convoy center in those days were equipped with radar. But at night, with the guide ship a couple of miles away and invisible, no distance measurements were possible, and a very approximate station had to be kept by bearings on the nearest merchantman when she could be made out and educated estimates as to range.

On her first convoy the 692 was assigned the starboard beam, with another SC ahead on the starboard bow, two others in opposite stations to port, and a fifth in the lead, dead ahead of the middle column of three freighters. With darkness, the escorts moved in from three thousand yards to two thousand in accordance with the operation order to maintain visual contact with the convoy and each other. That first night, with no moon and a high overcast shutting out the stars, no other ships at all were visible from the bridge, even from two thousand yards, presenting the fledgling escort with a dilemma: to stay at two thousand yards as ordered and risk getting very badly off station, or close to visibility range, even though it would be well inside where she was supposed to be. With the conscientiousness born of her recent and repeated training, she elected to compromise, staying out in the dark for twenty minutes, then easing in until assured that the convoy was really still there, and running back out to station again.

The compromise worked well enough until a scheduled course change early on the mid watch, signaled by two blasts of the freighters' whistles. The 692 came to the new course on signal, but on her next run-in to close the convoy she found only the empty blackness of the night sea. With radio silence in effect and all ships darkened, a problem now existed. The CO and the XO conferred at the chart table. It was probable, we decided, that the convoy was somewhere out ahead of us, since it was unlikely we could have crossed ahead without seeing at least one of the nine big ships or the four small ones. Therefore the logical action would be to station an extra lookout and proceed on the new base course at two knots over the convoy speed of eight. But what, we wondered, would prevent us from running clear past on a parallel course and finding ourselves somewhere over the horizon ahead at daylight? Then Charlie remembered the smoke.

All the way out from Key West a couple of the older merchantmen had been smoking heavily, to the great displeasure of the convoy commodore and the escort commander, who preferred not to advertise the position and movements of the force to any U-boat within thirty or forty miles. But when night fell they were still belching black smoke, which rose high into the evening sky and drifted downwind over the other ships and the screen. That was it! The convoy course was now roughly southeast. The brisk northeast trades had been and were still blowing that smoke straight out to starboard. The 692's station was on the starboard flank. We would know when we were abeam of the convoy when we smelled the sooty, sulfurous fumes of that stack smoke.

After half an hour of standing out there on the darkened bridge with the captain, exec, and two lookouts staring into standard navy issue 7 × 50 binoculars and sniffing like a pack of hounds, we picked up that distinctive and welcome stench and changed course thirty degrees to port. At 0145, three-quarters of an hour after the turn, we made out the bulk of the last ship in the starboard column and slowed to parallel her course, now keeping her firmly and continually in sight.

On the following two nights that the convoy was at sea, the 692 moved in, not to two thousand yards but as close as necessary to maintain visual contact: the SC, we figured, was far more useful for the protection of the merchantmen, on her proper bearing but a little close, than wandering around somewhere in the dark. Late on the afternoon of the fourth of March the five escorts lined up at the fuel dock in Guantánamo Bay, refilled their depleted tanks, and moved over to the section base for the night.

There was no time to explore the beautiful bay with its palm-lined fingers of green land reaching out from the hills. The men got ashore to stretch their legs for a couple of hours and take in a movie on the base, and the officers had time for a cold bottle or two of strong but delicious Hatuey Cuban beer at the club. Liberty and shore leave expired aboard at 2200, and at 0730 the next morning the five sub-chasers of Task Unit 91.1.2 (SCs 540, 541, 711, 692, and 1030) were once again under way to screen the sortie of another group of freighters bound back to Key West.

The return run was almost a pleasure cruise and nighttime visibility good enough so that the 692 was able to keep proper station at or close to the specified two-thousand-yard distance. At 1015 on March eighth a pair of big silver blimps from the Naval Air Station at Boca Chica came sailing over the horizon ahead, and at 1400 one of them signaled they would assume responsibility for the convoy. By 1600 the 692 was snugged down at her berth at Craig Docks with a third escort mission to her credit.

But at NOB her men learned that the two-month-long idyll of Key West was over. Orders were in to proceed to the Merrill-Stevens shipyard at Miami for a major refit and modernization, including replacement of the 3-inch/23 and the installation of radar, before assignment overseas.

The next day the SC's officers hosted their wives at lunch in the wardroom. The table that folded out from the forward bulkhead between the two bunks to port and the single to starboard was covered with a linen cloth and set with silver and with china plates, cups, and saucers. The young ladies arrived, tanned and in flowered summer dresses, entered the pilothouse, and with a chuckle or two negotiated the vertical ladder while their husbands looked politely elsewhere.

In due course, Mess Attendant Cleveland Hodge Ray arrived to serve, but that was not as routine as it sounds. He arrived descending the ladder with a large, gray wooden box held by a brass handle at the top, in which a series of shelves held the meal, which had been prepared back in the galley, at the bottom of another vertical ladder. It was a pleasant lunch with talk of the Guantánamo convoy and the experiences of other ships as learned from other wives at the Casa Marina, and conjectures as to the forthcoming stay in Miami. But unspoken was an undercurrent of anxiety and a touch of sadness at the end of something that would never come again.

Nor was there ever a lunch like that again. Ray was far too valuable a man to waste in service to a wardroom mess of three, and the galley and crew's mess far too convenient for officers standing four on and eight off to retain such formality. But that one time it felt right and was entirely fitting to mark the end of a chapter, the turning of a page in the life of a little ship and in the course of a war.

We got under way the next evening just at sunset on the now routine and easy run up to Miami. On our arrival at the familiar Pier Two at nine the next morning, there were two pieces of bad news. The Merrill-Stevens yard was full and could not take us; the work would be done at the Norfolk Naval Shipyard at Portsmouth. And off Alligator Reef, even as we had been making our solitary 12-knot passage up from Key West, although we were never able to get the details, PC 1123 had mistaken SC 1470 for a sub, rammed, and cut the wooden subchaser almost in half.

Instructors at SCTC had warned of this very thing. An SC with her long, low, flush deck and boxy little pilothouse, could look very much like a surfaced submarine at night or in poor visibility, and the 1470 was not the first and would not be the last to suffer from that resemblance.

Yet in defense of the PC in this case, the crews of antisub ships like PCs and SCs had every reason to be prompt and aggressive when they encountered anything resembling a submarine in sight or sound, out of the well-known sanctuaries and transit lanes established for friendly subs. This was especially true in these coastal waters where only months ago the blood-red flames of burning tankers had lighted the shops and homes along the beach. And if the memory of those U-boat depredations were not enough, the sailors on those little ships were painfully aware that a surfaced enemy sub with her guns manned and ready for action was superior in both speed and fire power, so that to hesitate to attack could well be fatal.

CHAPTER TWO

NORFOLK

There was not a man on the 692 who was happy at the prospect of spending two weeks in Norfolk rather than Miami, but at 0830 on the eleventh, in company with YMSs 62 and 69, the little ship stood out of Government Cut for the last time and pointed her sharp bow northward. On that three-day passage it seemed that every time a man came on deck to stand his watch, the air was colder and the sky darker with clouds than the last time.

Just after noon on the second day, off Cape Fear, with the SC third in column astern of the two sweepers, the familiar muttering and splashing of the twin exhausts and the comforting below-decks rumble of the diesels both suddenly fell silent and the ship lost way. Ham Morton was in the engine room within thirty seconds and a minute later reported that water in the fuel had caused the filters on both engines to shut them down. It took twenty minutes to change filters and clear the lines, then came the familiar jolt of the compressed-air starting system, and the SC was once more under way and answering her helm.

31

On the final afternoon the little column was some thirty miles east of Hatteras. There was no wind, but a heavy, oily ground swell was rolling down from the north. The ships were climbing up the slopes of the huge waves and sliding down into the troughs with an easy and not unpleasant motion when a few hundred yards to seaward, one of those twenty-foot rollers towered up, crested, and broke, sending thousands of tons of cold green water crashing down its front. It took just about the expected minute for the signal flags to go up on the leading YMS, "Turn Nine," and as one the three warships swung ninety degrees to starboard and held that course until they were five more miles to seaward of the shifting bottom sands of that treacherous cape that long ago earned its somber nickname, "the graveyard of ships."

In midmorning of the third day the tall, striped tower of the Cape Henry light was abeam to port and the ships stood down the long Thimble Shoals Channel, turned to port with Fort Wool to port and Old Point Comfort to starboard to enter Hampton Roads. At 1445 the 692 moored port side to SC 712 at Pier Ten, NOB, Norfolk, Virginia. All hands topside were in foul-weather gear and gloves. A cold drizzle blurred the nearby ships and buildings. The temperature was forty-five degrees.

The next day, the Ides of March Julius Caesar was warned of in vain in ancient Rome, the 692 moved a few miles down the south branch of the Elizabeth River to the navy yard. It was there that her men realized for the first time the scope of the changing pattern of the war of which her movements in recent days had been a tiny part.

Besides the two sweepers with which they had arrived, several of the SCs from the convoy center at Key West were there, and they recognized the 535, which had been a school ship at SCTC and on patrol off Miami when the 692 had entered en route to Norfolk. It was apparent that the focus of the war had changed from the protection of shipping to something more important much nearer to the enemy homelands, from the defensive on the high seas to the offensive at the doorsteps of the aggressors. The Allies had landed in North Africa in the fall and it looked as though that whole strategic coast would be secured by spring. Momentum would have to be maintained. There would be another assault, another slash and thrust against Hitler's "Fortress Europe," and when it came, the SC and her sisters would apparently be there. Otherwise why this accelerated, high-priority "maximum matériel improvement" that so many of the little ships were now caught up in?

That program shifted at once into the highest gear. On the sixteenth the 692 moved down to the ammunition depot at Saint Juliens Creek and turned in all ammo, explosives, and pyrotechnics, and at noon on Saint Patrick's Day, the big crane ship *Kearsarge* moved ponderously into position, attached a couple of heavy slings, and, as though she were a toy boat in a bathtub, ignominiously hoisted this commissioned warship of the United States out of the water and set her on the dock adjacent to Berth 43.

For three days up there on blocks, and for six more after that back in the water at Berth 42, yard workmen swarmed over the little ship. They cleaned and repainted her bottom, shafts, propellers, and rudders. They removed the short-barreled 3-inch/23 forward, replaced it with a far more modern and effective gun, and installed new ready boxes to store the different ammunition. They removed her depth-charge racks and installed new ones. They removed, recalibrated, and reinstalled the WEA-1 sonar. And best and most important of all, they installed an SF surface search radar, with its antenna in a little beehive-shaped antenna housing at the masthead and a console with the operating controls and two small circular scopes in the pilothouse on the port side. To support the additional weight of the radar antenna, the mast was braced with heavy pipe supports slanting forward to the main deck and braced athwartships above the bridge. To operate and maintain the new radar, a new man was added to the crew, Myron Robert Wells, a slim and pleasant young man, all of nineteen, just out of radarman's school and very serious and conscientious about his work and his gear; a most welcome man with a most welcome attitude, because after the uneasy nights with the Caribbean convoys, the value of the new radar was instantly apparent to every officer and man aboard.

By late on the twenty-sixth, to everyone's huge relief, the matériel part was over, the yard workmen left the ship with their electrical cables and air hoses and tool boxes, and we had a chance to clean up and make things shipshape, to take back possession of our ship and our home. When that had been done she looked like a different ship. In place of the high and stubby little 3-inch/23 on the foredeck, there was now a low and businesslike dual-purpose Bofors 40-mm, with the cone-shaped flash guard at the end of its long barrel extending almost up to the mousetraps at the bow.

The new gun alone nearly doubled the ship's effectiveness. It could hammer out its 2-pound explosive projectiles at a rate of more than one a second at both surface and air targets from the horizontal to the zenith. The ship's silhouette was further altered and her fire-power further increased by the addition of a third 20-millimeter on a raised platform aft of the other two, where it could engage a target on either side as well as astern. The two long depth-charge racks were gone from the fantail, replaced by six individual type-C racks along the deck edge on each side. And above the bridge, the new support structure and radar antenna housing at the masthead gave the ship a whole new look.

For the next three days the 692 was busy running up and down the Portsmouth-Norfolk waterfront; to Craney Island for fuel, back to Saint Juliens Creek to reload ammunition, to NOB for provisions, to the degaussing range for demagnetizing, and out into Hampton Roads to compensate the compass. With the month winding down and departure time approaching, there were just two days out in the lower Chesapeake to get used to the new sensors and weapons, firing at target sleeves towed by planes from the Naval Air Station and at canvas targets rigged on sleds well astern of the tugs that brought them out from NOB both night and day.

Then, inevitably, there came a final day. It began with a classified convoy conference in the wardroom of Commander, Service Squadron Five at NOB, where information on convoy composition, cruising dispositions, screening stations, and sortie and entrance plans were distributed on legal-sized mimeographed sheets and discussed at length. Destination: Bermuda. Convoy: 37 landing craft, infantry (LCIs); 31 landing craft, tanks (LSTs); two salvage tugs; and one net tender. Screen: five destroyers, three large minesweepers (AMs), three small minesweepers (YMSs), two PCs, and six SCs. Convoy speed: 8.2 knots. In the event an enemy surface raider was encountered, the destroyers would peel off and attack, while the convoy, protected by the remainder of the screen, took evasive action (at 8.2 knots!). All ships would get under way around 1730, anchor in assigned berths in Lynnhaven Roads just inside Cape Henry, and sail for Bermuda, six hundred miles to the south-southeast, at 0630 on 1 April.

The USS SC 692 had a real problem with that 1730 schedule. Although the radar had been installed, it was not yet working, and the captain was not about to sail without it. Likewise the Mark 14 gun sights for the 20-millimeters, which were supposed to compensate for target motion. And there were still two life rafts to come aboard as well as several crates of spare parts for the guns and the main engines and generators.

We spent the rest of the day trying with varying degrees of success to get those things accomplished. By 1730 all was ready for sea except the radar, on which three yard technicians were hard at work.

The author wishes he could be sure this is SC 692 under way at flank speed after "maximum matériel improvement" at Norfolk in March 1943. It probably is not. But this SC is identical in every topside respect and serves to show precisely how she looked. (National Archives and John Higgins)

At 1800 a messenger arrived from ComServRon Five. The hard-nosed old captain in that job had been keeping track and wanted to know why the 692 was not under way for Lynnhaven Roads in accordance with his orders. Through the messenger we reported that the ship would be under way as soon as the radar was operational and hoped that there would be no confrontation. I was really not going to sail without a working radar, considering it was my responsibility as commanding officer to assure as far as possible the safety and survival of the ship and her crew. I hoped there would be no direct order to the contrary that would create an impasse, and I didn't think he would force one, because it would take longer to find a new CO than to get the radar working.

At 2000 the technicians reported they had found the trouble and would have the gear functioning in a couple of hours, and half an hour later Mrs. Washer, Mrs. Coffey, and Mrs. Stafford arrived in the shuttle boat from Old Point Comfort to say goodbye. The last boat back to Old Point shoved off at 2130, and on the dark little float with the motor launch idling alongside and its crew standing by, we said our final goodbyes. My wife's kiss held all its usual magic, and as we parted her grip was strong on my arm with a message of reluctance to leave but confidence in me and whatever the future held, which with the baby and the war was very much indeed.

In what must have looked to an objective observer like a little ritual of separation, the three wives boarded the launch, and the three officers turned together and walked back up the dock to the little ship that was now truly home and upon whose sensors and weapons their lives would now depend.

The radar scopes were alight and showing targets by midnight, and a reprieve came down from NOB; get under way in time to join the rest of the force as it departed the anchorage and formed up.

CHAPTER THREE

THE ATLANTIC

With the dockside floodlights creating an island of illumination in the full dark of 0445 on the first day of April, the 692 singled up her lines and prepared to get under way. Charlie Coffey with Chief Murphy were in charge forward; Washer with big, capable Charlie Nader aft; Roughan on the wheel as usual; and Chief Morton at his station between the two big diesels in the engine room. I was happy that he was there, because when the last line had been snaked ashore by the sleepy sailors from NOB, and before I could give the first order to helm and engines, the starboard engine suddenly began to go ahead and the port engine to back.

"All stop!" I hollered down the voice tube. "What the hell are you doing down there?"

"Nothing, sir," Roughan answered in an injured tone. "Engine controls are on 'stop.'"

One of the advantages inherent in such a small ship is that the unaided voice can be heard from bow to stern, and I made use of that advantage to bellow at young Frank Hagan, fireman second, the youngest and most junior of the engineers, whose head I could see

37

poking out of the engine-room hatch. By that time the ship was swinging implacably to port, the bow only a yard or two from a barge tied
up ahead, and the starboard screw guard pressing against the pilings
of the dock.

At my "*All stop, dammit!*" Hagan's head vanished below, where he
apparently relayed that urgent message, because in a few seconds the
swirling water at the stern quieted and the situation returned to normal. Morton had acted just in time to correct a maladjustment in the
pneumatic system that controlled the diesels' transmissions.

Out in Hampton Roads it was dark and cold as the 692 groped
her way toward the Bay. In a few minutes we could see the distinctive
angular shape of a net tender ahead. She was the *Pepperwood,* one of
the ships in our convoy. Cartwright blinked over and asked her to
turn on her stern light, which she did, and we followed her gratefully
out of the Roads and into Thimble Shoals Channel. At the entrance,
with the low outlines of Fort Wool to starboard, the Chamberlain
Hotel was a dark block of masonry against the now noticeably lighter
morning sky. Somewhere behind those unlighted windows slept my
wife and my mother. I noticed Coffey and Washer eyeing it too and
knew their wives were also there. No word passed between us.

In the long channel out to Lynnhaven Roads we passed our fel-
low escorts from Miami, YMSs 62 and 69, and when we arrived, the
shallow Virginia end of the Chesapeake was full of ships. In the early
light they lay in five orderly rows roughly parallel to the shore with all
their bows pointing seaward into the flooding tide. Most were LCIs,
with knobby bows and thin cylindrical bridges amidships like the
battlements of medieval castles, but close to shore at the far end of the
inner row we could make out the larger shapes of LSTs, like small
tankers with their flat decks and aft superstructures. And in the outer
lines were a scattering of SCs, YMSs, a couple of big AMs, and a fleet
salvage tug, the *Narragansett.* Here and there along the rows of ships
a few were beginning to stir, with anchors coming up and running
lights flashing on as they eased drowsily toward the channel and the
sea. The 692 joined the first of the departing ships and continued on
to seaward.

By 0700 on Thursday, the first day of April, the whole group
was under way and standing out through the swept channel in a long
double column. At 1000 the last LCI passed the black-and-white-
striped lighthouse of Cape Henry on its bare and lonely strip of sand,
and at noon the force began to form up as a convoy.

That process took all of an hour, with signal lights flashing between ships and flag hoists soaring to their yards, pausing a minute or

two and plunging back into their bags. When it was all over the result was a moving rectangle of massed landing craft, seven columns of five with three hundred yards between columns and two hundred yards between ships in column. At the head of the center column steamed the *Narragansett,* acting as formation guide and looking very much like a mother duck with her brood closely in company. Two miles dead ahead a 220-foot minesweeper (AM 104), the *Pilot,* had the lead and the same distance directly astern a smaller sweeper, the *Direct,* brought up the rear. Ahead of the *Narragansett* and astern of the *Pilot* was LCI 87, flying the broad pennant of the Task Group Commander. At equal intervals on the flanks and front of the rectangle, five SCs and the net tender *Pepperwood* provided protection against submarines. SC 692's station was on the starboard quarter of the landing craft formation, with the *Narragansett* two miles broad on our port bow, SCs 535 and 680 ahead, and YMS 69 on our port beam at the rectangle's opposite corner. Two other subchasers listed in the operation order were no-shows; one, the 534, for reasons never determined, and the 503, which reportedly hit a channel buoy on the way out, bent a shaft, and returned for repairs.

Shortly after 1300, the convoy, collectively and officially known as Task Group 68.2, was in position on SC 692's new radar. Our course was 120 degrees true, speed 8 knots, with the escorts making 10 knots and patrolling back and forth in their assigned sectors, sonars probing below, radars searching the surface, and lookouts on full alert.

The radar on the 692 got a lot of use that first day of the first leg of the long voyage to the war. It was important that every man aboard knew how to use it and thus how to provide his ship and his shipmates with information their lives could very well depend on. And by nightfall every man at least knew how to recognize a target and how to get a range and a bearing on it. It was a start.

Also by nightfall the weather had turned nasty. All afternoon the clouds had been gathering, the wind increasing, and the sea building. Worse, the sea was on the beam, and the little SC, newly laden with stores, many of them of necessity topside, rolled her deck edges under repeatedly to the huge displeasure and discomfort of her crew. Electrician Bennie Braverman, Machinist's Mates Charlie Casey and Curt Christman, and Sonarman Senecal spent much of their time leaning over the new taffrail (while being careful to maintain a solid grip), and even Seaman Hawn and Fireman Posey, who from Key West to Guantánamo and back to Norfolk had never once been sick, were forced to join them. With the foredeck continuously wet with spindrift or solid water it was impossible for the men who lived for-

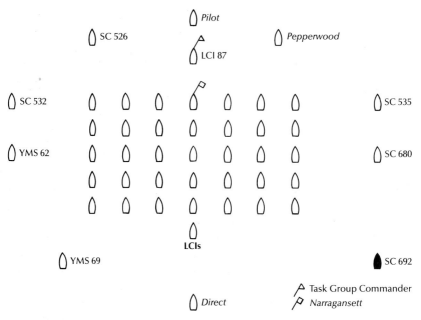

Convoy Disposition, Task Group 68.2, Virginia Capes to Bermuda, 1–4 April 1943

ward to come aft or to return to their bunks without a thorough drenching in cold Atlantic water.

To add to the general aggravation, the newly provided and presumably watertight galley hatch delivered a steady and copious drip on the mess table, and a hole inadvertently left open when the new galley blower was installed admitted seawater by the bucket into the after crew's quarters. Even the old leak over the captain's bunk, which a yard workman had collected two hours pay to fix, turned out not to have been fixed at all, and I was forced to move to the bunk of whichever other officer had the watch. About the only comfort that remained was the radar, which continued to show the position of every ship in the convoy in a night so black that the lookouts could not see for a hundred yards.

The blackness of that night and the steadily worsening weather took its toll of the convoy too. I had the morning watch (0400–0800), and when daylight came, on a howling gale under a heavy overcast, six LCIs, the YMS 69, and SC 680 were missing. But they had simply become separated in the dark and the storm and came straggling back in during the day.

At noon the sonar quit. Kidwell and Senecal went to work on it but to no avail, and we reported the casualty to the escort commander by flashing light. The wind increased slowly but steadily all afternoon and instead of going down with the sun as the old axiom states, it continued to increase after dark.

Shortly after 2000 I turned in to Charlie Coffey's bunk to try to get a few winks before relieving him for the mid watch. At 2315 I was jolted awake by the shrill screaming of the lube oil alarms indicating low pressure in one or both engines. My first thought, given the forty or fifty ships wallowing around in the immediate vicinity, was of an imminent collision. But topside Charlie reported that the port life raft had been torn loose by a sea and was towing alongside by its sea painter. I took the conn while he went aft to supervise its recovery. He was back in about thirty seconds. It seems the toggle that secures the sea painter had slipped through its eye with the thrashing of the ship and the cresting seas and released the raft. For about ten seconds I considered going back to locate and pick it up, but in the black fury of the night, the risk to the ship and her people was not worth the cost of the newly provisioned and equipped raft, and we increased speed and resumed station. Professionally, I fervently hoped we would not have occasion in the next few days to crowd all thirty men aboard the remaining starboard raft. Very unprofessionally, I could not help thinking what a find that raft would be for some kid on some New Jersey, Virginia, or Carolina beach.

The loss of the raft was not our only problem that night. Just as the watch changed for the mid watch the radar scopes went dark. Kidwell was routed out, and with Wells pointing a flashlight at the schematic with one hand and holding on with the other, he went to work on the set. After a couple of hours he had to admit defeat, and the 692 had to report another casualty. The situation was grim and the SC a highly ineffective little warship with both her primary sensors down, but it could have been worse. After his experience with the stragglers of the previous night the task group commander had wisely ordered shielded stern lights illuminated on all ships, and thus when another blustering dawn arrived the 692 was still approximately on station.

Yet the hours before that dawn were as wild as the little ship had yet experienced. Repeatedly she rolled down more than halfway from the vertical, often much more. Men were flung from their bunks and bruised and scraped on various hard objects. One man, Seaman Arnold Kapfer, lacerated his scalp to such an extent that for the first time my tenuous talents as medical officer were required. Trying hard to display a confidence I was very far from feeling, I washed the blood out of his hair and cleaned the two-inch wound with soap and water.

Then, with both doctor and patient holding on as best they could, we managed to get the area around the cut clipped and shaved, dust in a heavy coating of sulfanilamide powder, pull the edges of the laceration together with little strips of adhesive, and slap a bandage on top. With the bleeding stopped and the wound closed, Kapfer seemed to feel he was okay, but I took him off the watch he was scheduled to stand in a few hours and told him to lash himself in his bunk and get what rest he could.

While the operation was taking place in the wardroom, on one particularly violent roll, the long mess table, with several hundred pounds of provisions secured to its underside, broke loose with a crash and jammed athwartships in the aft crew's quarters, which already had several inches of salt water and assorted loose gear sloshing back and forth across its decks. In their soggy bunks around it the dirty and exhausted off-watch crew just opened an eye for a moment and thought to hell with it.

But an hour or so later there was another heavy roll and solid green water came pouring down the hatch close to Charlie Casey's bunk. Short stocky Charlie, dog-tired and dreaming troubled dreams, awoke to the careening ship and cascading water and concluded the worst had happened. Out of his bunk he came, sounding the alarm—"This is it, boys! This is it! Topside, boys!"—and mounted the vertical ladder like a cat, dragging his life jacket behind him. In a minute or two he was back, having determined that the 692 was still on the surface and under way, to the raucous merriment of his mates who were not too tired or ill or dirty or uncomfortable at 0300 to sit up on their sodden mattresses and laugh tears onto their stubbled cheeks, repeating with fresh laughter each time, "This is it, boys! This is it! Topside, boys!"

Casey, not at all abashed, rolled back up in his blanket, announcing, "To hell with you bastards! Next time you can all drown." But the next morning he was in a better humor and when Ship's Cook Rees observed that it was a good thing the port raft was not towing alongside when Casey arrived on deck because he sure as hell would have been on it, Charlie laughed and admitted he was right.

That same morning showed that the heavy seas that had torn away the raft and aroused Casey's instinct of self-preservation had also demolished the little 8-foot rowing pram, which was the ship's only tender. The next victim of the storm was the diesel-fired galley range, and the 692's men were denied even the comfort of what hot food they had been able to gulp while holding fast to whatever fixed structure was handy. So for breakfast there were cold sandwiches, and sandwiches for lunch, and for dinner, sandwiches, all joyfully washed down with hot coffee from the big electric urn.

By evening of the day of the sandwiches, which was Saturday, the third of April, while it abated not a bit in strength, the wind began to shift, and by midnight it was definitely astern. Although that made it tougher on the helmsman, the worst of the rolling stopped. But the relief was short lived. The next morning formation course was changed to starboard and that set her to rolling once more.

At 1100 on Sunday a signal from the task group commander relayed through the SC 532 reported the convoy only thirteen miles from its destination. Since my dead reckoning (in the absence of sun or stars for the entire voyage) showed us nearly fifty miles away, I climbed up the new radar tripod to have a look.

Of course the commander was right. Land was clearly evident ahead, lumpy against the sea horizon—the storied islands of Bermuda, Shakespeare's "still-vexed Bermoothes," happily not vexed at all this day but dark green and gently rolling. And that landfall had an almost magical effect. As soon as it was reported all the men off watch came crowding up to see, and what a seedy lot they were. For four days it had been either unsafe or impractical or grossly inconvenient to shave, and washing at all had been difficult. Most had made the effort to change clothes only when soaking with sea water had made it necessary, but the salt remained caked in the stubble of their beards.

As if on signal, within five minutes of landfall, the sun broke through and reminded us of our new latitude with its welcome warmth on our backs. Under the sudden sunshine the Atlantic turned from cold gray to clear and sparkling blue. The sea subsided as we approached the land, and thirty minutes after landfall Braverman reported the galley range repaired. With the welcome prospect of a hot meal after all those cold sandwiches, and with the green island looming warmly under the newfound sun, man after man disappeared below to emerge in ten or twenty minutes shaven, combed and clean, and in fresh dungarees and chambray shirt and immaculate white hat. It seemed a different crew that came back up from below that morning.

But the voyage was not yet over. As luck would have it, the entrance plan, which specified among other things the order in which ships would enter, named the SC 692 the last ship to do so, the forty-fifth ship of forty-five. So for some two hours we patrolled back and forth in a vicious, breaking chop as the rectangle of landing craft changed to a single file and threaded into the long channel between the island rocks and the reefs offshore.

When it was finally our turn to enter, there were still fifteen miles to go and the weather had changed again. Although there were still periods of brilliant sunshine, they alternated with violent rain squalls, and with both sun and rain came a wind that drove long parallel lines of spindrift along the surface of the sea, that pressed the 692 over in a ten-degree heel and tore the words from men's mouths, whipping them to leeward so that it was impossible even to shout upwind. We estimated the wind at forty knots; we learned later that the Naval Air Station had recorded gusts to sixty-five.

Once in the anchorage adjacent to the Naval Air Station, the 692 was again one of the last ships to be assigned a berth and it was 1830 before I was able to speak those welcome words, "Secure the bridge. Secure the engines." Five minutes later, my friend Prent Horne of the 535 brought his ship alongside with unintentional drama. He forgot to allow for the added momentum imparted to his ship by the weight of stores, spares, fuel, and water and came in so fast he needed full power astern to keep from ramming us.

The SC 692 was finally secure, in the first of many foreign ports in her long, one-way journey to the war. Later that evening, mellowed by the sheer delight of a quiet, secure, steady, and dry ship, big, tough Seaman First Charlie Nader remarked, "Boy, this duty sure gives a man an appreciation of the little things!" He had in mind, as we all did, a hot shower, a hot dinner, and a long deep sleep between the sheets in a dry, clean, motionless bunk. No truer words were ever spoken.

In the admittedly parochial view of the little SC 692, one of the most welcome attributes of Bermuda was the presence there of U.S. Navy Construction Battalion Forty-nine. Our list of necessary repairs and alterations was presented to their commanding officer the morning after our arrival, and in minutes a score of enthusiastic, skilled, and hardworking Seabees were aboard and turning to. In no time the faulty galley hatch was raised eight inches and thoroughly caulked, the hole left from the galley blower installation plugged, the sonar repaired, the radar fixed by the simple replacement of a vacuum tube, and work begun on the construction of a new pram to replace the one smashed by the seas the night the raft was lost.

At the same time, and despite the blustery squalls, the crew went to work with a will repairing the myriad minor ravages of the passage, fighting rust, scraping, wire-brushing, priming, and painting. Below decks Morton's engineers tore down and overhauled the port generator, which had been a source of trouble since Norfolk. There was no word on how long the Bermuda stopover would be, so work went forward at full speed.

On Wednesday, 7 April, the crews of all three 20-millimeters were bused over to the nearby gunnery range where they spent the morning hammering away at towed sleeves, a morning that would soon prove to have been well spent. At 1515 the same day a gray truck pulled up to the dock and unloaded a new raft to replace the one lost at sea. Just five minutes later the 692 was under way for a welcome change of berth. At 1630 she put over her mooring lines again, but this time she was nested right in the heart of Hamilton itself, just across the main street from the busy shops, restaurants, and bars of Bermuda's capital city.

In that nest of small escorts awaiting the word to sail to war were four SCs and the two YMSs of the Norfolk-to-Bermuda convoy. The 692 was the third ship from the dock, with the SCs 526 and 532 inboard. Outboard were SC 535, YMS 69, and YMS 62. As if that ideal berthing arrangement were not enough, word came the same day that the convoy for Africa would not be sailing until the twelfth or thirteenth. Almost another week in port. Time to get the ship as ready as she could be made. Time even to see something of these storied islands. Time also for some of the crew to get in trouble and for others to be transferred and lost to the 692.

While we were at the Naval Air Station, liberty was granted to the crew at 1300, expiring aboard at 1830, by order of the senior officer present afloat (SOPA). On the very first day, Casey and Posey went ashore in their dress blues promptly at 1300. By 1900 Posey had not returned. But a few minutes later two husky shore patrolmen with nightsticks, white belts, and blue and gold "SP" brassards on their arms delivered him aboard, along with a typed and signed form charging him with visiting an off-limits area, attempting to elude the shore patrol, and resisting arrest.

"Rebel" Posey, a clean-cut country boy from Rome, Georgia, with regular features and until now a clear record, looked the very embodiment of the charge. His white hat was missing, the sleeve of his jumper was torn, one of the knees was out of his bell-bottom trousers, and he was generally rumpled and dirty, although apparently sober. I took official custody of the culprit, the SPs departed, and in the relative privacy of the wardroom (Charlie and Washer were ashore), I asked for his side of the story. He protested earnestly that he was not aware of being off-limits until the SPs raided the bar where he was drinking beer and becoming acquainted with the local patrons. When my expression must have indicated skepticism, he sought to back up his statement: "Captain, if you don't believe me, just ask Casey!"

When Casey appeared from aft, showing a few scratches but clean and sober, and noticeably displeased with his shipmate for having spilled the beans, the full story came out.

The two sailors had wandered around Hamilton, stopping at pubs here and there, eventually winding up at a second-story bar on a remote back street. Whether or not they were aware that the area was off-limits when they arrived, any doubt should have been removed by the arrival of a pair of shore patrolmen on what was apparently a routine check. Casey and Posey, having no desire to end in the brig on their first day ashore, made an instant decision for flight. The problem was that the only access or egress to or from the bar was a steep and narrow staircase, where they could hear ascending the clumping footsteps of the SPs. Undaunted, the two SC sailors, both rather short and stocky with the law of gravity on their side, made a frontal assault down the stairs, bowled over the startled SPs, and escaped out the front door with the law in pursuit.

In the strange town, in the gathering dusk, they sprinted down the nearest narrow alley only to find it a dead end, necessitating a second successful charge past the patrolmen. At that point they separated and in a second blind alley Posey was finally caught and overpowered. But Casey was luckier. He vaulted a high wooden fence, landing in a patch of rose bushes on the far side (which accounted for the scratches), and made it safely back to the ship. He had cleaned up and was congratulating himself on a successful conclusion of the adventure when his shipmate inadvertently fingered him.

The following morning at mast both men were restricted to the base for the remainder of their stay in Bermuda—a punishment that lost most of its sting with the change of berth to downtown Hamilton two days later.

There were two other personnel problems to be dealt with while in port. One turned out for the best, the other decidedly did not. One of the 692's youngest, least able seamen habitually became of even less value under way due to chronic seasickness. On the rough passage just completed, I had literally feared for his life. He had not been able to keep anything down, even water, and had spent most of the time lashed to the deck aft of the pilothouse with the dry heaves bringing up nothing but his gastric juices as he grew progressively weaker. In an atypical burst of initiative in Bermuda, he located another seaman on the air station who wanted very badly to go to sea. Their request for an exchange of duty was approved without hesitation both ashore and, especially, afloat.

At the same time the 692 lost without replacement one of her ablest and most valuable men, Newton Cartwright, her only rated signalman. Cartwright, a likeable, sociable second class from Nashville, had been handling all signal duties—flashing light, semaphore, and flag hoists—handling too much as it turned out, because his striker, just out of signal school, was in no way yet qualified to replace him. Cartwright, we were informed by the medical officers ashore, had developed an unglamorous but advanced case of hemorrhoids, which would require surgery and several weeks of hospitalization. The orders that took him ashore specified "for transfer to this vessel in whatever port she may be, upon completion of treatment." But apparently those orders, issued by a reserve "jaygee" commanding a very minor warship, lacked effective authority, because Cartwright never set foot on her decks again.

The loss was serious because it effectively handicapped the SC's ability to communicate, much as a speech impediment would affect a human being. Less serious but a loss affecting the ship's composite personality, was the tear left in the web of her social structure. Cartwright had been not only the voice of the 692 to the outside world, but a respected and popular petty officer who pulled his weight and with whom it was a pleasure to stand a watch. All three officers and bright, personable young Archie LaFlamme, the striker, turned to in earnest to improve their signal abilities, especially in flashing light, by which most communications were sent and received at sea.

With the ship's work completed and the personnel problems settled for better or worse, a couple of days in the middle of a war were somehow left for pleasure and a chance to enjoy the beautiful islands that had inspired Shakespeare's *Tempest*. Thus on one sunny, breezy afternoon, Charlie Coffey, Prent Horne of the 535, and I rented bicycles ($1.50 for the half day) and set off to see the country. It felt glorious to be out of uniform and temporarily out from under the cares and responsibilities of our ships. The sun was warm on our faces and the soft breeze filled with the dry, sweet scent of the land. We were three young men in our midtwenties, sightseeing in one of the beauty spots of the world, and the war seemed very far away. With no particular destination in mind at the start, we somehow found ourselves on the road to Saint George, sixteen miles away from Hamilton beyond the end of the principal island, Bermuda, on Saint George Island. We marveled at the neat white and pink homes with their sparkling white roofs, green lawns, and bright flowers. We crawled through a hole in a shoreside hibiscus hedge, sat on the rocks where a tiny, clear blue tongue of the sea licked into the land and fired in a desultory way at the translucent purple sails of passing Portuguese men-o-war with .22-caliber target pistols. Halfway there we stopped in a little bar and refreshed ourselves with the local lukewarm beer. We visited the famed aquarium and its adjacent zoo. At Saint George we rested on a deserted terrace overlooking the little harbor, where an anchored YMS and an SC reminded us of the temporary nature of our tourism, and speculated lazily on the desirability of duty on this lovely island.

It was midafternoon when we started back. The pleasant breeze had increased considerably and now blew from dead ahead, combining with the many hills to make the return trip into something of a chore. It was then that I got to know Charlie Coffey better. In his quiet, rational lawyer's way, he announced that since this expedition had been planned as a pleasure but had now changed into something approaching physical torture, he found no reason to continue and at the next station would put his bike on the train and *enjoy* the trip back to Hamilton. And that is exactly what he did, impervious to and entirely unruffled by the gibes of his two companions.

Prent and I pushed on, but we adopted what we had observed to be the sensible local custom of walking, not pedaling, up the hills. Saving our energy in that way, we arrived back in town simultaneously with Charlie, who spoke with measured eloquence for some time on the scenic restfulness of his own journey. Since dinner was long over on both ships, we all settled for large quantities of chilled, canned fruit cocktail in the galley of the 692.

On our final shore leave, Charlie and I shopped for Wedgwood articles for our wives and mothers in an immaculate little shop just across from the ships. We were so successful that afterward we lacked even the fifty cents required for admission to the officers' showers at the USO. Not to be denied a final hot bath, we shifted into dungarees, borrowed white hats, and luxuriated in the free enlisted men's facility.

On Monday, 12 April, a conference of commanding officers of the new convoy was held at NOB. A motor launch picked up the six from our nest at Hamilton, and when we arrived the big briefing room was crowded. We quickly found out why. There would be sixty-eight landing craft (thirty-seven LCIs, and thirty-one LSTs) in the group, plus eighteen escorts, the tanker *Kaweah* (AO), the net tender *Pepperwood* (YN), and the fleet tug *Narragansett* (AT). A few of the LSTs would be flying the white ensign of the Royal Navy.

We received detailed instructions on night and day formations, emergency maneuvers, communications, fueling schedules and procedures, and a series of noon positions through which we would pass, all backed up by mimeographed sheets marked "SECRET" in red block letters. But there was no mention at all of the destination of this considerable force. Back aboard the 692 that afternoon, we plotted the noon positions on the chart and joined them. The result was an irregular line running generally eastward, terminating some seventy miles due west of Casablanca.

The next day the Bermuda intermission ended. At 0600 on a cool and windy morning, the thirteenth of April, the last line snaked aboard from the 532, the whistle sounded, the jack came down, the steaming colors soared to the gaff, and the SC 692 resumed her passage to the war. Astern of the 535 and the two YMSs, she left Hamilton's sheltered little bay and joined the stream of other ships forging down the long, narrow channel toward the sea.

The operation order called for the escorts to establish an antisub screen for the landing craft as they sortied and formed up, so we cranked on extra turns, passing ship after ship, entered open water well ahead of the first units of the convoy, and went about the business of setting up the screen. It seemed the blue seas were full of escorts that morning, five destroyers, three of the big minesweepers (AMs), three PCs, the two YMSs, and five subchasers. After many flashing lights and a few flag hoists, a moving half circle of warships emerged, with the destroyers to seaward and the smaller escorts on the flanks. Into the open side of that semicircle poured the landing craft, forming into columns as they headed eastward. It was a fairly straightforward operation but complicated and made arduous for the smaller ships by the weather.

That thirteenth of April off Bermuda was the sort of day that is beautiful ashore and in appearance but vicious in practice at sea. Under a warm blue sky, unmarred by even a single cloud, the sea was a deep, clear blue set off by the pure white of breaking wave tops. The problem for the SCs and YMSs was that those pretty, pure white wave tops were on the crests of eight- to ten-foot seas driven by some forty knots of wind, and most of them came aboard the small ships with a crashing, soaking violence that belied their visual appeal.

It took until 1500 for the eighty-nine ships to form their cruising disposition, and for that eight and a half hours the 692 and her sister SCs stood first on their bullnoses and then on their fantails, then, with a course change, rolled their deck edges under, wallowing and thrash-

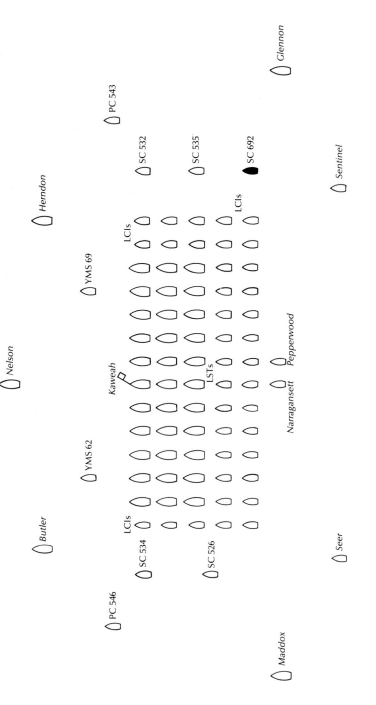

Convoy Disposition, Bermuda to Casablanca and Gibraltar, 13–31 April 1943

ing and soaking even the new beehive radomes at their mastheads with the heavy whitecaps.

Aboard those ships the crews worked hard merely to maneuver their vessels and maintain a watch on their sensors. Topside the men were repeatedly drenched and half blinded by spindrift, spray, and solid water. In the pilothouse and below, whatever a man was doing had to be done with one hand while the other grasped a rail or stanchion or any other fixed structure to hold him in position. After ten days in port, most of the 692's sailors had lost their sea legs, and only a few stalwarts went aft for the noon meal. There, if a man let go of his tray for an instant it was gone; if a container was more than half full of any liquid, it slopped over. In their bunks the men off watch tried vainly to doze while being tossed from one side to the other and lifted and dropped as if by a faulty elevator. We were lucky that the enemy did not see fit to challenge that sortie from Bermuda during those hours, at least along the flanks guarded by the smaller escorts, because he would have encountered little opposition.

Despite the weather, as dusk descended on the mid-Atlantic, the convoy was in order and the escorts more or less on station. With 500 yards between ships in column, 600 yards between columns, the leading destroyers 4 miles ahead, the trailing escorts 6 miles astern, and those on the flanks 4 miles from *Kaweah* (the formation guide), the disposition was 14 miles across and 12 miles fore and aft, covering 168 square miles of ocean and forging eastward at 8 knots.

So broad was this moving mass of ships that destroyer *Maddox*, twelve miles to port, guarding the left rear corner, and *Nelson*, in the lead, with the screen commander embarked, were hull down from the SC's little bridge, with only their stacks and top hamper showing above the sea horizon. In our own relatively small tactical world of the right flank, three SCs steamed in column one thousand yards apart and two miles from the righthand column of LCIs. The 532 was in the lead followed by Prent Horne's 535, with the 692 astern and abeam the last LCI, a comfortable station, it seemed, with little risk of either collision or inadvertent separation.

Outboard of the line of SCs, and four miles from the convoy flank, the destroyer *Glennon* patrolled reassuringly back on our starboard quarter, matching the position of her sister ship *Maddox*, and "Silver" Silverstein's PC 543 was on station equidistant from the convoy but ahead and to starboard of the leading SC. Six miles astern of us, the sharp bow of AM 113, *Sentinel*, was diving deep and throwing water, and across the stern of the formation PC 562 and two more big sweepers, *Pilot* and *Seer*, formed the rear guard. Exactly opposite our station, leading the pair of SCs on the left flank, was Tommy Lincoln's 534, which had missed the sailing from Norfolk but caught up at Bermuda.

On the same day, 13 April 1943, while the SC 692 and her sisters were laboring to set up their screen around the landing craft, far ahead in occupied Algeria a decision had been made, a date less than three months away selected on which those ships and men now struggling eastward would make the first assault on Adolf Hitler's "*Festung Europa.*"

The first three days out of Bermuda were as miserably uncomfortable as the four that had brought us there. The weather abated not a whit—clear skies, unlimited visibility, bright sun, and bright stars—with gale-force winds and the tall, savagely cresting seas marching day and night from horizon to horizon.

But in SC 692 the routine was now slightly different. Until Bermuda, the three officers had stood officer-of-the-deck (OOD) watches, each at the head of his own watch section, standing four hours on and eight off with the rest of the crew. Experience since the halcyon days of Miami and Key West had shown that as CO always on call, I had spent a disproportionate number of hours topside; on occasion, having been roused from a deep sleep after just coming off watch, I had not been at once as alert as I would have liked. Accordingly, Chief Murphy had been standing with me as junior officer of the deck (JOOD) under training, beginning with the passage from Miami to Norfolk. Now he took over my watch section, leaving me free to supervise, respond, and assist whenever circumstances required.

This change, planned anyway, became especially useful after the loss of Cartwright in Bermuda, since in practice at sea I was at least initially also the 692's most competent signalman. Repeatedly, in the first ten days or so out of Bermuda, the little whistle at the head of my bunk would sound and an urgent voice come down from the bridge: "Captain, the *Glennon* [or the *Nelson* or some other destroyer] is trying to send us a message and it's coming in too fast for me!" I would scurry topside, man the light, and with young LaFlamme at my side (another training program, now high-priority) receive and acknowledge a message of often fifty to seventy groups. Although our sister SCs, who knew of and understood our problem, would send at a reduced rate, the "big brother" DDs had no such patience, and the escort commander was given to sending long messages to be relayed around the screen.

There were also other changes in the developing personality of the subchaser. As the result of a brief ceremony at quarters abaft the pilothouse while we were in Bermuda, bright, capable John Roughan, the ship's only yeoman and her best helmsman, was now a first class; Lou Rees, ship's cook first class; leading Radioman Kidwell was a second class. Even Frank Hagan, the junior man in the engine room, had advanced from fireman second to fireman first; and good-natured, prematurely gray, Pennsylvanian Bill Hawn, from seaman second to first.

The third day out of Bermuda was fueling day for the small escorts. For the 692 it was the first time, except for a single practice in the sheltered waters of the Chesapeake after her refit in Norfolk. We left our station back on the starboard quarter of the convoy on signal, cranked on 1100 RPM for about 12 knots, and threaded our way forward between the columns of landing craft to where the *Kaweah* had pulled out a mile ahead.

The scene reminded me of the lines from Tennyson's poem "The Revenge."

> Thousands of their soldiers
> Looked down from their decks and laughed,
> Thousands of their sailors
> Made mock of the mad little craft.

On the relatively huge LSTs and even on the LCIs, soldiers in khaki fatigues and sailors in dungarees looked down, pointing and shaking their heads at the little gray ship plunging past throwing white water in all directions, their gratitude and relief not to have been assigned to such a tiny ship apparent even from three hundred yards. The one-hundred-ton SC approached the ten-thousand-ton tanker from well out on her port quarter to avoid the turbulence of her wake, then angled gingerly in toward her port side amidships, slowing to match the big ship's speed of 8 knots. Gingerly, because she was approaching a vertical gray steel cliff the top of which was just about even with the radar antenna housing at the highest point of the SC's mast. And that cliff was forging relentlessly through the long Atlantic ground swell at nearly ten miles an hour.

About thirty yards out the subchaser turned a little to port and paralleled the tanker's course. A few seconds later the monkey fist of a heaving line thumped down on the wet wooden deck just abaft the ground tackle. The other end of the heaving line led well forward on the big ship, and when Nader, Ridgeway, and Sadler took it in, they hauled across the eye of a 6-inch manila towing hawser. With the eye on the heavy towing bitts at the deck edge just opposite the 40-millimeter, the tanker crew took a strain with their clattering steam winch, the hawser pulled taut, and the SC was held in place alongside the oiler, now about ten yards abeam.

The trick now was to keep her there by the judicious use of helm and engines while other heaving lines brought over fuel and freshwater hoses and a high line for the passing of provisions. What made the maneuver difficult was the 8-knot stream of seawater being pushed outward from the tanker's huge bow. When that stream impinged on the SC's port bow, it tended to drive the smaller ship in toward that menacing steel cliff, made only slightly less dangerous by the big fenders *Kaweah's* crew had rigged. When it pressed more on the starboard bow the little ship was forced away from the big one, stretching and threatening to break the connections between the two.

In the hour and five minutes it took to fill the 692's tanks and take aboard a case of freshly baked bread, we learned that just a little port rudder against the tug of the towing hawser would keep the bow dead into the current. But even with Roughan on the helm and big, capable Curt Christman on the throttles to answer rudder and engine orders, it was a job that left the SC's captain wet with sweat when the welcome moment came to cast off and return to station. Although it was necessary to fuel every third or fourth day and although with practice we gained confidence, it was always an evolution requiring careful planning and total concentration by all concerned.

Between fuelings, an at-sea shipboard routine developed and became familiar and habitual. The watch changed every four hours except for the dog, or split, watches from 1600 to 1800 and 1800 to 2000. Morning general quarters came half an hour before sunrise, usually around 0600. Breakfast was at 0730 for the forenoon watch and a few minutes later for the off-going morning watch. At 1000 it was time to observe the sun for a morning sun line and work out the time of meridian passage, or local apparent noon (LAN). Lunch came at 1130 for the afternoon watch and later for the off-going watchstanders. LAN came usually around 1300, and after that observation, the morning sun line was advanced to obtain a running fix for the noon position. Around 1400 we closed the convoy sufficiently to read the official noon position from flag hoists and compare it to our own. Around 1700 we closed the convoy again to read course changes scheduled for the night. Supper was at 1715 and evening GQ about 2000. The first evasive course change was usually executed an hour after sunset, or about 2130, and the second, back to base course, just before midnight.

Occasionally the routine was enlivened by the unexpected. On the evening of the sixteenth, freshly fueled and provisioned, the 692 was steaming over a reasonably calm sea, her men at their battle stations for evening twilight, when surface craft are still visible but a periscope is not, when sonar reported a contact broad on the port beam at two thousand yards. That was a very long range for her relatively primitive WEA-1 sound gear, but she came quickly to attack speed and swung her bow toward the echo. The next range was close in—250 yards and closing—too close for an accurate attack. We opened the range, turned and came in again, but now the data seemed to go haywire. The longest range was three hundred yards and the bearings all over the ocean.

After half an hour of chasing that phantom echo we gave up and increased speed to rejoin. By then we were about eight miles astern of the convoy and in the vicinity of the PC 562 in trail position. As we straightened out in pursuit of the force, the 562 was about five hundred yards ahead and crossing from starboard to port. Apparently, although we had been watching her for several minutes, she had not seen us until that moment. She turned suddenly and headed straight for us on a collision course, white water curling at her bow as she increased speed, her men running to battle stations. I remembered the fate of the SC 1470 off Alligator Reef and the warnings at SCTC that with their low silhouette, flush deck, and boxy pilothouse, SCs are easy to mistake for surfaced subs. With unpleasant mental images of being fired on at point-blank range with a 3-inch/50 and then rammed by a sharp steel bow, we turned away at flank speed, flashing the day's recognition signals full at her with an unshielded 12-inch light—blinding in the late twilight. We repeated the coded letters until, dangerously close aboard and still at high speed, she sheered away and without comment headed back to station.

In the 692 we resumed breathing and, operating entirely by radar, rejoined and took our assigned position. That night, in a pattern of motion-induced material failure that began west of Bermuda and was to become all too familiar, the radar died. We could expect the sonar next, then the galley range and the refrigerator. As before, the best efforts of Wells and Kidwell over some six or seven hours failed. The effect was to blind the ship during the hours of darkness. With our assigned screening station 4,000 yards, or two miles, from the nearest ship of the convoy, and the distance at which another ship could be made out at night 1,500 to 2,000 yards, we were left with a familiar choice: leave the screening station and close to visibility distance, or remain on station and hope we would not get too far off by morning. With several evasive course changes, planned and unplanned, occurring each night, as in the Straits of Florida we took the first choice—the same choice we had made on the convoy to Guantánamo—trading a degradation of our antisub capability for the assurance that we would remain with the force on the assigned bearing ready to assist in other ways.

But having made the choice and accepted the trade-off did not mean that the nights without radar were easy for the subchaser's OODs. As darkness came on, the ships ahead and to port faded and lost their silhouettes as the horizon blurred and disappeared. With radio silence and darkened ships, the convoy executed unscheduled turns on whistle signals relayed across and down the close-packed columns—signals inaudible over the night sea noises on small ships low in the water and miles away. A continuous condition of maximum alert was required and a sixth sense would have helped. If those dim shapes barely visible through binoculars seemed to grow shorter or longer, we could assume that a turn had started. Then we had to turn to what we hoped was the new course and to adjust RPM as the ships increased or reduced speed, depending on the direction of the turn. Often that involved a 360-degree turn or a reversal of course in order to remain even roughly on station. And while the 692 was thus blindly groping, barely able by her utmost efforts to stay approximately where she was supposed to be, the force that she was assigned to protect was steaming across an ocean patrolled by hostile submarines and dotted with wolf packs awaiting only a contact report before launching their deadly surface torpedo attacks.

After four such nights, on Tuesday, 20 April, a week out of Bermuda, we fueled from *Kaweah* again, and three hours later the sonar died. Gamely, Senecal and Kidwell broke out the manuals and the schematics and took the console apart. That evening while they were up to their elbows in tubes, condensers, wires, and relays, Rees reported the refrigerator warming up. The only surprise was that the galley range was still operative. The progression of failures was slightly out of order. Chief Morton himself went to work on the refrigerator but hours later could only announce a tentative diagnosis of leaking Freon lines.

After two days of ineffective attempts to make repairs, it was time to ask for help. A message flashed over to the screen commander in the *Nelson* requesting the appropriate technicians be put aboard to lend a hand, "before entering more actively hostile waters."

The message worked. The next morning, the twenty-fourth, a sparkling day of dark blue sea, light blue sky, white clouds, and white wave tops, the SC came alongside the *Nelson* at her station well out ahead of the ordered mass of splashing, thrashing landing craft. The operation was much like fueling but with two rather daunting differences: there would be no manila hawser to hold her in place, and that place would not be ten yards out but close enough to permit a man to jump from ship to ship. At about 12 knots the destroyer turned to a heading that put the wind and sea slightly on her port bow, and the subchaser eased up on her lee, or starboard, quarter.

A couple of big fenders wrapped in gray canvas had been rigged slightly aft of amidships where the destroyer's deck was lowest. With Roughan and Christman in the pilothouse responding to orders from topside coming down through the vacuum-cleaner hose and the voice tube, the little SC slid docilely in until the heavy wooden rub rail along her port side bit into the two fenders. Docilely, but throwing a lot of white water, most of which splashed down on the *Nelson*'s decks and poured back out through her scuppers. The little ship shuddered slightly as she bumped against the fenders, then steadied as a touch of left rudder held her solidly against them. In rapid succession a chief and two sailors jumped across the fender-wide space separating the ships, the rudder was put gently a little to starboard, RPM increased by one hundred turns, and as easily as they had come together, the small ship and the large one parted company.

One of the men who had jumped aboard from the *Nelson* was a chief radio technician; the other two were radar technicians. The chief was lean, intense, bespectacled, with ears that turned forward and a quiet air of knowing exactly what he was doing. He tore methodically into the inert and silent sonar while the other two men attacked the radar. By noon they had done all they could do and reported gloomily that the radar was not repairable. It had, they said, a burned-out transformer, which probably could not be replaced "until you get back to the States."

The chief worked on the sonar all day, littering the pilothouse with parts and tools, breaking only occasionally to go topside and be sick, an indignity that he obviously resented, having served some fifteen years in destroyers with no such problem. The motion of a subchaser in a seaway, we assured him, was different.

At day's end the sonar remained dark and silent, and in a repeat of the morning's maneuvers, we put the three men back aboard their ship, the chief, not to be thwarted, vowing to return and finish the job next day. But the next morning he came aboard again, again worked (and was sick) all day and returned reluctantly to the *Nelson*, defeated but promising that if we ever hit the same port at the same time he would be back and fix that gear, whatever it took.

Thus, in midocean, the SC 692 was bereft of both her sensors, her search capability comparable to that of HMS *Victory* on the night before Trafalgar, except that given her superior freeboard, the *Victory* must have given Lord Nelson with his telescope a greater range of visibility than that provided the 692's OODs and lookouts with their binoculars. Still, once an enemy was sighted, neither radar nor sonar would be required and she could fight as well as ever. To that end we secured the mousetraps, set the stern-dropped charges to shallow, readied armor-piercing ammo for the 40-mm, and made fully ready for surface action. At the same time, we continued during daylight to patrol our assigned screening station with vigor, giving at least the outward appearance of a fully functional antisub escort.

Apparently the screen commander considered that since this particular SC was less than effective in her antisub role but seemed competently handled, she could profitably be used for other purposes. So while the chief from the *Nelson* was spending his second day aboard, the 692 fueled again and then delivered official mail in waterproof canvas packages to two LCIs in the port outboard column of the convoy and to the AM *Seer,* three and a half miles astern. In each case the SC would approach from the lee quarter of the other ship, move up so that her bow was approximately opposite the recipient's waist, and get over a heaving line. Bent to the heaving line would be a light messenger with the package secured at its midpoint. The other ship would haul the package across, the SC sailors would retrieve messenger and heaving line, and we would be off to line up the next approach. It was good experience in shiphandling and seamanship and a welcome break in the routine.

But with the long passage almost over there came a break in the routine that was not so welcome. The night of Tuesday, the twenty-seventh, when the force had been two weeks at sea, was exceptionally dark, with no moon and the stars obscured by a high overcast. The 692 had moved in even closer than usual to maintain even marginal visual contact. The watch had just changed at 0400 when Bill Hawn on port lookout reported a light ahead. It grew brighter and broke up into a cluster that proved to be a neutral merchantman bound southwest down the bulge of Africa but very far offshore. Unwittingly she was headed straight into the mass of blacked-out landing craft and warships on the opposite course. When it looked from the 692 as though she would pass right through the convoy, radio silence was suddenly broken with the single order, "Starboard! Starboard! Starboard!"

By the terms of the op order that meant a forty-five-degree simultaneous turn by all ships, that heading to be maintained until further orders. Obediently SC 692 came right and steadied up, increasing speed at the same time to keep clear of the big ships. After several minutes we slowed again to drop back toward the convoy, which had faded from sight. When no ships came in sight, we reversed course searching. Still no ships, no convoy and no further radio transmission to resume base course. Like a hound that has lost the scent, the SC circled, binoculars sweeping the sea, to no avail. There was nothing to do but resume base course and speed and wait for daylight.

Dawn came in about an hour, the east brightening almost imperceptibly, then the light increasing under the high clouds, until finally the sun broke bright red up out of the sea to shed its light across an ocean occupied solely and exclusively by one small gray U.S. subchaser muttering dutifully northeastward. It was a morning about which I had long had unpleasant premonitions, premonitions that had multiplied since the failure of first the radar and then the sonar. But my presentiments were nothing compared to the reality. The emptiness of "the lonely sea and the sky" was awesome. All that huge expanse of gently rolling ocean and nothing on it, not even a mast poking hazily over the horizon, however hard we searched. I even climbed to the radar platform at the masthead, binoculars slung around my neck, and searched methodically the full circle of utter nothingness.

Added to the hollow feeling in my stomach was the knowledge that this was fueling day; the diesel oil remaining in our tanks was not sufficient to make port. Any port.

After the hollow feeling came the urge to action. While waiting for the sun to climb sufficiently for a usable sun line, we plotted our DR (dead reckoning) position, broke out the table of noon positions in the op order, set course for the coordinates listed for the twenty-eighth, and adjusted speed to arrive at that position precisely at 1200.

At 0730 our never ceasing visual search turned up first one and then two ships well off to starboard. Assuming they were the fringes of the force, we joyfully cranked on additional RPM and came to an interception course. As we drew closer we could recognize the *Narragansett* and a single LCI. LaFlamme was just manning the light to ask directions to the task force when the big tug's own light began to flash. "W-H-A-T," it spelled out inquiringly, "I-S C-O-U-R-S-E T-O C-O-N-V-O-Y?"

LaFlamme gave her the heading we had figured out. She concurred and the SC continued the interception, joined up ahead of the tug and landing craft, and without sonar or radar simulated a protectively screening escort. An hour later a destroyer came in sight ahead, then an AM, another destroyer, an LST, and eventually the whole force. By 1100 we had rejoined the convoy in our assigned station, and at 1300 we took our normal turn at fueling. No one had even missed us. No one that is except ever vigilant Prent Horne in the 535, who blinked over irreverently, "Where the hell have you been?"

We learned later that the force had never turned at all. The "Starboard!" order had apparently been transmitted by another convoy far away but on the same frequency, and by a quirk of ship distance and atmospherics only our little receiver had picked it up.

As the crossing neared its end (the linked noon positions on our chart were nearing Casablanca), the men of the 692 presented a different appearance from that on sailing. As a small step toward maintaining morale on the long, arduous passage, the regulation requiring all hands to be clean shaven had been relaxed, and now the variety of facial hair that appeared with each change of watch was wonderful to behold. Charlie Coffey made one think of either Sir Francis Drake or Henry Hudson with a lank mustache and goatee, and the sight of him peering seaward from under a sou'wester, his deepset brown eyes alert, was something to treasure. Washer quickly achieved a small, neat, closely trimmed mustache that suited him so well he seemed always to have had it. I simply let the whiskers on my upper lip grow with no attempt at cultivation and they were rapidly achieving a fairly luxuriant reddish bushiness. Roughan's full beard was uniform in thickness but chaotic in direction, not a success. Morton's on the other hand was satisfyingly black but thin and skimpy on the chin and at the jaw points. But the unchallenged champion beard belonged to Charlie Nader; black, thick, curly and perfectly uniform, it combined with his bulk and his body hair to give him something of the look of the Saracen warriors in his blood line, a truly awesome figure of a man, a phenomenon of which we were later to make practical use.

Yet, while the upper parts of us flourished, the lower extremities were in extremis. The weeks of wet decks and watch standing and the constant sloshing of the sea aboard had devastated all our footgear, literally rotting the shoes off our feet. Several of the deckhands had sewn soles and uppers back together with sail twine, palm, and needle; others had just taken a few turns of small line around the entire shoe to hold it together.

In other ways the voyage had seasoned and improved us as a crew. Our daily sun lines and noon observations consistently came out close to the official position signaled by the convoy commodore, building our confidence as navigators. The loss of Cartwright in Bermuda, as wounding as it was, resulted out of necessity in the quick and effective progress of young LaFlamme as a signalman, and of all three officers as well. As the force approached Casablanca there were four men in the 692 capable, with a minimum of stumbling and repeating, of sending and receiving ordinary messages by flashing light, and LaFlamme was forging rapidly ahead on the way to full qualification.

The long Atlantic passage was nearing its end, and with it the minor drama we would all remember enacted each night at sea—

Charlie Coffey preparing to go on watch. Charlie was an inveterate and continuous smoker. In my bunk directly across from him, a light sleeper, I would hear the watch come down the vertical ladder from the pilothouse flashing a red-shielded flashlight around the dark wardroom until he located Charlie in the lower bunk on the port side. "Mr. Coffey," the man would half whisper, conscious of at least one other sleeping officer in the same compartment, "It's oh three thirty, Sir." (or 1130 or whatever the time was).

"Very well," Charlie would mutter, very military and alert at once. When the man had gone, Charlie, apparently by braille, would switch on the reading light at the head of his bunk and, with eyes tightly closed against the glare of the little light, fumble along the adjacent shelf for cigarettes and matches, shake out a cigarette, get it in his mouth, and light it, still all by touch. Not until the first puff was caroming off the bottom of Washer's mattress would he open his eyes.

A few seconds later he would swing his long, skinny hairy legs over the side and stand there in his droopy boxer shorts, scratching and groping around for his clothes. The shirt was easy, quickly donned and buttoned, with the cigarette drooping from Charlie's lips. The pants were different. You need to look down to get your legs in a pair of trousers and pull them up. And whenever Charlie looked down, the cigarette smoke curled into his eyes. So he would attempt the nearly impossible, trying to get his legs in the trousers while looking up at the overhead. Once in a while, if the sea were calm, this worked. Most often it didn't and he would be thrown against the bunk or bulkhead muttering ungentlemanly blasphemies until he removed the cigarette from his mouth and found a place to put it. Before he had completed dressing, the cigarette had usually rolled off onto the deck and had to be swiftly retrieved and returned to his mouth, where it stayed as he clapped on his hat and mounted the ladder to take over the watch.

A couple of days out of Casablanca, for the first time since Bermuda, the lookouts reported an aircraft in sight ahead. After a minute or two of tension, we could see it was a B-24 Liberator type, which, out there alone, obviously on antisub patrol, would be the navy version, a PB4Y. An hour later it was joined by the familiar parasol-wing, twin-engine shape of a PBY Catalina flying boat. They were with us off and on during daylight every day thereafter, circling reassuringly along the horizon, keeping down (and therefore harmless) any subs that might have been around.

As though relenting after the pounding and the misery it had dealt us earlier, the Atlantic subsided as we approached its eastern lit-

Ensign (later Lieutenant, junior grade) C. S. Coffey, Jr., the 692's executive officer, and then her captain for eight months. (Mrs. C. S. Coffey, Jr.)

toral and became a vast, flat liquid plain shining harmlessly in the sun. What a blessing those days were. No water on deck. No need to hang on always with at least one hand. No need for fiddle boards on the mess table, no need to crouch and run from hatch to hatch topside, or on watch to shelter one's binoculars from flying spray. I was even able to take down the shower curtain I had rigged above my bunk to keep out the persistent leak that saturated my bedding on every starboard roll.

At the end of one of those halcyon days came a perfect picture: a destroyer on dusk horizon sweep sharply silhouetted broadside at the far intersection of a flaming sunset sky and its reflection in the tranquil sea, as though to show that the majestic natural beauty of our planet remains unspoiled and unaffected by the petty beings who squabble on its surface. And in the night that followed, the feel of the ship and the sea was a languorous ballet, the bows dipping with gentle grace, the mast tracing a shallow arc against the stars, the dark water sliding down the sides, and always the throbbing and muttering of the big diesels driving her inexorably toward whatever lay in store.

Increasingly during those days the ever-present question occupied our minds. Where were we going? What would we do when we got there? The most common guess was Casablanca and short coastal escort jobs from there in the manner of Key West. But on the day before our chart showed we would be there, the 692 was ordered back to the *Kaweah* for fuel. Alongside the tanker we received six packets of official mail to deliver. One was addressed to us and it answered at least the first question. Although part of the force would indeed go to Casablanca, the remainder was ordered to a scattering of ports with unfamiliar names. Our port, and that of two LSTs and SCs 534 and 535, was called Nemours. A check of the chart showed it just across the Moroccan border in Algeria, about one day's run inside the Mediterranean from Gibraltar.

At 0900 on 29 April the LSTs and LCIs for Casablanca peeled off to the eastward with their escorts. Not, however, before the 692's out-going personal mail had been passed to the LST 355 for delivery to the fleet post office there.

That night it appeared that the force commander must have had reports of subs in the area, because immediately after dark we made a series of five course changes that took us in a wide sweep to the westward and then toward the Straits on a heading of due east.

At 0605 on the thirtieth we made landfall, the high dark bulk of Cádiz looming on the port bow against the brightening sky. Cádiz, whence Columbus himself had sailed in wooden ships much smaller than ours to find the world from which we had just come. At noon we entered the Strait of Gibraltar, the fabled Pillars of Hercules, and on the bridge of our tiny warship, busy as we were screening the flanks of seventy ships as they shifted to a double and then a single column, a sense of history blew over us on the warm Mediterranean breeze. I saw Charlie Coffey stare at the Rock of Gibraltar as its unique angular summit emerged from behind Tarifa Point, then across at the cloud-topped crags of Africa, then back to the Rock and I could read his mind. He was imagining the biremes and triremes of Phoenicia oaring through these waters millennia ago, the Roman galleys, the ships of the line of Nelson and Napoléon, the *Constitution*, the *Philadelphia* and Commodore Preble's frigates, the Great White Fleet of Teddy Roosevelt, and all the seamen of all the nations who had made this passage between the continents in peace and war. It was as though eastbound between the capes, with Gibraltar growing large before us, we and the sturdy little structure of New England juniper beneath our feet somehow gained kinship with those ships and sailors of other times and other lands, who must also have looked up at Gibraltar in awe.

Since the orders we had received from *Kaweah* had not even mentioned Gibraltar, it came as a surprise when the head of the long column swung to port, and ship by ship, the entire convoy headed into Gibraltar Bay. The other small escorts were as much at a loss as we and blinked back and forth in quest of answers while we dutifully patrolled the flanks of the column as it entered port. As the last ships were entering, a message came by flashing light from the *Glennon.* "Small escorts proceed to Gibraltar, take on fuel from *Kaweah.*"

The big tanker was anchored in the middle of the bay where a sizable ground swell was running. When the 692 arrived several SCs were already alongside, rolling heavily against each other. We needed hardly any fuel, having topped off the previous day, but we did need lube oil, so we made the starboard side of the 535. Before we could get our oil and get clear we had lost a yard of our port lower rub rail to a splintering contact with the 535's cast iron davit that the Luders yard insists on building into their SCs outboard of everything on the starboard side.

While alongside the *Kaweah* we learned for the first time that we would remain in Gibraltar at least for the night—welcome news after eighteen days at sea. From *Kaweah* we steamed directly into the inner harbor with the 535 and at 1610 tied up outboard of her in the lee of the high stone breakwater.

With her engines quiet and motion stilled under the loom of the Rock on that late April afternoon, the SC 692 was four weeks and a day out of Norfolk, with three weeks at sea and some 3,500 miles astern. In the unfamiliar silence her bewhiskered crew climbed topside to scratch prosaically and look inquiringly around. They sensed the closing of a door astern, the opening of another one ahead. They were poised on a threshold of their lives as they were on the threshold of this ancient sea, and deep within, unspoken, each man wondered uneasily what lay ahead.

CHAPTER FOUR

NORTH AFRICA

First priority at Gibraltar were radar and sonar repairs; second priority was shoes; and minutes after the diesels had shut down, the skippers of the SCs 535 and 692, Prent Horne and I, were on our way ashore in search of the U.S. Navy liaison officer, who, according to word from the *Kaweah*, was the man to see. A jeep ride with a couple of hospitable British army officers took us within easy walking distance of the U.S. Consulate, but the liaison officer had left for the day. Reached by phone at his hotel he provided another clue. Wait, he said, until after the convoy conference tomorrow, and he would be able to arrange repairs; he didn't know about the shoes. A conference the next day meant departure a day later so it was apparent we would have two nights and a day at Gib.

The conference was held 1 May in an austere stone building at dockside with yard-thick walls that appeared to have been built to withstand cannon balls. Departure was scheduled for 1300, 2 May, the force to consist of twenty-seven LSTs, seven LCIs, and the *Pepperwood*, escorted by two AMs (the *Seer* and the *Sentinel*), three PCs, two YMSs (our old friends the 62 and 69), and three SCs (the 534, 535, and 692). Two LSTs and the three subchasers would drop off at Nemours; others, which didn't concern us, at other ports along the coast of North Africa. Escort commander would be Commander A. F. Block of the *Seer.*

When the conference broke up I cornered Commander Block and reported our problems with radar, sonar, refrigeration, and shoes, and he agreed to send over technicians to work on the sonar and refrigerator. The shoes he would look into. The liaison officer gave me the name of a Royal Navy officer who could help with the radar. I found him, a lieutenant commander, in a bare nearby office and he agreed immediately to "attend to it."

Feeling greatly relieved, I walked back to the ship with Prent Horne, taking a roundabout route as our last chance to sightsee. My remaining impressions are of steep and narrow streets with closely packed overhanging buildings; a curious odor of bakeries, spices, foreign tobacco smoke, and manure from the open fields behind the Rock; hundreds of British soldiers in khaki; old Spanish crones with black shawls over their heads; and over and above all, the huge mass of the Rock, bristling with gun barrels and agitated by radar antennas ceaselessly sweeping sea and sky. Overhead the sky was loud with warplanes, mostly Hudsons and Spitfires, climbing steeply out or letting down for landing, wheels and flaps hanging awkwardly.

Back at the ship two British technicians were already at work on the radar and two men from the *Seer* had the sonar all apart. Aft, Chief Morton and another *Seer* sailor were elbow-deep in the recesses of the refrigerator. That work went on all day and well into the evening. At 2000 the *Seer* people reported progress but no final fix and returned to their ship anchored out in the harbor.

Not so the Brits. About the time the *Seer*'s sonarmen were going home, the lieutenant commander who had promised to "attend to it" came aboard, rolled up his sleeves, and dug into the radar himself. It was nearly 2300, when (my journal for that date records) "Oh happy sight, targets were beginning to appear beautifully on both screens and the gear was working again." In celebration we had the officer in the wardroom for conversation and coffee, and coffee for his men aft where Charlie Casey entertained them in his good-humored, earthy, down-home Alabamese. If there was a communication problem, no one mentioned it. We were very grateful for the long hours of hard, skilled work those Brits had put in, but had we known what the immediate future would bring, we would have been more grateful still.

The second of May arrived with wind and rain. The *Seer*'s people came back early and worked all morning, finally getting the sonar into marginal working condition before having to return to their ship to get under way. At 1224 in a light drizzle and a howling wind, the 692 and her sisters stood out from under the shadow of the Rock to screen the big boys as they sortied in single file. In the 692 the feet of most of the crew were visible through an assortment of makeshift footwear.

It took the better part of three hours for the LSTs and LCIs to get clear and form up on the base course that would take them and us into the bitterly contested Mediterranean. In the 692 the watch was changing for the 16–18 when all was in order, the gray bulk of Gibraltar fading into the drizzle astern.

This force was a junior version of the one we had come to know so well between Bermuda and Gibraltar. It was considerably broader across the front than deep, with nine columns of three LSTs each, the ungainly *Pepperwood* taking the place of the third LST in one column and the seven LCIs making the fourth ships in the middle columns. Commander Block as screen commander in the *Seer* had the lead escort position, eight thousand yards ahead, with a PC on each side and the two YMSs on the convoy's port and starboard beams. YMS 69 had the port beam, which we noted with care, since after the failure of our refrigerator she had been kind enough to store our fresh meat in hers. Appropriately on this operation her assigned voice radio call was "Steak." Another AM, the *Sentinel,* held station astern of the port YMS, matched to starboard by a PC. The three SCs screened the stern sectors with the 534 on the port quarter, the 535 directly astern, and the 692 on the starboard quarter. All escorts were eight thousand yards, or four miles, from the nearest ships of the convoy.

In the 692 this screening plan found whole-hearted approval, since it put her in position to keep the convoy always in sight ahead and able to respond appropriately to scheduled and unscheduled turns and yet be outside the massed wakes that masked any sonar echoes. The danger of being rammed by the ponderous big ships was minimal, and our proximity to the 535 allowed for unofficial consultations and joint action should that be required.

But the 692's station assignment was the only good thing that happened to her on that first day in the Med. The weather was foul, with a nasty, high, breaking sea, which is the worst kind for a ship of her size. All afternoon she stood first on her bullnose and then on her fantail, shaking the green water off her decks and hurling it up over the radar antenna. And the heavy black clouds stacked up ahead promised no relief any time soon.

About 1900, just as it was beginning to get dark, we got our first taste of the war in the ancient Mediterranean. Without signal or warning, the *Seer*, far out ahead and eight miles away but plainly visible, turned hard to port and raced across the front of the force laying down a pattern of big, 600-pound charges. Even at that distance the deck jumped under our feet as the water hammers hit the hull.

Before there was any chance to figure out what was happening, whether an attack was in progress by a wolf pack or a lone sub, whether an emergency turn had been ordered (a logical possibility), the 692 went mute and motionless. Almost with the booming of the first *Seer* depth charge both generators fell off the line, and before control could be shifted to the engine room, both main engines stopped. The sudden silence and loss of forward motion at the first moment of danger was heart-stopping. The sonar died in mid-ping. The radar screens went dark. Lights on engine instruments and the steering compass winked out, and as the ship lost way the helm became mushy, threatening to drop us into the trough of the angry sea.

In the engine room the watch worked fast by emergency lighting and the engines quickly came back to life and throttled up to eight hundred turns, more than enough for steering control. The 692 returned to base course in an instant, but it took a long and uncomfortable ten minutes to get the generators back on the line, minutes with no contact with the screen or the convoy and therefore with no knowledge on which to base our own actions except what we could see. We could tell that the convoy had changed course forty-five degrees to starboard and we followed.

With power restored we blinked over to the 535 for news but they had heard nothing by radio and were as much in the dark (although not as literally) as we were. We found out later that the *Seer* had acquired a good echo, attacked, lost it, and continued on. Why she didn't stay and prosecute the contact, or detail another ship to do so, remains a mystery.

Fortunately for the comfort of all the little ships plunging eastward into the Med that evening, the wind and sea subsided to acceptable levels as darkness fell. But when darkness finally came it was total. With a low overcast obscuring even starlight, it was the blackest night imaginable. A hundred times before daylight we blessed those British technicians at Gibraltar, because the radar was our only eye and with it we maintained position and patrolled our assigned sector as though visibility had been unlimited.

Apparently that was not the case for the 535. When dawn broke she was nowhere to be seen. Prent Horne, the self-styled old master, was lost. About ten o'clock he came straggling up over the horizon astern and slipped quietly into station, obviously nursing the illusion that he had not been missed. In a saintly exercise of restraint, the USS SC 692 permitted that illusion to remain intact, at least while we both remained at sea.

According to navigational data distributed at the Gibraltar conference, we were due at Nemours at 1700. Our own plot showed our ETA to be a couple of hours earlier. So about 1430 the 12-inch light was just beginning to clatter out a message requesting permission to make the YMS 69 and retrieve our fresh meat, when, without the pre-arranged signal, the two LSTs for Nemours peeled off to starboard and headed for the coast, whose high, rolling green hills had been in sight all day.

There was nothing to do but sacrifice the meat and form the three SCs into a screen around the landing craft for the short run to port. In the lead of that little formation, with the two LSTs wallowing astern, the 534 on the starboard flank, and the 535 to port, the 692 approached the first of many ports she would make along the northern coast of Africa.

The circumstances of our arrival were symbolic of conditions in the port. About two miles from the breakwater an LCVP came roaring up alongside, bearing an ensign who carried himself like an admiral, and a signalman. The ensign ordered curtly through a megaphone, "Follow me in!" We explained with careful patience that we would be screening the LSTs as they entered and would follow them in. At that the ensign/admiral registered total amazement. "Oh!" he shouted up. "Are they coming in too?" When we confirmed, he churned off hurriedly in pursuit of the LSTs, the blunt little boat bouncing and throwing white water in all directions.

In due course our charges passed inside the small harbor and it was our turn to enter. As in most ports on this almost harborless coast, shipping was sheltered by a long breakwater circling out from shore south and then west to join, except for the gap that forms the entrance, a pier making straight out from the land. At the end of that pier in those days was a single 40-mm identical to the one on our own foredeck, but camouflaged, sandbagged, and manned around the clock. As we passed close aboard, the army gun captain hollered over, "Go to Condition One! Red alert!"

Since it is not possible to man battle stations on such a small ship and have men left over to bring her alongside, we settled for a careful watch of the sky and went to GQ as soon as the lines were over, which was at 1530. We could have saved ourselves the trouble. There were four more red alerts that afternoon, but no enemy appeared, and we quickly adopted the policy of manning the guns when and if enemy planes actually appeared. It was our first adjustment to the basically fouled-up nature of the place.

Nemours was a sleepy, dusty little town at the foot of high, bare coastal hills, inhabited, it seemed, by a few well-dressed Frenchmen and a great many native Arabs in badly soiled burnooses and heelless sandals that the American sailors promptly labeled "go-aheads." Its primary excuse for existence was the railroad, which ran along the waterfront and which had made the town a coaling and fueling station. The docks were cordoned off with concertina wire, but plainly visible close across the wire was the local version of Main Street, with a few shops and a café with tables out on the grimy sidewalk, which we quickly learned sold "vin blanc," "vin rouge," and "muscatel," all three of grossly inferior quality. In the hills above the town was an encampment of U.S. Army Rangers and a small unit of British troops. The small U.S. Navy detachment operated out of a row of barrackslike wooden sheds just back from the docks.

In addition to intelligence about the local café (the "Cercle Civil"), we learned, first, that we were to be allowed four days for rest and repairs after the long voyage; second, that the three SCs would then be operating out of Nemours for a while under the command of Commander Block of the *Seer;* and last, that there was no mail and no immediate prospect of any.

With the radar working and the sonar marginally, our priority in Nemours was shoes. It was there that the practical procurement policy developed that stood the ship in good stead throughout the Mediterranean. It developed quite naturally. I sent Washer to the naval base with a list of sizes to draw thirty pairs of shoes. He reported that the base had none to spare but he did manage to acquire enough one-piece army fatigue uniforms to outfit all hands. He was next dispatched up the hill to the Rangers, who were sympathetic but unable to help since what spares they had would be needed badly in their next march, presumably on foot. The British next door were as kind as always and genuinely wanted to assist but were worse off and had the same requirements as the Rangers.

No shoes. But there had to be an answer. Even a naval unit as lowly and junior as a wooden SC with thirty men commanded by a reserve jaygee should not be expected to fight the war barefoot. In desperation a scouting party was sent out under Charlie Casey for an unofficial check of warehouses, supply tents, and stock yards. Within an hour Casey was back. On a railroad siding adjacent to the docks he had located an entire *boxcar* of shoes.

This bonanza, we thought, must have been overlooked by the base support people whom Washer had contacted. He went back over and was told rather brusquely that those shoes were strictly for "base personnel," a classic example of a base established to support operating forces subordinating its mission to the support of itself.

A brief council of war was held in the wardroom and afterward appropriate oral orders were issued.

At the stroke of eight bells to begin the mid watch, a detail of ten men left the 692. They were dressed in the newly issued army fatigues and the olive-drab liners of their battle helmets. The man in charge, a reserve jaygee wearing no insignia of rank, carried a rifle with fixed bayonet. With military precision, the detail marched down the dock, stopped briefly at a utility shed to pick up a couple of wheelbarrows, and continued across the main tracks to the railroad siding and Casey's boxcar. The car was unlocked and Casey jumped up with a flashlight and the list of sizes. Hawn and Fields swung up behind him and the wheelbarrows were lined up at the door. The man with the rifle stood at parade rest adjacent to the scene of action as security for the detail. As Casey called out sizes, his shipmates located the appropriate boxes and passed them down to the wheelbarrows, two each of every size, sixty pairs of rugged, regulation high-topped new shoes.

In ten minutes the job was done, with hardly a dent made in the carload. The detail, in proper cadence, and except for the loaded wheelbarrows, looking like a squad on parade, marched smartly back across the tracks and down the dock to the 692, where they fell out and carried their cargo aboard. The two wheelbarrows were returned and the operation was over.

A pragmatic precedent of procurement had now been established. "Try the Navy. Try the Army. Try the British. Liberate." And for the final step, Charlie Casey had earned a new rating: "Chief Thief."

With all feet at last suitably shod, we took advantage of our opportunities to enjoy the warm North African spring and recharge our energies after all those weeks at sea. Liberty was normally granted from 1300 to 1900 and the primary activity during those afternoons was softball in a small informal league made up of the 692, 535, 534 and the *Seer*. With rare exceptions every officer and man on every ship took part at one time or another. The sights and sounds of the American sandlot diamond, the baseball chatter, and good-natured vocal

"Ever-willing, affable, sociable, and multifarious Charlie Casey," mechanic, welder, cook, and "Chief Thief" when the occasion demanded, in a formal pose just before joining the 692 and becoming motor machinist's mate first class. (C. D. Casey)

abuse—so out-of-place and anachronistic on that parched and antique coast—were nostalgic and touching, bringing thoughts of home.

Thanks almost entirely to the skilled pitching of Cleveland Hodge Ray, age eighteen, the 692's only mess attendant and only black, that little ship remains undefeated to this day. Ray was also the best lookout, quick, alert, and willing to take on any task assigned. The assignment of a mess attendant to an SC, especially in a combat area, was a nonsensical hangover from bigger ships in peacetime. After that special farewell luncheon in Key West, Ray was never again required to perform the duties of a steward: dishing up the officers' meals back in the galley; stowing them in a special shelved box with a handle on top; and transporting the box up the ladder from the galley, along the deck, and down the ladder into the wardroom where the meals were served. After Key West, Ray was incorporated into the crew as a valued watchstander who pulled more than his weight. And at softball he was a true champion.

One early May afternoon, Prent Horne and I buckled on our .45s and went exploring. We climbed to the top of the line of bluffs behind Nemours and from there could see the high coast stretching away to the eastward, the surf white on the steep shore and the blue Mediterranean spreading far away to the horizon. The country gave an impression of antiquity, of being worn out from millennia of use and war. We wondered if Hannibal had passed this way en route across the Straits and the Alps to Italy, or during his campaigns in North Africa. Here and all along that coast there was not a hill, however small, without at least the remnants of fortifications. The military value of high ground had apparently always been well known here.

On 7 May, while the men of the 692 were enjoying the last of their port relaxation, a decision was made that would affect their lives in the most direct and personal way. The Anglo-American high command selected the beaches across which would be launched the most massive invasion in the history of war.

When our four-day respite had passed, all four warships of the "Western Unit, Escort Sweeper Group, North African Waters" were ordered thirty miles eastward to another small breakwater port to take on fresh water, that at Nemours not being potable. The port was Beni Saf, a slightly larger version of Nemours, and the 692 would see a lot of it.

On this first Nemours–to–Beni Saf run, we were honored by the presence of Commander Block himself, Western Unit boss, who came aboard demanding to know whether we had a broad command pennant, his "flag," and was obviously displeased when he found we did not. For the entire passage of two and a half hours over a glassy, windless sea, he kept the three SCs busy with flag hoist drills, the bright flags soaring to the "dip," pausing for duplication and understanding by the other ships, rising to the "two-block" position, then plummeting to the deck for the "execute."

The 692's first visit to Beni Saf was less than auspicious. As we approached the docking area we were accosted by a stocky little officer with a megaphone who assigned us the worst berth imaginable for a small wooden ship, across the ends of two stone-and-steel-finger piers in a dead-end corner of the harbor. Then, no sooner were we there, after a certain amount of effort and some trepidation, than he changed his mind and ordered us to back down to another pier where he assured us there would be deeper water.

Five seconds after the order "Starboard back one third," we felt the starboard propeller bite into something, followed immediately by a vibration that rattled the decks under our feet. At least a bent blade and possibly a bent shaft, suffered while obeying instructions from this officer who was supposed to know the port! I could feel the color rising to my face and in the seconds it took to assert control I heard myself yelling something like "For Christ's sake! Do you know what you're doing? I've just bent a prop!" The man with the megaphone appeared not to hear, although my voice is not known for its softness. Which was just as well because he turned out to be one Commander Bell, the commander of the base at Beni Saf.

At the new berth we took on water to our full 1,600-gallon capacity and Morton checked the damage. It appeared that the shaft was okay. The effect of the bent blade would have to be determined under way.

There was not long to wait. The freshwater tanks had no more been filled than Commander Block came puffing down the dock with orders for all three ships to shove off at once for Nemours, where he would return to the *Seer* and lead us in a search for a submarine sighted eighty miles offshore. On the westward run we found that vibration from the damaged starboard prop occurred only at speeds around 900 RPM, an annoyance but one we could live with until repairs could be made.

We were alongside at Nemours for exactly ten minutes and then followed the *Seer* to seaward. The sun was just setting as the four ships formed a line of bearing and headed for the scene of the sighting. And as the sun went down, the wind and sea made up. The requirement to arrive at the sub's last reported position as quickly as possible forced us to drive at full speed through the rising seas directly into a gale-force north wind that turned out to be the ill-famed mistral, born of a sudden pouring of cold and heavy air down the steep slopes of the Maritime Alps and out across the sea, which has plagued Mediterranean sailors since the days of the Phoenicians.

The little task force arrived at the datum point in the middle of the mid watch and began an expanding square search that continued all night, all the next day, and the following night under the continuous lashing of the mistral. As in the worst days of the crossing, nearly all hands were wretchedly sick, exhausted from the need always to hold on hard and never to sleep properly, soaked and chilled while on watch and weary of cold food bolted with one hand. And never once during that time did one ship get one return echo from the continual pinging of four sonars. The sub's crew, as I conjectured in my journal, were "probably peacefully tied up alongside some quiet Italian dock, snickering, while we beat ourselves to death all over the Mediterranean."

It was nearly noon on 10 May when the 692 came to rest once more, starboard side to the 535 in Nemours. There an official letter was delivered designating the commanding officer of the USS SC 692 as "Commander Subchaser Section, Western Bases and Training Group." That evening Prent Horne and I tried to determine whether that entitled me to fly the broad command pennant that Commander Block had so badly wanted. "Subchaser Section, Western Bases and Training Group" comprised SCs 692, 535 and 534, commanded respectively by me, Prent Horne, and Tommy Lincoln, all lieutenants (junior grade) in their middle twenties.

Prent and Tommy presented a study in opposites. Prent, a graduate of Deerfield and Amherst, was bright, personable, conscientious, and thorough, although a reservist, as competent and competitive as any regular officer of his age and grade. Tommy, on the other hand, although likable enough, was casual to the point of carelessness, expending each day the minimum amount of effort required to get by.

On a chance visit to the pilothouse of the 534 shortly after arrival in Nemours, I was startled to find his bulky radio direction finder screwed down tightly in the middle of his chart table. "Jesus, Tommy," I asked, "where do you do your navigating?"

"What navigating?" was his matter-of-fact response. "We're always with a convoy or a bunch of other ships. Who needs to navigate?"

I thought immediately of the morning we had found ourselves alone on the face of the Atlantic and wondered if Tommy would ever have been seen again had he been in our place. I suggested in the strongest terms that he find another place for the RDF and break out his charts. But the 534 had already been stamped with her skipper's casual complacence and was never seen to change. Like her captain, she always got by, but she was always the slowest at flag hoists, semaphore, and flashing light; always just slightly out of position in formation; always the last to get the word and act on it.

With that futile antisub sweep began a full month of patrols, searches, and coastal escort runs along the shores of northwest Africa, while farther to the east, Anglo-American forces steadily built their strength for what even the men of the 692 could see would be a major assault on the underside of Adolf Hitler's Europe.

On 7 May, the last of the 692's four days off at Nemours, the last major Tunisian city, Bizerte, fell to the British, and on the thirteenth the last German soldiers in North Africa surrendered. It was apparent to the least informed bluejacket in those busy waters that a use would shortly be found for all the LSTs and LCIs with their shiploads of troops and weapons he had been shepherding across the Atlantic and screening along the coast. The questions in all our minds in those days were direct. Where would the assault take place? When? What would our job be when the big day came? There were of course no answers but plenty of conjectures. The consensus in the subchaser fleet seemed to be that it would take until September to get things in North Africa sufficiently organized to mount an assault, which would take place in October. Where? Sardinia had its champions, as did Corsica, Sicily, and Italy proper.

The guessing was easy and entertaining, but in the meantime there was work to do. Commander Block had established patrol lines ten miles long off both Nemours and Beni Saf. For eight nights, from sunset to sunrise, the 692 ran back and forth off Nemours, steering 075 and 255 degrees true. On one of those nights a tiny radar blip popped up a mile to the north. It had all the earmarks of a periscope: faint, appearing and disappearing. Almost gratefully after so much inaction the crew ran to battle stations. The diesels revved up to flank speed and the SC charged in to ram. Strangely, Senecal could get no sonar echo from the bearing of the blip, so the mousetraps were out, but the stern-dropped charges were set shallow, and in we came. Forward, the 40-mm was loaded with armor-piercing rounds and fully depressed, Gunner Walter and his crew straining their eyes into the darkness ahead for the first sign of a target. They saw nothing as we swept across the spot at 15 knots. But on the port 20-mm, Kapfer made out our target outlined close aboard in the white water of our wash. It was a drifting sonobuoy, its slim vertical antenna poking up to catch and reflect the radar beam. Suddenly let down from the tension of battle alert, the men secured from general quarters, established the regular steaming watch, and we swung around to pick up our "periscope" and returned it the next day to the sound matériel lab ashore.

On another night we observed suspicious lights moving and flashing along the coastal hills and reported them by radio for the Rangers to investigate. But that was as near as we came to action off Nemours. Three times for a total of six days we patrolled the coast from Nemours to Beni Saf and back with the PC 624, the senior PC in the area, commanded by a Lieutenant Commander Lowther and having aboard as gunnery officer a Dartmouth classmate and fraternity brother of mine from what seemed very long ago.

When not patrolling we screened groups of LCIs and the smaller

LCTs as they transited eastward between the two ports. Once we patrolled to seaward of a group of LCIs as they dropped their stern anchors, ran ashore, extended ramps on both sides of their bows, and practiced landing and reembarking troops.

It was the little LCTs that required the most tending. Each was in the charge of a reserve ensign, most of whom seemed to have been assigned without adequate training, at least in seamanship and navigation. Early one morning in May, the 692 was ordered out of Beni Saf on short notice to locate two LCTs that were several hours overdue on an overnight eastward run from Nemours. It was early afternoon before radar picked them up twenty miles north of their ordered track, churning purposefully along on a nearly northerly course that would, if maintained and their fuel held out, have taken them to the vicinity of the historic but unfriendly neutral port of Cartagena, Spain.

We pulled alongside the leading ship and provided the course and distance to Beni Saf, which was approximately one hundred degrees to the right of what the skipper was then steering. After a minute or two of startled disbelief, he swung around to the new course, the second craft splashing along in the leading LCT's broad wake. We cranked on turns and returned to port, leaving the LCTs to follow at their top speed of 8 knots.

The next day in Beni Saf I inquired as to how they got so far off course. I found out that the ensign in charge, the night dark with the coast lost to view, had decided to steer by the stars, a phrase he had read somewhere but had not entirely understood. Instead of picking out the essentially stationary North Star, in that latitude about a third of the way toward the zenith, and keeping it broad on his port bow to maintain the required northeasterly heading, he had simply picked a convenient but unidentified bright star dead ahead and kept his bow on it. As the star moved across the sky from east to west (as stars are wont to do), it pulled his bow around to the north before fading into the dawn, a course to which this ensign had steadfastly held until the 692 providentially arrived.

Out of those weeks of patrol, escort, and odd jobs in the western Mediterranean, out of the pragmatic realities of the duties assigned us thus far, where the few friendly subs transited in well-advertised moving "sanctuaries" and operated in closely defined areas, the 692 developed her own equally pragmatic doctrine for dealing with a hostile submarine should the need ever arise. It was derived from the rather daunting knowledge that any German or Italian sub we might encounter would, once she surfaced, be able to both outgun and outrun us. We would therefore have to use the tactics of a short, stocky boxer matched against a quick, long-armed puncher, staying inside and hitting hard and often.

Ideally we would acquire sonar contact in time to attack with mousetraps. Even one mousetrap hit, firing on contact, would be likely to force the sub to the surface before she flooded and sank. But since in practice we seldom obtained a sonar range of more than five hundred yards, very close for an effective mousetrap attack, we would most likely have time only to turn toward the contact, make a quick estimate of her course and speed and lay down a pattern of stern-dropped charges. If we were lucky, that too would bring the enemy to the surface, at which point everything would depend on quick, close-in aggressive action on our part. The 692 would close to point-blank range, our "main battery," the 40-mm, pumping armor-piercing rounds into the enemy pressure hull while the twenties swept his decks and prevented him from manning his own guns. All the while, we would be reporting the action, urgently requesting assistance. Since the success of those tactics, not to mention our own survival, depended on keeping the sub crew from their guns, we all agreed that the more firepower we could bring to bear, the better. Accordingly, Washer, as gunnery officer, was appointed to see about the acquisition and installation of a couple of light machine guns for mounting atop the pilothouse, where they could be manned by the two lookouts.

Although about half the hours during May were spent at sea on one job or another, the other half permitted limited activity ashore. Liberty and shore leave in Nemours and Beni Saf normally expired before dark for the safety and well-being of all concerned. Thus most activity was more or less wholesome and out-of-doors. Pleasant, secluded beaches lay within a short hike of both towns, and it was a pleasure to walk the rolling coastal hills, then wash off the dust in the clear, cool waters of the Mediterranean and dry off in the warm sun while theorizing as to the time, place, and outcome of the imminent invasion. The beach just southeast of Beni Saf was especially attractive, with little restaurants along the shore where you could walk in directly from the surf and enjoy a glass of white or red or muscatel or kirschino, none of them very good (in fact the red would invariably leave a powdery pink high-water mark when the glass was tipped) but welcome just the same. Washer and I walked over there a couple of times, but the real adventure was by sea with Charlie Casey.

The day was warm and bright and the little harbor calm, a good afternoon to row over in our eight-foot wooden pram, which the Seabees had made for us in Bermuda. As I was climbing down into the

The foredeck of an SC at general quarters with the 40-mm main battery manned and ready to fire. Just forward of the gun is the hatch to the forward crew's quarters, and forward of that the eight launching rails for her antisub mousetrap rockets. (National Archives)

pram from the fantail, Casey was leaving across the gangway for the same destination. I offered him a ride and after a moment's hesitation he accepted.

Outside the breakwater it was no longer calm, with perhaps four-foot waves over which the little pram rose and fell in a fairly dramatic fashion. But the waves were smoothly rounded and not breaking, which, I kept assuring Casey, would make for a perfectly safe passage. I could sense that Casey was not fully convinced.

We made a rather spectacular landing, riding a breaking sea in through the surf, jumped out, hauled the pram up above the line of wrack, weed, and driftwood that marked high water, and walked down the beach for a swim and a drink. Almost at once we acquired a third party, a ragged Arab boy who had six fresh eggs to trade. Casey, who to this day has never met a stranger, fell joyfully into the spirit of the bazaar, but the kid was a shrewd bargainer. First he wanted a cake of soap for his eggs, then half a cake and a pack of cigarettes. Finally he settled for a half a cake and three cigarettes and ran off in triumph. Cradling the six eggs, Casey joined a bunch of his shipmates on the porch of one of the restaurants, and after a dip in the surf so did I. Boats, Walter, Hoffner, and Rees were there, with the exception of Morton, pretty much the enlisted elite of the 692—the chief boatswain's mate, the leading gunner, a first-class machinist's mate, and the ship's cook.

Our departure after a glass of wine provided several minutes of rare entertainment for the assembled SC sailors. The shore break was running high and the pram was not designed as a surf boat. Three times the men ashore gleefully watched their CO and his passenger get swamped and ducked, haul the pram out, dump its load of water, and relaunch. On the fourth attempt, with Casey bailing vigorously, we made it, to sustained and raucous cheering from ashore. Miraculously, Casey's eggs remained intact.

Once clear of the breakers we found that the chop had built up to respectable dimensions and it was going to be a long row home. That problem was solved by a friendly French fisherman, who must have been more worried than we were. He insisted on taking us (and the pram) aboard his fifty-foot diesel trawler and deposited us safely in the placid waters inside the breakwater only a few yards from the ship. But for Casey our rescue had been a mixed blessing. The scramble from pram to trawler had also scrambled two of his closely guarded eggs.

Back aboard we found the galley packed with bushels of fresh fruits and vegetables, the product of a trading expedition to the hills behind the town led by Roy Washer. The price of all that luscious looking produce—two (soiled) cotton mattress covers.

At both Nemours and Beni Saf, rifle and pistol ranges had been set up, plenty of practice ammunition made available, and the ships' companies encouraged to improve their marksmanship, "just in case."

We all spent a lot of hours doing so and many qualified as "expert rifleman" and "expert pistol shot." As we learned in the first days at Nemours, softball contests between ships drew large numbers of enthusiastic and highly partisan participants and spectators, and the sport expanded and flourished with the arrival later in the month of additional convoys and their escorts.

But as in all wars and all times there were less salutary activities ashore than swimming, softball, and target practice. Both harbor towns swarmed with legions of skinny, dirty boys much like the small entrepreneur with whom Casey traded for his eggs. Their English consisted of phrases learned at the ungentle khaki-clad knees of recently arrived American tankers, Rangers, and infantrymen. One of their milder offerings was something that sounded like "shoeshinesonovabitchgoddam?" All spoken in one breath with an ingratiating rising inflection and grimy smile.

The problem was that they had more to sell than a shoeshine or a few eggs. They would sell anything, including their sisters, and often even the sisters of their friends and neighbors, with or without prior arrangements. An unwary sailor or GI, having paid his "agent" the negotiated price, would be led to the door of a particular shack or hut on the outskirts of town where his knock would coincide with the disappearance of his guide. Often the woman who opened the door would be a veiled and perfectly respectable wife and mother to whom (and to whose husband) the American's obvious expectation and intent were quite unwelcome. Blood was shed and some lives were lost in this way before warnings got around and action was taken by those in authority.

One of the actions taken—unwritten, unofficial, anonymous, but realistic and effective in its time and place—was to set up in each town a "GI House." A score or so of prostitutes from Oran or Algiers were bused in, examined for communicable diseases, and if found healthy established in the house. Then a traffic pattern was set up. An entering customer was required to register and pay at a desk manned by a serviceman on duty. Opposite his name was entered the name of the woman he would visit, in case of problems later. He was issued a condom and given fifteen minutes. The only exit after his time was up was through a lavatory of sorts where he was required to give himself a prophylactic treatment under the supervision of an on-duty medical corpsman who logged him out by name and rate.

Insensitive, mechanical, animalistic, degrading. But a line of one hundred men stretching around the block in the blasting North African sun was not unusual. And with MPs and shore patrol enforcing the closure of all other known similar establishments, the VD rate plummeted to near zero.

Only one incident marred the success of this innovative concept during the stay of the 692 in those waters. A burly sailor from a PC docked at Beni Saf, made impatient and combative by a quart or so of the terrible local vin rouge, worked his long way through the line, paid and registered, and then, perhaps because of his semi-inebriation and his brutish appearance, was at the last moment refused. What followed was ten minutes of astonishing violence that can only be described as a one-man riot. The PC sailor knocked the woman cold with a single punch and then threw all the room's scant furnishings out of the second-story window and into the street, without opening the window. The few pieces too large for the casement he quickly made small enough. When the room was bare he kicked down the light partition and went to work on the one adjoining. When two SPs rushed up the narrow stairs to restore the peace he threw them both back down again. It took a four-man detail with billy clubs to subdue and lead him away to the brig, still struggling and cursing at his captors and the world.

Fortunately, given the opportunities for trouble ashore, far more time was spent by the 692's crew aboard and at sea. Three nights out of four the ship patrolled the familiar courses off one or the other of the two ports or ran down the long track between them. Days under way were spent on ship's work and various drills to sharpen skills, help the crew, and prepare as best we could for whatever the future held.

One calm afternoon motoring eastward leisurely five miles offshore—radar, sonar, and lookouts searching the empty sea and sky—I rashly decided to lend a little realism to the drills that were beginning to become routine. Tony Curato, the striker I had noticed working on the twenties on my first visit to the ship, now a rated gunner's mate, was forward, greasing the heavy recoil springs of the 40-mm. He was shirtless and sweating in the sun, since the only breeze was provided by the 8 knots of the ship's own passage. I knew Tony was a strong swimmer and I walked around to where he was working. In a voice no one else could hear I asked him how he would like to go for a swim. He knew from my tone that something was up and the plan was concluded in less than a minute. A few moments later, back on the bridge where Chief Murphy was rather lackadaisically handling the duties of OOD, I casually removed my cap and scratched the back of my head. Instantly from up forward there came a heavy splash, followed at once by the genuinely alarmed shout of the port lookout, "Man overboard! Man overboard! It's Curato!"

Boats came instantly alive and looked inquiringly at me but when I showed no intention of taking over, he swung into action. "Left full rudder!" he ordered, swinging the stern and the dangerous port prop away from the man in the water. "Man overboard! Man overboard!" he yelled fore and aft, sending the men topside scurrying to their stations, then perhaps remembering the famous message at Pearl Harbor, "This is no drill!" (Only Curato and I knew it really was.) From the depth-charge station aft a life ring flopped into the water near Tony, who was beginning to swim in any easy circle, enjoying himself in the clean, cool blue water.

Expertly Boats brought the ship around in a tight circle to port, slowed, and stopped with Tony about twenty yards abeam. Charlie Nader had rigged and released the Jacob's ladder so that the bottom rung was well below the surface. I was congratulating myself on the realism of the exercise and the crew's swift, professional completion of the drill, when I noticed that Curato was no longer stroking in easy circles but making for the Jacob's ladder in desperate haste, his arms slashing the water and his feet kicking up a wake like a PT boat. Then, with a gasp of horrified disbelief, I saw why.

Out beyond Tony, perhaps another fifty yards, a tall, triangular dorsal fin was cutting through the water, throwing a little spray, and leaving a line of froth astern. It was headed straight for the crewman I had ordered into the water for a drill. There was no time to grab the rifle we used to guard against sharks at a planned swimming call. It was down in the pilothouse. I should have thought of that.

There was no time for anything but watching the final seconds of the race between man and shark. Big Charlie Nader and equally husky Curt Christman were at the head of the ladder yelling encouragement and reaching down to grab. Curato's face was a pale mask of terror and the muscles in his back and arms corded as he dug with all his strength at the water. He never touched the ladder. Nader and Christman grabbed his arms and jerked him out of the sea as though he weighed 15 pounds instead of 150. His feet had barely hit the deck when the fin slashed past the foot of the ladder and we could see the deadly, streamlined shape of the ten-foot shark, half over on its side as it turned away and vanished beneath the surface, robbed of a sure meal.

I don't know who felt worse when that drill was over, the gunner's mate who almost lost his life, or the captain who had needlessly put him at risk. As commanding officer, it would have been my duty to explain to his next of kin. What would I have written? "Dear Mrs. Curato, I regret to inform you of the death of your son, Anthony. I told him to jump overboard and a shark ate him." Or this? "Dear Mrs.

Curato, I regret to inform you of the death of your son, Anthony, in the line of duty. At my order he was bravely acting as a man-overboard dummy and a shark bit him in half." More than four decades later the events of those moments are as clear in both our memories as the day they happened. There were no further realistic drills in the SC 692.

In one welcome break toward the end of May the SC broke out of the patrol routine for a run, in company with the *Seer*, to the major Algerian port of Oran, some sixty miles east of Beni Saf. It was the biggest city the crew had seen since Gibraltar, with the French naval base of Mers el-Kébir adjacent. The point of the visit was to check on mail for the Nemours–Beni Saf ships; we had received no mail and no pay for weeks.

No mail and no pay materialized, but a benefit for me came of that port call. Rounding the port side of the pilothouse from the fo'c'sle the next morning, the twenty-third, I found an old and good friend standing between the 20-mm guns, inquiring for me of the gangway watch. He was George Steele, a classmate during my one year at the Naval Academy and again at the Reserve Midshipman's School in the USS *Prairie State* in New York, where we were commissioned together on 16 September 1941. I had not seen him since that day, and I quickly learned that I was lucky to be seeing him at all. While I had been languishing for a year as an instructor aboard the *Prairie State* and at the Officers Indoctrination School at Newport, George had been out fighting the war from the deck of a destroyer in the Pacific. About the time I joined the 692, George's destroyer was torpedoed in a night battle off the Solomons and later sank. He was rescued, sent home on sixty-days leave, then to PT boat school at Melville, Rhode Island. He was now skipper of a PT, the 215, which had been deck-loaded to Gibraltar, then run on her own bottom with the rest of her motor torpedo boat squadron (MTBron 15) to Oran en route to Bizerte, where the squadron would be based.

As we parted, George presented the ship with a huge box of chocolate bars and allowed that we would probably meet again "up the line a ways." He didn't know how right he was, or how far up the line, or how hairy the circumstances would be. The 692 arrived back in familiar Beni Saf and tied up alongside the PC 556 at 1710 that same day.

At the end of May, preparatory to the coming action (whenever and wherever that would be), higher authority decided that the time had come to repair the 692's starboard propeller, damaged three weeks before by the misdirections of the base commander at Beni Saf. The decision was the easy part of an operation that extended over two weeks and eighty miles of the North African coast.

We would be hauled on a marine railway at Beni Saf used to haul the fishing trawlers that worked the coast in peacetime. But we had a problem. We would have to get our draft aft down to three and a half feet, the depth of water at the submerged end of the tracks. Our normal draft at the stern was seven feet. To the SC's three officers, none of us engineers, the requirement appeared impossible to meet. But we had been trained to follow orders and to have confidence in the judgment of our seniors (in this case commander, Western Bases and Training Group; commander, Beni Saf; and a lieutenant in the Civil Engineer Corps who was his resident expert). So all hands, including the three officers, turned to with a will to transfer all movable heavy objects from all the way aft to all the way forward. We emptied the crammed lazaret, manhandled two dozen 300-pound depth charges the length of the ship, pumped all after fuel and water tanks empty and those forward full. A mobile crane from the base drove up alongside and lowered two gigantic two-ton propellers onto the fo'c'sle. Then we checked the draft at the stern. It read five feet eight inches.

The powers that be consulted again and decided to try to haul us anyway. It took a solid week of all-day efforts by highly vocal mixed gangs of Frenchmen and Arabs to get the cradle under our stern, during which it broke and was repaired twice. Cables snapped and others wrapped themselves around the propellers of LCVPs pressed into service as tugs. Finally, amid urgent pleas by the 692's CO, whose ship was at risk, the project was declared a failure.

The logical next step, it seemed to the worn and frustrated crew of the SC, would be to send us to Oran, where we had observed a commodious, fully operational dry dock. But that was not the official decision. Nemours also had a marine railway, reportedly somewhat more capable. We were to try again there. So back down the now familiar coast steamed the little SC, light at the stern and down by the bow where lashed tarpaulins covered a ten-foot pile of assorted heavy gear that reduced the 40-mm's field of fire to broad on either beam. It was well that the sea was calm and the enemy elsewhere.

At Nemours it was refreshing to find a cool and logical expert after the prolonged fiasco of the week before. He was only an ensign but he knew his business. He looked the ship over carefully, made a few quick measurements aboard and ashore, and declared that it would be a waste of time and labor even to try to haul us. A message to that effect clattered out to Beni Saf, and a response ordering us to Oran came swiftly back. Joyfully we got rid of the huge propellers, stowed the rest of the gear back where it belonged, and shoved off, back in proper trim and at our best speed.

On Friday afternoon, 4 June, the 692 steamed slowly down the long harbor at Oran—lined on both sides by freighters, warships, tugs, barges, and cranes—and backed carefully into the flooded dry dock, already occupied by the SCs 691 and 530. She was just in time. As soon as we were in place, big pumps began to thump and by 1530 the ship was resting high and dry on her blocks on the bottom of the dock. The wonder was that it all happened so fast, given the swarms of workmen and the dozens of bosses all yelling in French at the same time.

The 692 was dry-docked for a week. The work accomplished could have been done in two days but the other two ships had more. The ship's force ground a few small nicks out of the blades of the damaged prop and scraped, cleaned, and refinished her bottom with antifouling paint—a hard, messy, malodorous job. Washer came up with a couple of Hotchkiss .303-caliber machine guns for the bridge, with several cases of ammunition and one stand. They were very rapid-fire guns and when installed would add significantly to the SC's ability to keep a sub's decks clear while the 40-mm punched holes in her hull.

That week in the dock had both its advantages and its disadvantages. For the first time since Bermuda and the one-day stop in Gibraltar, the crew found themselves in a fair-sized modern city with restaurants, bars, and movies, and half were allowed ashore each evening. With the exception of a couple of false alarm GQs, all hands could and did sleep well all night.

Even more important to the morale of the SC's men, the mail finally caught up with us. There were bundles of letters, both conventional and V-Mail, and even a few packages very much the worse for their long journey and rough handling. One of the packages was for me and in it my thoughtful mother had included a pint bottle of Listerine antiseptic, presumably in case her son were to catch a cold.

There was also one treasured letter from my wife, acutely welcome but disappointingly solitary after all that time. Not so for Roy Washer. He must have had twenty or thirty, one for each day since we had left the States, each with a pink mouthprint in lipstick on the back. He luxuriated in the quantity, and spent some time sorting the letters according to their postmark dates. For an hour after I had memorized mine, I watched as he lay in his bunk in his skivvies with those letters lined up in order beside him, reading and smiling, until sheer, uncontrollable envy drove me up on deck.

On the negative side, the U.S. First Division was in town, fresh from the front in Tunisia, and crowded most of the restaurants and bars with khaki. A sailor pretty much had to take what was left. Aboard, fresh water was in short supply and of course the heads could not be used. To wash or brush your teeth meant standing in line at a water tap at the bottom of the dock. A visit to the head, unless you didn't mind going public, involved a hot and dusty mile-long hike through the busy traffic of the waterfront.

One memorable evening in Oran I took time out from the 692 for a brief visit to another planet. A friend from training days, now flag lieutenant to an admiral, came aboard for dinner and then invited me back to the quarters he shared with his boss. It was on the fourth floor of a first-class apartment house on Front-de-Mer, the hilltop, seafront avenue overlooking the harbor. There were thick Moroccan rugs; deep comfortable chairs; a big new radio with perfect tone playing lovely, familiar music; a sea chest stocked with the best of Scotches, bourbons and blends; and three mess boys to keep the place in order. We sat around and drank the admiral's whiskey and shot the breeze all evening. He practically had to throw me out at 0100.

Throughout the 692's stay in dry dock, LST after LST stood in from the eastward, their decks packed solid with prisoners of war, both German and Italian. As could be expected they were rumpled and unshaven, the Germans sullen and taciturn, the Italians smiling and loquacious. Some remained aboard under guard, others were loaded into trucks and halftracks, standing jammed together in the heat and the dust, and driven away. Although there was not much opportunity for conversation as the ragged POWs filed down the ramps of the LSTs and climbed up into the trucks, some of the Italians spoke a little English, and Tony Curato spoke fluent Sicilian. Between the two, the men of the 692 learned to their surprise that the Japanese had landed in California and were on the march toward Washington, D.C., and that both that city and New York were little more than smoking piles of rubble from repeated heavy bombings by the German Luftwaffe.

But the course of the war was not entirely one-sided. While the 692 was more or less safely in dry dock in Oran and her crew enjoying liberty in the ancient city, men were dying at sea not very far away, in waters to which the SC herself was shortly bound. On the day of the subchaser's arrival in Oran, PC 496 was entering the swept channel into Bizerte as an escort for a group of landing craft. Her skipper, who had been on his bridge most of the night, was in his bunk, the XO at the conn. At 1300 an exploding mine tore open the whole after third of the 173-foot steel ship. By the time the CO, a young man who moved fast, could get to the bridge, the PC was already tilting over in a fifty-degree list to starboard with the port shaft and propeller, bent ninety degrees from normal, extending grotesquely up into the air and the aft deck opened as though by a can opener. There was nothing left to do but order abandon ship, and three minutes after the explosion the PC went down stern first. The SC 639 picked up fifty-three survivors and the SC 638 recovered another seven of the crew of sixty men and five officers. Five men died in the blast of the mine.

With our relative liberty in Oran ended, early on the morning of 11 June the big valves were opened, the sea sluiced into the dock, and at 0755 the three SCs were once again most welcomely afloat. On the short run westward around the point to the naval base at Mers el-Kébir (MEK) we determined that the vibration of the starboard prop for which we had been docked was there precisely as before. But since it still occurred only in the immediate vicinity of 900 RPM we simply avoided that particular setting and lived with the problem.

The temporary duty of the 692 at the Western Bases (everything west of Oran) provided a kind of transition between peace and war, although, of course, the whole world was technically at war. West of Oran, nevertheless, the enemy's presence was either nonexistent or minimal from the limited perspective of the SC's crew. In the spring of 1943, while we were sloshing at 8 knots across the Atlantic Ocean, the Axis armies in North Africa were being cut up, captured, and pushed by the Allies into a final pocket where the Tunisian coast reaches northward as though grasping for the shores of Sicily. On the twelfth of May, while the 692 was patrolling off Beni Saf, the last units of the redoubtable Afrika Korps surrendered and came riding down out of the wooded hills of Cape Bon in three lanes of tanks, trucks, scout cars, and half-tracks to give themselves up. The long, bloody, back-and-forth struggle for the control of North Africa was over.

Although an occasional U-boat or Italian sub no doubt lurked offshore and an occasional long-range plane scouted and took pictures, the threat of enemy action was not serious. East of Oran, nearer to enemy bases in Sardinia and Sicily, it was different. After her week in dry dock in Oran, the SC 692 never turned her bow back to the westward. Her men had seen the last of Nemours and Beni Saf and no tears were noticeable among them. The gathering momentum of the war was now to the east, and with scores of other SCs, PCs, AMs, and YMSs, that was the way she went.

The day after leaving the dock, orders came to load fuel and water to capacity plus provisions for thirty days and be ready for sea by the following evening, the thirteenth. In the ensuing hours not only were those orders carried out but two thousand additional rounds were procured for the new bridge machine guns and two large drums of lube oil brought aboard for the main engines. The always helpful British, this time aboard the repair ship *Vindictive* moored just astern, designed, manufactured, and installed pipe stops (which we had been trying to get from our own people since Norfolk) for the three 20-millimeters to prevent them from accidentally firing into each other or the bridge or pilothouse.

The *Vindictive* had a lot of countrymen in Mers el-Kébir, including the new battleship *King George V*, the big carrier *Formidable* with her armored flight deck, and half a dozen mean-looking Royal Navy destroyers. The British felt right at home in MEK. It was there three years before that the carrier *Ark Royal* and five battlewagons had stood off the breakwater and methodically smashed up the French battleships *Bretagne, Dunkerque, Strasbourg,* and several heavy destroyers to prevent their possible use by the Axis powers. At 1330 on Sunday, the thirteenth, Lieutenant Commander R. D. Lowther, the skipper of the PC 624 and senior escort CO, called a conference of the commanding officers of all small escorts present. We met in the PC 624, which was moored to the rusting hulk of one of the wrecked French destroyers. The information he gave us cast a beam of light one full week into the future, the longest distance we had been able to see ahead since arriving in the Med. We would get under way early Wednesday morning, he said, destination Algiers, 220 miles east, for three days of amphibious training and practice. Beyond that everything was classified. But it did not require a Phi Beta Kappa key to figure out that the real thing could be expected to follow the practice as promptly as possible in order to derive the maximum benefit from the training.

Even the enemy appeared to know what was up. That evening "Axis Sally," after her usual ranting about this being "a Jewish war but a Gentile's fight" and how sorry she was for the poor U.S. sailors and GIs, all of whose wives and girls back home were being unfaithful, concluded with "Come on, you Churchevelts, with your long-promised invasion! Europe is ready and waiting to give you a lesson you will never forget." Even usually mild-mannered, soft-spoken Charlie Coffey muttered uncharacteristically that he hoped she would be "on the beach to get that crammed down her goddam throat!"

The next morning at 0200 a red alert sounded. Air raid sirens shrieked and in all the ships men ran to battle stations. Unfortunately almost all the closely nested ships also fired up their engines. The result was a rising cloud of smoky haze, which at once obscured the sky for the gunners and provided a point of aim to enemy airmen, had any been around. Luckily no planes appeared and the all clear was announced at 0230.

As the sun was setting on the fourteenth of June, *King George* and *Formidable* got ponderously under way, stood down the harbor and out to sea behind a businesslike crescent of destroyers, the famed white ensign of the Royal Navy dramatically evident on every ship.

Tuesday would be the last day in Oran, and the little ship was busy running around the harbor to top off with fuel and water. The fuel came from the LST 380, whose cordial skipper invited me to dinner. It was an invitation I later regretted declining because the 380's CO turned out to be Marcus Goodrich, the author of *Delilah,* one of the great sea stories of this century. Water we got from the *Cardium,* a British tanker with a Chinese crew. Back at our berth, the obliging Brits from the *Vindictive* delivered the stand they had manufactured for our second Hotchkiss machine gun; and Casey, Hoffner, and Gunner Walter immediately installed it and mounted the two guns, despite an increasing northeast wind and sea that set the ship to rolling even behind the shelter of the breakwater. The 692's last official act in Oran was to deliver a letter to the CO of the *Vindictive* thanking him for all the good work done for us in such a prompt, expert, and friendly way. A copy was posted and drew the enthusiastic concurrence of the SC's entire crew.

At 0626 on the sixteenth, the last line came back aboard from the LCI 193, to whose port side the SC had been moored, and she was under way for Algiers. Like Nemours and Beni Saf, Oran and MEK were ports her men would never see again. Six escorts ran eastward in two columns at 10 knots to pick up forty LSTs and LCIs at Arzew just down the coast to the east. The AM *Steady* with the officer in tactical command (OTC) led one column with the SCs 692 and 690 astern. PC 624, LCDR Lowther, headed the other, trailed at intervals of five hundred yards by PCs 621 and 627. The *Steady* held flag hoist and formation drills all the way, the little ships curving around on cue to form echelons, lines of bearing, lines abreast, and a single column. After the weeks in port it was good to feel the deck lift under your feet, read the bright flags as they soared and dropped, to feel the rudder bite, the stern swing, and see the gray ships slashing the blue sea in perfect order.

Off Arzew the 692 was detached and ran in to lie off the breakwater to count and check off the numbers of the LSTs and LCIs as they came chugging out, their blunt bows pushing at the seas and their flags snapping in the wind. Two were missing and we could see why; they were broadside and aground on the beach just west of the harbor, the surf crashing against their sides and spouting into the air. A tug was in attendance and it looked as though they would get off okay since the beach was just soft sand and the sea moderate. But we couldn't wait. The other ships formed up in columns, the screen fell in around them, and the 624 set course for Algiers, speed 9 knots, the escorts patrolling station at 10. In those increasingly dangerous waters the SCs and PCs were at Condition II, half the crew on watch, half the weapons manned, four hours on and four off. Boats and I stood one watch, Charlie and Wash the other.

That night it was almost a pleasure to be on the bridge. The moon was well up in the sky ahead and nearly full before the sun set, flaming red, astern at 2130. It never turned really dark. The moon was bright on the water and the convoy easily visible to the naked eye at four thousand yards. The high, irregular coastal hills loomed clearly six or eight miles to starboard. Toward evening a PBY and two Spitfires appeared overhead and circled protectively for a couple of hours. Light began to appear in the eastern sky at 0530, and as the east brightened, the moon settled to the western horizon as though the watch had been relieved and it was turning in.

At 0600 the approach to Algiers began, the landing craft forming into first two and then a single column to enter port, the escorts in a semicircle to seaward pinging away, radars sweeping the surface, lookouts on alert, and the ready guns manned and trained out. The 692 entered and was tied up port side to the 694 by 1100. At 1600 we were ordered to shift berth and moored in a nest of other SCs along the starboard side of the British light cruiser *Sirius*. A few yards away was our own light cruiser the *Savannah* with the *Steady* and the PCs alongside. We felt very secure. In case of an attack, the nests of little ships would be protected by eight 5-inch/25s and twenty 40-millimeters on the *Savannah,* and ten 5.3s and numerous pom-poms on the *Sirius*. Our agreed tactic would be to "lay low" and let the cruisers do the shooting.

As soon as we were tied up, Casey and stocky, phlegmatic, but always willing deckhand Howard Ridgeway rowed the pram up to the head of the slip and brought her back loaded with fresh produce, courtesy again of our British allies. In the evening half a dozen 692 sailors enjoyed a "cinema" in the British ship.

The first full day in Algiers was eventful for the SC's crew. Casey visited in the *Sirius* in the morning and as usual made a lot of friends. As a direct result a leaking muffler on the port engine was spot welded,

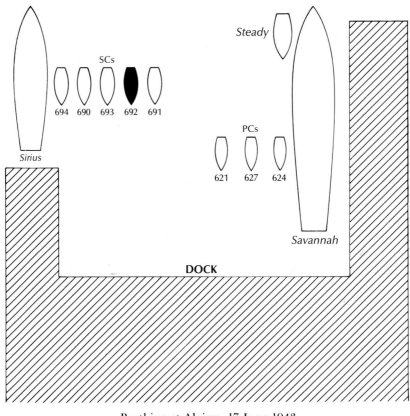

Berthing at Algiers, 17 June 1943

and Casey borrowed the welding gear to install a ready ammunition box on the bridge for the .303s.

Casey also arranged for another urgent service from the *Sirius*—the fumigation of every article of clothing and bedding in the crew's quarters of the 692, both forward and aft, and the thorough dusting with insecticide of every man who lived there. Ever since Oran, a plague of crab lice, known to the men as just plain "crabs," had been spreading through the ship and over the bodies of the crew. The tiny, tenacious, irritating little creatures, brought aboard (it was generally agreed and not denied) by Gunner Walter from one of the more unsavory districts of MEK, had not been content with their normal residence in the genital area but had spread their itching contagion and ugly little black spots through all the hairy parts of the body until some of the men even had them in their eyebrows. For some fortunate but unexplained reason, only the wardroom and its occupants had been spared, and the officers were not even aware of the problem until Chief Morton brought it tactfully to my attention as medical officer.

With the fumigating and dusting successfully under way on the first day in Algiers, Charlie Coffey and I went ashore and were rewarded with an unforgettable glimpse of General Charles de Gaulle striding like a giant through a public square surrounded by a running mob of people who appeared to come only to his waist and who seemed to be trying to snatch off his uniform in adoration. We also saw a movie, *Foreign Correspondent*, in English with French subtitles, and joined a bunch of PC officers for dinner at an army officers' mess: hot pea soup, fresh roast lamb, potatoes and peas, and glorious chocolate ice cream for dessert.

The SC 692 was in Algiers for ten days, during which signs of imminent action multiplied until the tension was almost palpable. More SCs, PCs, YMSs and AMs stood in daily, and the space between the cruisers was crammed with the nests of small warships. Among the YMSs were the 62 and the 69, with which we had been more or less in company since Norfolk. An army second lieutenant we ran into at the officers' mess ashore told us his unit (armor) had fired its last practice and drivers were on standby twenty-four hours a day awaiting word to embark.

On the evening of the twentieth the exec of the 693 came aboard to borrow some books. He was full of intelligence from a source he did not name. The landings he said would be in Sicily around the twenty-fifth, anyway very soon, and would be made with overwhelming air and gunfire support. He was sufficiently convincing to inspire me to walk around the ship and draw up a list of actions to be taken before coming under fire. They included rerigging the jackstaff forward, the flagstaff aft, and all the lifeline stanchions on the fo'c'sle to be instantly removable to provide clear fields of fire for the 40-mm and the aft 20-mm. Since it appeared that the major threat would be from aircraft, another item on the list was to turn in sixteen of our mousetrap projectiles and convert that stowage to ready ammunition for the 40-mm. Engine governors would be advanced to 1420 RPM, and just prior to action, mattresses would be lashed inside the weather cloths around the bridge, gun deck, and the aft 20-mm to stop or slow down splinters and shrapnel.

On the twenty-first, the *Sirius* got under way and the U.S. light cruiser *Boise* stood in and took her place, causing a major rearrangement of all the little ships in the vicinity. But good came of the inconvenience. There were friends on the *Boise* and that meant ice cream and movies for the SC's crew and hot showers and dinner in her spacious wardroom for the officers. Our old companion from the trans-Atlantic convoy, the destroyer *Nelson*, arrived with the *Boise* but anchored outside the breakwater.

On one of the final evenings in Algiers, Chief Bosun's Mate Murphy delivered himself of a practical joke that left many of the men wondering about his overall rationality. He had come back from liberty just drunk enough to fuel his natural aggressiveness and found a card game in progress in the after crew's quarters. Suspecting, not without some reason but without any evidence or proof, that gambling was involved, he attempted belligerently to break it up. Strong words were exchanged (Boats was not popular with several of the crew), and he eventually retreated, threatening darkly to break up the game permanently by dropping one of the ship's small, bright yellow fragmentation grenades down the hatch.

The game continued after the interruption, but some ten minutes later, Boats's flushed face again appeared above. "Take that, you bastards!" he yelled, and flung a yellow, baseball-sized object down among the players, who erupted from the mess table to throw themselves on the deck, under bunks, behind lockers, the refrigerator, the galley range—anywhere to escape the inevitable lethal blast.

When a minute or so had passed with no explosion, someone had the courage to raise his head with utmost caution to see why the thing had misfired. It had not exploded because it was a lemon, one of a supply brought aboard that same afternoon and left in the cool night air topside.

Smiling with satisfaction, Murphy ambled forward to his bunk and turned in.

At 2000 on Tuesday, the twenty-second, there was a hastily called conference of COs aboard an attack transport, the *Barnett*. The transport was hard to find. When I headed over with John Hinkley, skipper of the 693, we walked along the docks for almost forty minutes only to find that the *Barnett* was across the narrow harbor, several miles around by land. We went aboard one of the LSTs beached bow-in in a long row along the waterfront and talked the OOD into running us across in his duty boat. The transport's huge wardroom was hot and smoky and filled with hundreds of officers, most of them fresh-faced and terribly young ensigns who, it turned out, were all boat officers in the LCVPs that would take the troops ashore.

There would be, we learned, a full-scale invasion practice the next night on a beach ten miles west of the harbor. The SC 692's job would be to rendezvous with the *Barnett* offshore, pick up one wave of troops embarked in half a dozen LCVPs, and guide them to a PC on the "line of departure," four thousand yards from the beach. We were then to return to the transport area and act as an antisub screen. All this would be done during darkness, but as long as the weather and the radar held up, it didn't sound too difficult.

Early the next morning the reality of the war was brutally brought home to the men of the 692. Between reveille and breakfast the SC 503 came in slowly and tied up just forward. Our men on deck had noticed when the other ship was a quarter mile away that something was wrong. Now we could see that her decks were literally covered with inert forms under bloody blankets, some on stretchers, some on the bare wood. The forms with faces were the wounded, those with faces covered were the dead. It took a long time to unload. The wounded, along with a few who could walk, went into ambulances, the dead into trucks. When all were ashore the 503's crew broke out hoses and brushes and began a scrub down.

We learned from the 503 that with four other SCs they had been screening two LSTs en route from Arzew to Bizerte and that just after sunset the evening before, a sub had managed to get through and torpedo both LSTs. The dead and wounded we had seen were from the LST 333, which had been hit in the stern but had been towed to shore and beached in order to salvage as much as possible of her weapons and gear. Most of the casualties were to the LSTs crew, which had been manning the bridge and control stations aft. Seventeen of the seventy-seven-man crew had been killed and thirty-one injured. Eight more men had been killed and another twenty-four injured of the more than two hundred troops aboard.

All thirty men of the 692 were abnormally quiet and thoughtful that sizzling African morning, their youthful conviction of immortality deeply dented. When the little ship got under way at 1300 and stood out of port to screen the big ships as they sortied for the rehearsal, they went seriously about their duties. It was as though they had suddenly and fully realized for the first time that their personal survival depended mostly on how well they did their jobs and fought their ship.

At the end of the swept channel well outside the harbor, the 692 joined with her twin sisters, the 691 and 693, and the PC 621. The big transports were already at sea, screened by half a dozen destroyers. We could see them silhouetted all along the horizon. About 1500 the LSTs and LCIs sortied. They were our charges and we patrolled to seaward up and down their starboard sides as they turned gradually to port in a long, sweeping curve to the south and east to approach the

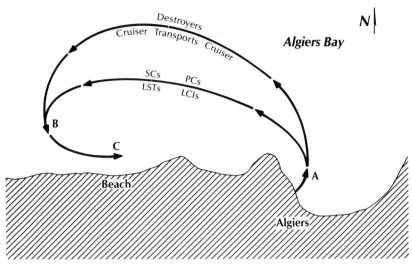

Approach Plan, Invasion Rehearsal, Algiers Bay, 23–24 June 1943

practice beach from the northwest. Farther out to sea, a long column of big transports, a cruiser leading and following, and destroyers along the flanks followed a similar curving course. They were faster but had farther to go so that the two groups would come together as they turned to parallel the shore.

When maneuvering was completed, the plan called for four parallel lines of ships to be lying to along the shore about seven miles off—two lines of LSTs inboard, then a single line of LCIs, and outboard the transports. Small escorts, when their work was done, would patrol to seaward of the transports but inside the destroyer screen.

That was the plan and it seemed a good one: clear, logical, and potentially effective. And it all went well at first. It was just becoming full dark as the two columns converged (at point B on the diagram). There the first flaw in the plan became evident. The small escorts had not been assigned any definite position during this maneuver, only to "continue screening the landing craft." That put them between the landing craft and the transports, which was logical since their duties involved the transports and they were still protectively to seaward of the landing craft. But a few minutes into the approach, as the columns began to come parallel to the coast, the line of LCIs, for reasons never made clear, cut hard to starboard, across the bows of their escorts. At that the lumbering LSTs appeared to hesitate. One group tried to get shoreward of the LCIs, where they belonged; the other group just stopped. Soon there were LSTs headed in every direction. Then the darkness became complete and from the 692 we couldn't see them anymore.

But we could certainly see the LCIs, which had now begun to crowd the line of transports, leaving very little room between. All this time the watch in the 692 had been assiduously keeping the transport *Barnett* in sight, both visually and by radar. She was easy to distinguish because of her long superstructure deck and her two thick crane masts well forward and aft.

When the LCIs crowded us we ducked through the transport column and patrolled along outside. The *Barnett* was dimly visible, well up on our starboard bow. When the destroyers moved in and took over the screening job, the SC headed for the *Barnett*, where her job was to be done. It was still, dark, and flat calm as we fell in with her, and we could hear from the huge black bulk of the transport the shrill whistle of the bosun's call and her loudspeakers ordering, "Load all boats." It was exactly midnight.

The 692 took station as ordered about one thousand yards inshore of the transport ahead of the *Barnett*, the *Oberon*, and stood by. The SC 691 was in the same position opposite the *Lyon*, astern of the *Barnett*, and the PC 621 was between the two SCs, opposite the *Barnett* herself. We could make out the bulking forms of the *Oberon* and *Barnett*, and the low, slim shape of the PC. The other ships were lost to sight in the midnight darkness.

About 0130 a swarm of squat, low shapes began to separate from the mass of the *Barnett* and make their way, bobbing and splashing, toward the PC. The sound of many engines came clearly across the night sea. In a moment the scratchy voice of a loudspeaker overpowered the background rumbling of engines. "This is the Red wave for Blue beach," it rasped. "Fall in astern."

At 0145 the PC picked up way and began moving shoreward, a string of LCVPs at unequal intervals in her wake. As they disappeared, the SC 691 came in sight and took the station just vacated by the PC. At 0158 she began to blink a dim blue light. At 0200 exactly she held the light steady and moved off toward the beach, with no landing craft anywhere around that we could make out.

As soon as the 691 was gone, the 692 went to GQ and eased over to take her place. We could see a covey of LCVPs churning in a circle between us and the *Barnett*. I broke out the big megaphone (we had no loudspeaker or bullhorn), pointed it in their direction, and yelled, "This is the Yellow wave for Blue beach; form column astern." In the weak starlight we could see the circle break up and several landing craft heading in our direction. At 0213, according to orders, we began blinking our blue light. This was a special device issued in Algiers just before the rehearsal. It looked like a very heavy-caliber rifle. The blue light was in a tube so that it could be seen only where it was pointed (the 691's light must have been unshielded) and the trigger was the on-off switch. At 0215 exactly we held the light steady, pointing directly aft; I hollered, "Under way," and off we went.

Down in the pilothouse, Wells had PC 621 on radar five miles dead ahead and four thousand yards offshore on the "line of departure." It was her job to assemble the various waves of troop-loaded LCVPs and shove them off for Blue beach according to schedule. Ours was to deliver the Yellow wave to her.

To the surprise of the SC's crew, as we approached the beach yellow flares began to appear in the sky, and a couple of searchlights came on and swept their long fingers across the water. Someone had taken the trouble to make this rehearsal as realistic as possible. With the flares and lights, we could see the PC at two and a half miles. At 0235 we ran up close along her port side and reported by megaphone, "Here is the Yellow wave." We were ten minutes early. "Very well," yelled back the skipper, a lieutenant named Ross. "Where the hell is the Blue wave?" We had to tell him we didn't know. Apparently the 691 had never found him. But when we turned and headed back out we found we had not six but twelve LCVPs astern. We figured the other six were the Blue wave that had missed the 691.

Back alongside the towering black bulk of the *Barnett,* shouting up at the darkened bridge, we held a conversation with an invisible someone shouting down.

"Ahoy the bridge!"

"Go ahead."

"We are the 692. We have delivered the Yellow wave to the line of departure and are proceeding out to screen the LSTs, unless you have further orders."

"Carry out that order." Then as we were moving away, "Did you deliver your wave on time?"

"Yes sir, ten minutes early at the line of departure."

"Very good."

The 692 spent the rest of the night running up and down outside the ranks of ships lining the shore, sonar pinging away and radar sweeping the sea. Dawn came with fog so thick it hung in bright beads along the lifelines. At the truck the steaming colors hung dank and limp as the SC spent the morning rounding up lost landing craft by radar and leading them back to their ships. At noon the fog cleared and all the ships got under way to return to Algiers. It was late afternoon before the 692 could enter port, but at that point she inadvertently put on a little shiphandling demonstration for the crews of two light cruisers moored parallel to each other about 130 feet apart, sterns to the dock. She came in close to the starboard side of the right-hand cruiser, the HMS *Euralyus*, swung hard to port, backing the port engine, and came neatly alongside the other big ship, the *Boise*. She had made the turn in a space only twenty feet longer than her own length. The 694 and the 690 tied up outboard having backed into position.

Three days after the landing practice a meeting of all officers and chiefs was held in the transport *Samuel Chase*, the flagship of one of three task forces that would take part in the landings, the one to which the 692 was assigned. Charlie, Wash, Boats, and I (Morton and Roughan were taking physical exams for warrant officer) arrived at 0930. The *Chase's* spacious decks were bulwark to bulwark and jack-staff to flagstaff with men in khaki, sweating and fidgeting in the African sun, already blistering at that early hour. At 1000, Rear Admiral John L. Hall, the task force commander, was piped aboard (it was he to whom my friend in Oran was flag lieutenant). We were close enough to see that he stood about six feet tall, trim and fit-looking with a rather long face, bushy eyebrows, and a strong, prominent nose. He wore just two rows of ribbons on his khaki jacket—no wings, no dolphins—a big-ship surface sailor.

The admiral climbed up to the port wing of the bridge where all hands could see him and made a short but articulate and straightforward little speech. He said he wanted the men of the amphibious force to know that those who put out the orders and drew up the plans were thinking of them, their living conditions and their general welfare. He said we had done a fine job so far, that he had full confidence in us, and assured us, in concluding, "For the rest of your lives you will be proud that you are wearing the uniform of the American navy." The way he said that last sentence would have made any man proud who was not already, and the rest even prouder. We could see why John Hall was an admiral.

On the way back to the ship we fell in with the skipper of LCI 17, his flotilla's flagship, and he came aboard with us to pick up six hand grenades. We didn't expect to get close enough to the beach to use them. He definitely did.

After an afternoon of running up and down the harbor taking on fuel and water, Charlie dropped me off at the *Nelson*, where I had been invited to dinner. On the long walk home after the meal and a movie I acquired a new realization of the size and power of the force of which the 692 was a real if not a major part, and I began to understand the imminence of the coming action. For at least a mile, the route lay along a seawall solidly lined with LSTs, bows to the shore and stern anchors out. There was less than twenty feet between them. Their bow ramps were down and their huge clam-shell doors swung wide, exposing the deep caverns of their holds. Under dim red lights, as far back as I could see, those holds were lined with tanks and trucks, three abreast. The long barrels of the tanks' guns gleamed under the lights, and everything was pointed forward, out, poised, powerful, ready. In ship after big gray ship it was the same, in a row so long I grew tired from walking.

As though that impression of immediacy were being confirmed, a message came in at 0900 the next morning, 27 June, to get under way as soon as possible and go alongside the PC 624, anchored outside the breakwater. Since Senecal, the mail orderly, was already ashore and Casey, with tall, easy-going Missourian Machinist's Mate Harold Fields, had gone to draw fresh meat, "as soon as possible" turned out to be 1115, about ten seconds after the steaks and chops were safely aboard.

The 624's communications officer gave us the operations order for the invasion and some rolled-up charts. Most of it was sealed and labeled "SECRET" and carried the stern warning, "Do not open until directed by task force or unit commander." LCDR Lowther invited us to tie up alongside but we declined and anchored close by. We had seen what happened to our wooden sides when nested to a steel ship in an open roadstead.

The 692 was not at anchor long. At 1230 a flag hoist went up on the PC, and the SC was under way to join the other small escorts in screening the landing craft as they poured out from behind the breakwater in a long, closely spaced gray column. By 1500 they were formed up and moving eastward again: eight columns of ships with a file of five LCIs on either flank, five columns of three LSTs and one LCI each, and one of two LSTs and three LCIs. Astern of the two outboard columns on either side were three YMSs, and astern of the middle columns, a little subformation of the *Redwing* (a repair ship), the big fleet tug *Hopi*, and four little yard tugs in line abreast. The AM 119 *Sustain* carried the escort commander dead ahead of the formation, flanked by PCs 624 and 625. The PC 621 had the port bow and the SC 692 the starboard. Convoy flanks were covered by SCs 694 and 676 to port, and 693 and 690 to starboard. The PC 627 was rear guard. All escorts were four thousand yards from the nearest ship of the convoy. Speed was 8 knots, the escorts patrolling back and forth in their assigned sectors, about thirty degrees either side of base course, at 10.

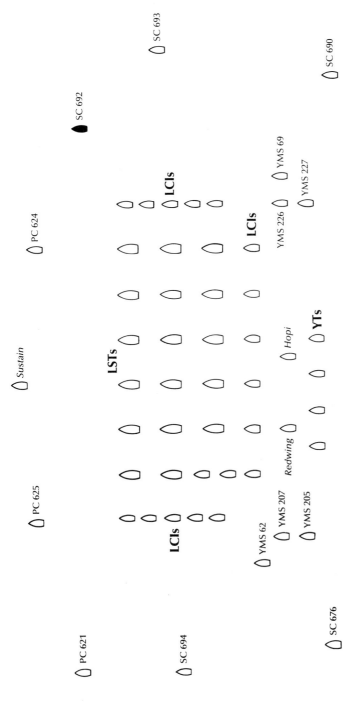

Disposition, Convoy "Arrow Six," Algiers to Tunis, 27–30 June 1943

This large block of eastward-moving ships, officially designated "Arrow Six," did not escape the notice of the enemy. At 1800 a single plane flew over very high, the 40-millimeters of several ships reaching vertically and vainly after it, and disappeared to the north. The 692 did not fire. The enemy was well out of range and she might soon need her ammo for more threatening targets. That same evening there was a further reminder of the danger lurking in these placid waters as the convoy passed the wreck of the LST 333, beached and broken at the foot of high coastal hills, her torn, charred stern awash.

Summer nights along the northern littoral of Africa are short and the periods of twilight very long. That night, sunset was at 2120 and there was still light in the western sky at 2230. At 0430 the east began to brighten and sunrise came at 0615. All night the broad box of landing craft and its bordering square of escorts ghosted eastward over a flat, calm sea. From the bridge of the SC 692 we could clearly see the high, rolling coastal hills to starboard, and to port and astern the lumpy black shapes of the LSTs appeared almost motionless on the still water. The night was moonless but so clear and calm that several bright stars drew silver paths between the ships. The only sounds were the steady throbbing of the diesels, the bubbling of the underwater exhaust, and the gentle hiss of the water sliding along the sides. At its setting and its rising again the sun was just the same, a round, red, hot ball. At least here our experience disproved the ancient adage "Red in the morning, sailors take warning." Here all the days were perfect.

All the next day, the twenty-eighth, the little force crept eastward at 8 knots into increasingly dangerous waters. The chart in the pilothouse of the 692 showed enemy bases in Sardinia only 120 miles away, thirty-minutes flying time for a fighter. And the operation order warned of mines along the route. To reduce that danger by presenting a narrower front, the OTC ordered the landing craft into two long columns, with the escorts ahead and along both flanks, and *Redwing*, the repair ship, in the trail position midway between the columns.

The new formation took effect at sunset, but late in the afternoon the 692 requested and received permission to leave station and investigate an object bobbing high and light, well off to starboard. It turned out to be an empty aluminum aircraft drop tank and we took it aboard for delivery ashore at our next port.

About 1000 on the twenty-ninth another ship was lost and five more sailors killed when a mine blew out the bow of the *Redwing*. The repair ship had dropped back five miles astern during the night to take the four struggling yard tugs in tow, escorted by two YMSs and a PC, and had just signaled to the YMS 62 that she had rejoined, when

Sustain

LCI 17

SC 692

LSTs,

LCIs,

Escorts

YMSs,

Escorts

and

Tugs

Redwing

Convoy "Arrow Six," Reformed to Avoid Mines, Algiers to Tunis,
28–30 June 1943

the explosion tore her apart. The tugs tried gamely to take her in tow, but only three and a half miles from where she had been hit she sank in twenty-seven fathoms, to the considerable detriment of small-craft maintenance and repair all along the busy coast in the throes of invasion preparations.

The sinking and the deaths reminded the SC's crew once more of the terrible danger of mines, moored or adrift, in these waters. Moored mines were of course invisible, but with luck they could be

The repair ship *Redwing* sinking in twenty-seven fathoms after hitting a mine en route from Algiers to Tunis, 29 June 1943, in a convoy escorted by the 692. Five men forward were killed when the mine blew out her bow. (Ted Dicecco, Avondale, Pa., U.S. Naval Historical Center)

avoided if your navigation was precise and you stayed in the swept channels. Drifters could be seen and avoided during daylight, but at night the life of the ship and the crew depended on pure, blind luck alone. No one wanted to think about the effects of a mine on a little wooden ship in which a dozen men bunked forward.

With some twenty ships in each column and five hundred yards between ships, the *Redwing* had been more than five miles astern of the 692, and the SC sailors saw neither the explosion nor the rescue; their only information came from the busy TBX voice radio in the pilothouse. As precautions against suffering the repair ship's fate, we were already doing all that could be done: an extra lookout stationed right at the bullnose during the hours of darkness and relieved every thirty minutes; radar and sonar alerted for tiny targets and weak echoes from ahead; and, I suspect, some fervent prayers offered frequently.

The day of the *Redwing*'s loss continued to be full of surprises. At 0745, while Boats and I were relieving Charlie and Wash for the morning watch, three twin-engine aircraft appeared low on the water off the starboard bow. With the land behind them, they were in to about three thousand yards before we saw them, coming directly at us at high speed, the spinning disks of the props growing larger every second. None of us had ever seen a torpedo attack but this looked like a textbook illustration. I yelled down to the 40-mm to commence firing, hit the switch to sound the general alarm, and got a belt into the starboard Hotchkiss all in about three seconds. I could hear the men running along the deck to their battle stations as I lined up the lead plane in the open sights of the machine gun, mouth dry and palms wet, waiting a few more seconds for the range to close. My finger was just tightening on the trigger to squeeze off the first burst when my target flipped up and to his left—and on the underside of his wings we could clearly see the red, white, and blue circular insignia of the RAF.

All guns were manned and ready when the three planes circled and came in for another practice attack. The gun crews tracked them for our own practice while our pulse rates slowly returned to normal.

Around 0900 the long columns of ships swung to starboard and into the Gulf of Tunis. We had only been on the new course for a few minutes when the port lookout reported an object in the water a couple of hundred yards on the port bow. That placed it just about ahead of the starboard column of landing craft forging along astern. As we headed over to take a look at it, a message came flashing over from the *Sustain*, "Keep clear of object ahead of you." Then a minute later another signal, "Investigate cautiously." Did she think we were going to dash over and ram it?

We investigated cautiously by running by, dead slow about thirty yards away. It was not one but two mines, ugly, rusty three-foot spheres with protruding horns, wired to a couple of equally rusty metal floats. The 692 circled around and positioned herself between mine and convoy, her 12-inch light flashing "Mine. Keep clear. Mine. Keep clear."

It was our first experience with live mines. We knew we were supposed to sink them but unsure how to go about it. When the convoy was clear, we opened up on them with .30-caliber rifle fire, but nothing happened. Apparently it was necessary to hit a detonator in one of the horns, and they were difficult targets. We tried a shallow-set depth charge, running past and firing the port K-gun. That produced a satisfyingly thunderous roar and a tall fountain of seawater but had no visible effect on the mines. Finally we just sank the floats with rifle fire and they took the mines to the deep botton with them. It took us an hour at 1100 RPM to regain our place in the screen.

By noon the force was in the approaches to the port of La Goulette at Tunis and reformed to a single column to enter. But the 692 did not enter Tunis that day. A megaphoned order from the PC 624 sent her, with the 693, to twenty-four hours of harbor-entrance patrol. The patrol line was roughly northeast and southwest, seven miles long—between the site of ancient Carthage, the scene of a thousand years of wars, and rugged, hilly Cape Bon, where the Afrika Korps had made its last stand only seven weeks before. The two SCs ran back and forth, in line abreast, one thousand yards apart, all night and half the next day. There were no sonar echoes, no suspicious floating objects, and except for the bright, sharply defined masses of the land, the radar screens were clear. At 1300 they were relieved by the PC 625 and SC 694 and proceeded into La Goulette for fresh water and a look around.

There was plenty to look at, all of it more or less grim. The narrow harbor was an obstacle course strewn with rusted sunken and half-sunken ships lying at every conceivable angle. A recently entered LST was hung up and hard aground on one wreck attempting to get herself off with a wire cable right across the channel, closing it. The one- and two-story buildings fronting the harbor were chipped and broken, pocked with bullet holes. There was not a window in sight that was not shattered. We took on water from another LST, and while the tanks were filling, a few of the men went ashore to look around. They came back with German magazines, machine pistol clips and spent 88-mm brass as souvenirs. All day the skies were busy with high-flying formations of aircraft, mostly twin-engine B-25 Mitchells. We counted a total of eighty-eight, almost all returning from the direction of Sicily, a fact in which the SC's crew took considerable comfort.

A week of patrolling out of Tunis followed, the patrols interspaced with a variety of administrative and recreational activities, while all the crews of all the scores and hundreds of assembled warships and the troops embarked waited apprehensively for the seemingly long-overdue order that would launch them against the underside of Europe.

In the SC 692, a letter went back to the Bureau of Naval Personnel certifying Charlie Coffey as qualified for command; another, at his request, recommending that Ray's rate be changed from the useless mess attendant to fireman; and a third recommending Roughan, yeoman first, for warrant officer. Examinations were held for advancement in rate, and as a result at quarters on 3 July, Charlie Nader became boatswain's mate second, Tony Curato gunner's mate second, Archie LaFlamme signalman second, Myron Wells radarman third, and Elmer André quartermaster first.

Almost always, when not on patrol, the SCs and PCs anchored in three or four fathoms out in the Bay of Tunis. There it was quiet with a cool sea breeze to offset the fiery African sun, and the clear waters were ideal for swimming. When the ship's work was done, swimming

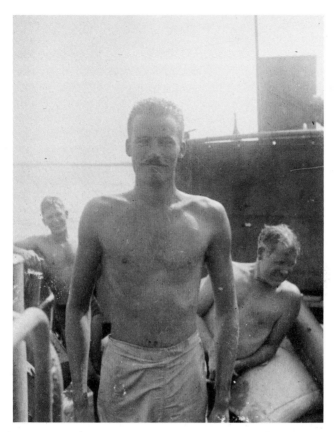

The 692's CO (center) after swim call in the Bay of Tunis, showing the mustache begun on the long Atlantic crossing from Bermuda to Gibraltar. On the left is Charlie Casey and right, Bill Hawn.

call was announced and young sailors and officers cavorted in the bay as young men of all lands and nations are wont to do.

In the 692, swim call usually included the launching of our inflatable eight-man raft (acquired in Beni Saf under dubious circumstances with the explanation "a soldier give it to us") and the little pram. A dozen sailors would overcrowd the raft, falling overboard and climbing back in to displace others while two or three in the pram made hit-and-run attacks with hurled buckets of seawater. Always, after Curato's experience, one man stood shark watch on the bridge with a loaded rifle.

Out there in the floating community of small warships there was much visiting back and forth via pram between the SC and PC skippers and XOs. Although the visiting was primarily social and comradely between brothers-in-arms with much in common, including especially the imminence of their first action with the enemy, an important result was a highly constructive cross-insemination of ideas on all aspects of the operations of their ships. Formed under the pressures of the times, friendships established in the bay off Tunis, and later in the big lake anchorage at Bizerte, were to last a lifetime. For the immediate present it was simply good that personal relationships and understandings were established between young officers who would have to work closely together under stress at sea.

Friendships between the officers of the little ships were confirmed and strengthened by a series of evening and late-night bull sessions that branched out from subjects of immediate concern to long-range goals and ambitions; philosophies of life; and exchanges of views on love, marriage, and children—of special concern to men at war in their middle twenties.

People could be divided into three general categories according to their views on marriage and children: those who believed a young man in the armed service should on no account get married in wartime since it was manifestly unfair to expose the prospective bride to the chance of becoming a young and early widow; those who said it was even more important to be married in wartime so that at least some time and some happiness might be shared even if the worst should happen, but under no circumstances should children be born until the war was over, since it would be unfair to both mother and child to risk leaving them without a husband/father; and those more daring or less caring souls who considered it urgent both to marry and have children so that forever, no matter what their personal fates, the children and grandchildren of their bodies, born of a shared love, would live and breathe and walk the earth.

In such discussions and in hours of others, John Hinkley of the 693 (our sister ship, built by the Yankee shipwrights at Manchester on adjacent ways and commissioned two weeks later), Roger Robinson of the 694, Chuck Highfield of the 1030, Silver Silverstein of the PC 543, Lee Brekke, XO of LCDR Lowther's PC 624, and of course Prent Horne of the 535 and Ben Partridge of the 978 were primary participants and special friends of the 692. Ben was slightly older and wiser than most of us, having graduated from the University of Florida back in '37 and married in '39, and his always thoughtful and well-chosen words were heard with more than usual attention.

It was after one such extended bull session that I returned to the ship with my throat feeling a little scratchy from overuse and remembered the bottle of Listerine received from my solicitous mother, back in Oran in early June. Just before turning in, I stepped into our little head, tipped it up, and took a swig to gargle. But I never gargled; the taste that filled my mouth was definitely not Listerine. Unless my taste buds were deceiving me, I had a mouthful of an excellent grade of Scotch whisky, a commodity so rare along that parched and pillaged coast as to be practically priceless. I promptly returned the Listerine to the medicine cabinet, and only later took it out and shared it with my astounded and envious brother officers.

One evening on the 693 John Hinkley told an incredible story of an incident that had occurred on his ship during shakedown off Boston, before the 40-mm had replaced the old 3-inch/23. On one gunnery run, the 3-inch/23 misfired—when the firing lanyard was jerked nothing happened. Under the supervision of the assigned gunnery expert from the training command ashore, the lanyard was pulled twice more, resulting only in dry clicks. At that point, according to Hinkley, the shore-based expert opened the breech, removed the two-foot-long fixed ammunition cartridge, shook it, listened to it, turned it this way and that inspecting it, found nothing obviously wrong, inserted it back into the chamber, and closed the breech. The gun fired of its own accord two seconds later. John reported that a fraction of a second after the "expert" opened the breech, he was totally alone on the fo'c'sle.

Hinkley also reported on the rumored peculiarities of a couple of LST skippers. One, reputed to be the author Marcus Goodrich of the 380 (whose dinner invitation I had regretted declining earlier), was demonstrating to his XO the correct way to pace the quarterdeck, in full uniform and with a long glass (telescope) held firmly under the left arm. Ten paces to port, turn, ten paces to starboard, and back. At the time the 380 was one of the long row of LSTs moored bows to the dock in Algiers. Apparently by prearrangement, the skippers on three or four ships on either side fell into step with the pacing figures on the 380. Only their attire differed. All were dressed solely in white regulation boxer undershorts.

One of the many topics of discussion in these sessions was the professional differences between U.S. officers and our Royal Navy peers. At the conference before the landing practice at Algiers, a British "subleftenant" (an ensign) had briefed us on gunnery matters in a way that clearly indicated a knowledge far beyond that of the most knowledgeable among us, and we had all been most impressed although somewhat put down. But then someone (it might have been Ben) made everyone feel better with the simple explanation that in accordance with long tradition, British officers specialize in a particular aspect of their profession—gunnery, navigation, aviation, submarines, engineering, and so forth—to a much greater extent than we do. In all probability, it was agreed, the young gunnery officer knew very little outside of his specialty and would have been hopelessly at a loss if required to perform such generalized duties as those required to command a small man-of-war.

The harbor patrols off Tunis were generally without incident and in the 692 we took advantage of that fact to train a fifth officer of the deck, Chief "Ham" (an acronym from his initials) Morton. He stood with Boats and me at Condition II and with Washer at Condition III and was a rapid learner.

Morton was on deck one afternoon with visibility poor in haze and distant showers when a lone LCT came in sight, steering what appeared to be erratic and indecisive courses. On sighting the 692, she angled over and came within hailing distance. Morton called me to the bridge. "Which way," the officer-in-charge hollered over, "is Tunis?"

I applied the parallel rulers to the chart and called back, "Two two zero, magnetic."

Surprisingly, that didn't seem to help. The sunburned young officer (he looked about nineteen) pushed his hat forward over his eyes, scratched the back of his head and then with a winning smile yelled over, "Which way is that?"

I glanced at the compass and extended my arm to the southwest. "That way!" I called over.

"Thanks a lot!" he yelled and with great relief swung the square bow of the LCT in the indicated direction and went churning away, now on a steady course for his destination.

One afternoon of the last week before action, the men of the 692 tasted their first Mediterranean "sirocco." We had just anchored after returning from patrol when the wind began to increase to fifteen or twenty knots from the south. But what a wind! It was as though somewhere nearby the door of a cosmic blast furnace had been flung open, or a hurricane had risen up out of hell. The scorching wind tore at your clothes, sucked each molecule of moisture from your flesh, and desiccated the skin. It was far hotter in the shade and the wind than in the sun and the lee. We instantly held swim call and all hands except Washer, who volunteered for the shark watch, went over into the cool sea. In life jackets at the ends of trailing lines we floated with the gentle current until in an hour or so the sirocco moderated and we could go back about our duties. Later we learned from the meteorologists ashore that the sirocco originates deep in the Sahara and blows clear across the Med to bake the coasts of Spain and France and Italy.

On 4 July, Independence Day, Boats and Hawn (with Hawn rowing) took the pram over to a long white beach directly astern and there a ragged little Arab boy told them that the Americans would land in Sicily "in a couple of days." Two nights later, on patrol, the 692's crew saw their first air raid, just as the watch was changing at 0400. It began with a shifting triangle of distant searchlight beams to the northwest in the direction of Bizerte, thirty-five miles away. As we watched through binoculars from the SC's bridge, a thin, pale curtain of flame rose quickly to fill the triangle formed by the beams and increased in brightness. It was a moment before we realized that what we were watching was a tremendous, sustained barrage of antiaircraft tracers. Washer and Morton had the deck and they reported that a twin-engine aircraft had flown over, very slowly, just a few minutes before the fireworks began. It had seemed to come from the general direction of Bizerte. Armed with that information we went to general quarters and trained the guns out toward where the tracers were still lashing upward, to be ready for any other planes that might be coming our way. But none did and after about an hour, with a new day beginning to lighten the east, the distant firing stopped and we went back to Condition II.

At sunrise the LCIs, their topsides dark with troops, began to pour out of Tunis with a pair of PCs screening ahead. I knew from other skippers who had peeked into their secret packages of orders that the sailing of the LCIs was scheduled for four days before the landings, or D minus 4. As the landing craft formed up and headed seaward we counted sixty aircraft in echelons and wedges flying high and fast toward Sicily. If our bootlegged information was correct, the SCs and PCs remaining at Tunis, including the 692, would be sailing in two days, on 8 July. Late on the afternoon of the sixth the radar died.

Early the next morning, the seventh, we took aboard a radar technician from Hinkley's 693. He and Wells and Kidwell worked until 1700 and gave up. We dropped the radarman off at his ship and picked up another, reputed to be the best around, from the 691. While the radar was under the knife, in accordance with orders just received, we painted white diamonds on both sides amidships and "692" in white across the transom.

With the radar still under repair, we made the side of the *Sustain*, which was reported to have an electric bullhorn for us. She didn't. Then inside the harbor to top off with fresh water. While we were there the 690 came alongside. Weber, her skipper, came aboard to ask that we make a "gentleman's agreement." In the event that one of us does not return from the coming operation, the other agrees to

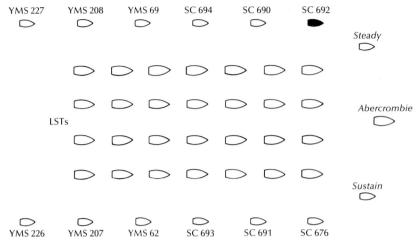

Force Disposition, Dime Section, Tunisian Joss Medium Convoy, a Component of Task Force 81, the Gela Attack Force, Bound for the Invasion of Sicily, 8 July 1943

visit the widow and advise her of the circumstances. I thought of my lovely young wife, now eight months pregnant, decided I had to be immortal, but reluctantly agreed since he seemed so serious and sincere. We duly exchanged addresses.

It was deep dusk and moonlight when we stood out of the harbor, tanks full of water, the radar back in operation. Every man aboard knew that a working radar could very well mean survival within the next forty-eight hours. When we returned the 691's technician to his ship he could have been elected emperor of the world by the SC's crew.

All that final week we had been anxiously awaiting instructions from our "task force or unit commander" to open the secret package, which was obviously the operation order for the landings. When I turned in that night that instruction still had not come in. We knew from unofficial information among the little ships that 8 July, D−2, was departure day for the 692. Reveille was scheduled for 0530 and orders left to make it earlier if there were signs of activity in the harbor before that.

At 0545, with anchors coming up all around us, we opened the op order. The SC 692 was under way at 0550. At 0600 the LSTs sortied and formed up, twenty-eight of them in a rectangular formation of four columns ringed by escorts. In the lead was the awkward-looking but powerful monitor HMS *Abercrombie*, with her two monstrous 15-inch rifles jutting from a high single turret forward. She was flanked by the *Steady* and the *Sustain*. SC 692 had the port bow opposite the leading rank of LSTs.

At 1100, clear of the land and in the "Tunisian War Channel," we fell in behind another force of landing craft. Still another joined from astern. My personal journal describes the immensity of the invasion and the uncertainty of our future.

> The narrow seas are filled with ships. This is the largest invasion
> armada . . . in the history of the world. Our objective is the
> beach just east of Gela, Sicily. Our duties are to be as in the
> practice. . . . I expect no action until tomorrow. I am putting
> this journal with the secret publications to be destroyed if the
> ship is lost.

As the mighty assault force fell into line and moved off toward the enemy, I thought of King Henry's words on the eve of the Battle of Agincourt in *Henry V:*

> This day is call'd the feast of Crispian:
> He that outlives this day, and comes safe home,
> Will stand a tip-toe when this day is nam'd,
> And rouse him at the name of Crispian.

GELA

Even the irrepressible SC sailors stared in awe at the magnitude of the force of which they were a part. Casey said it best in his inimitable Alabamese, looking around and scratching his head in wonder: "If those poor guineas only knew what was in store for 'em!"

The op order made it clear that a lot indeed was "in store for 'em." The SC 692 was part of Task Force 81, the Gela Attack Force. Our twenty-eight loaded LSTs were just one component of that force, "Dime Section, Tunisian Joss Medium Convoy." The myriad ships ahead and astern were other units of the same force. And there were two other task forces of similar size and composition: Task Force 86, which would land at Licata just west of Gela, and Task Force 85, attacking Scoglitti an equal distance to the east. Those three armadas composed the mostly U.S. Western Naval Task Force. But there was also an Eastern Naval Task Force of mostly British ships and troops sailing from Alexandria and other eastern Mediterranean ports. They would attack four groups of beaches on both sides of the Pachino peninsula at the southeastern corner of Sicily at the same instant as the U.S. landings.

Ben Partridge's SC 978 comes alongside the destroyer *Buck* en route to the invasion of Sicily, July 1943. After shooting up enemy shore batteries during the landings, the *Buck* sank an Italian submarine and captured its captain but was herself torpedoed and sunk with heavy casualties off Salerno in October. (National Archives)

Altogether, the 692 was part of a force of nearly 3,000 warships carrying 160,000 troops, 14,000 vehicles, and 600 tanks, covered by some 4,000 aircraft. All the ships were now at sea, converging for the assault.

At 1400 the long rectangle of LSTs passed close aboard the high wooded headland of Cape Bon and turned south, the sunbaked, recently captured island of Pantelleria in sight thirty miles to port. All afternoon, as they steamed southward at 10 knots along the African coast, and Pantelleria faded slowly back into the haze on the port quarter, large formations of aircraft passed back and forth overhead, coming and going from Sicily. In the 692 they were a welcome sight. The sun when it set on that momentous evening was blood red and the sea picked up its color to remind us of Homer's "wine-dark seas" and all the men who had sailed and fought on them before us. At 2300 course was changed due east for Malta, and all night the ocean-ful of darkened ships continued their approach.

The next morning, as though to disprove the rosy prediction of the sunset, a wind came up with the sun. By noon it was above force four and increasing. The LSTs bucked and rolled like cattle in a wallow, and aboard the 692 all hands were forced to hold on hard to maintain their feet while the little ship thrashed and tossed and threw solid water. It was as though impartial nature had taken the enemy's side. The invasion force had run into another of the sudden violent winds peculiar to the land-locked Mediterranean, this time a full-fledged mistral, the exact opposite of the sirocco—cold and northerly rather than hot and southerly.

This mistral had arrived just at the worst of all possible times. On the SC's bridge we brushed the salt spray out of our eyes with one hand while grasping the rail with the other, wiped our binoculars with lens paper for the hundredth time, and remembered the weeks of calm, hot days stretching back to April off Nemours and Beni Saf and Oran and Algiers and Tunis. Days of short, routine patrols when the weather was only a minor factor. Now, it was critical, perhaps even decisive, to the success or failure of the mightiest amphibious assault ever mounted. We looked over to starboard through eyes smarting with salt at the wallowing LSTs and thought of what it must be like in their crowded, unventilated interiors for the hundreds of seasick soldiers who were expected to charge ashore through the surf and fight that very night. Then we remembered the much smaller LCIs also at sea and shook our heads in sympathy.

All afternoon the wind continued to build. The only cheering sight from the SC 692 was the formations of friendly planes that continued to shuttle back and forth between Africa and Sicily. By 1500 Malta was in sight, its high coast stratified in brown, like stale chocolate layer cake. The force turned northwest to the rendezvous point five miles west of the chalk cliffs of Gozo, now tinged pink by the lowering sun. Speed was reduced and that eased the violent motion of the ships a little. We hoped the wind would reverse the phenomenon of the morning and go down with the sun, but it did not.

Ó Steady   Ó Sustain

                    Ó YMS   Ó YMS

                                Ó LCI 17
    Ó LST 381   Ó LCI 188   Ó Savannah
                                Ó LCI 189

    Ó LST 338   Ó PC 624   Ó Dickman
                                Ó SC 676
    Ó LST 312   Ó SC 690   Ó Prince Charles

    Ó LST 311   Ó LCI 233   Ó Prince Leopold
                                Ó LCI 192
    Ó LST 313   Ó LCI 193
                                Ó LCI 190
    Ó LST 344   Ó LCI 191   Ó Oberon
                                Ó LCI 76
    Ó LST 370   Ó LCI 75   Ó Barnett
                                Ó LCI 46
    Ó LST 308
                                                            Ó Monrovia
    Ó LST 480   Ó PC 621
                                ● SC 692
    Ó LST 345   Ó SC 691   Ó Lyon
                                Ó SC 693
    Ó LST 337
                                                            Ó Chase
    Ó LST 346   Ó LCI 236
                                Ó LCI 40
    Ó LST 371   Ó LCI 41   Ó Betelguese
                                Ó LCI 42
    Ó LST 380   Ó LCI 235
                                Ó LCI 238   Ó Thurston
    Ó LST 382   Ó LCI 234
                                Ó LCI 220   Ó Stanton
    Ó Orziba   Ó PC 625
    Ó Chateau   Ó   Ó PC 627   Ó Boise
      Thierry   Ó Yard   Ó SC 694
    Ó Brant   Ó Tugs
    Ó Hopi   Ó

    Ó YMS   Ó YMS   Ó YMS   Ó YMS

Note: *Steady, Sustain,* and the two YMSs were sweeping eleven miles ahead of the other ships.

Dime Attack Force Approach Disposition to Gela, Sicily, 9–10 July 1943

Off Gozo, the op plan called for a change to approach disposition; three long columns of ships with minesweepers in the van, eleven
transports in the starboard column with the light cruiser *Savannah*
leading and the *Boise* following; a column of LCIs, with groups of SCs
and PCs interspersed; and a port column of LSTs.

The disposition was logical, precise and orderly on paper, but in the howling wind and breaking seas off Gozo there seemed to be a minimum of order and precision. First, the force of transports and cruisers with their destroyer escort was nowhere in sight. Second, and of far more concern to the men of the SC 692, the long line of plowing, thrashing LCIs, which had joined up on schedule, had left no gap into which the small escorts could fit. As best we could, the SCs and PCs made an on-the-spot revision of the op plan. We moved out into screening positions on the starboard flank of the LCIs.

Just at dusk, with the last of the light and the wind still increasing, the *Savannah* came in sight off the port quarter at the head of the transport column. The short, steep seas that were punishing the smaller ships posed no problem for the big ones; with a kind of serene contempt, on even keels, they sliced right through, rounding the stern of the laboring landing-craft formation and charging up the starboard side so that for a few minutes, the disposition looked pretty much like the diagram in the op plan.

War correspondent Ernie Pyle was aboard the transport *Samuel Chase,* the flagship, and in his report filed later from Sicily, he described the scene: "The little subchasers and infantry-carrying assault craft (LCI's) would disappear completely into the wave-troughs as we watched them. The next moment they would be carried so high they seemed to leap clear out of the water." We watched in awe the gyrations of the adjacent SCs and PCs as they leaped and plunged, attempting to keep pace with the heavy ships, into the wind and sea, half of their red antifouling-paint bottoms indecently exposed time after time, huge sheets of white water flung up from their bows and pouring down on their decks and bridges; knowing full well that we looked exactly the same to them. The PC directly ahead stood up so straight on her fantail that we could see her 3-inch/50 main battery just forward of her high pilothouse.

By the time it was full dark, the *Savannah* and two of the transports had passed us close aboard to starboard and the transport column was steadily pulling ahead. That provided us with a serious problem to add to that of the weather, the problem of rendezvous off Gela with "our" transport, the *Barnett,* whose boats, as in the rehearsal, we were to lead ashore. For a while we could make her out in the moonlight (she was number five in the column), but as we plunged and thrashed, she forged sedately ahead and we lost sight of her in the darkness.

In the multiplicity of targets all around, radar was unable to pick her out and hold her. But that problem had to wait. First we needed to assure our arrival off Gela in operational condition. The danger of collision was very real. In the wild darkness, the column of huge transports was only a few hundred yards to starboard, the line of plunging iron LCIs the same distance to port. Survival depended on careful helmsmanship and sustained power. But with the SC 692's twin rudders and propellers frequently out of the water, both were difficult. The little ship would plunge from one breaking sea into the next, shooting solid water in torrents over every inch of her topsides, drenching the bridge watch, making binoculars useless, the salt burning in our eyes like acid. The most dangerous position was directly between two ships, a transport to starboard and an LCI to port. We would fight to pull ahead a little, abeam of the intervals between ships in the two columns, where we could breathe more easily, but just as we began to have room, the subchaser would bridge two seas, and the cooling-water intake for the diesels along the keel amidships would get a shot of air, setting off a siren and stopping one or the other engine. Charlie Casey, on watch in the engine room, leaped like a high hurdler from one engine to the other, throttling back, restarting, and throttling back up time after time. But in the three minutes or so it took to restart, we would fall back between the two ships again. Even without an impending invasion that would have been a very bad night.

But would there, *could* there be an invasion in that weather? Could the troop-laden LCVPs make it to shore? If so, could they beach in such surf? How could we cover them with gunfire while bouncing around in such a sea? We knew there was a plan for a twenty-four-hour delay. But that would inevitably involve the loss of surprise so essential to an amphibious assault and risk the failure of the operation. Which would be worse, the loss of men and equipment to the sea tonight, or to the enemy tomorrow night? As the SC 692 fought her way in the teeth of the mistral toward Sicily, even in our anxiety and discomfort, on the SC's bridge we shouted to each other that we did not envy the admiral who had that decision to make.

About 2245 there were parachute flares in sight ahead, orange-yellow blobs of light sinking slowly in the distance on both sides of the bow. A few minutes later red tracers began to string up into the sky and searchlight beams sprang up where the flares had been. According to the op plan that would be our airborne troops dropping down behind the beaches.

By 2300 the waxing moon, which up to now had been providing at least some badly needed illumination, was setting off to port, but the SC was not taking quite as much water. Apparently we were coming into the lee of Sicily, and from then on the wind gradually decreased and the sea subsided. Now we were back to the problem of finding the *Barnett*. Two factors helped: the fact that the transport column had pulled well ahead, and a series of air attacks that ignited half a dozen large fires on the land ahead. The op plan called for a straight-in approach to Sicily east of Gela, then a turn to the west to parallel the coast until the prescribed positions were reached.

We were still well at sea as the *Savannah* and then her transports made their turns and began the run along the shore. One by one each ship was revealed in sharp silhouette, backlighted in glaring red, as she slid silently past the burning towns and villages ashore. Each of the transports had a different silhouette and we knew that of the *Barnett* well, a long superstructure amidships and kingposts forward and aft. As she crossed the first fire, Wells picked her up on the radar and received the most emphatic orders conceivable from the bridge to disregard everything else, hold her at all costs, and report range and bearing every two minutes.

At that point, given the overriding priority of timely rendezvous with the transport, the SC 692 left formation and cut diagonally to port to intercept the *Barnett* as she came to anchor off her assigned beach. Our course was roughly the hypotenuse of the right triangle formed by the northward approach of the transports and their westward track along the coast.

The interception worked. Precisely at 0045 on D-day, 10 July, we slid past the high stern of the *Barnett*. Her anchor was down. Her boats were swung out. As we eased up her starboard side to take position off the bow, there came the familiar high-pitched whistle of her bosun's call and the order over her loudspeakers, "Commence debarkation!"

A little after 0100, three twin-engine planes came skimming out from Gela, where fires still burned brightly, black against the night sky, low on the water, but flashing recognition signals—friendlies. After that all was quiet in the darkened Gulf of Gela. In groups of half a dozen at a time the men of the 692 picked their way aft and ducked down below for hot baked beans, hot coffee, and fresh apple pie. It had been a long, rough night and it was not over. There was no point in fighting a war on an empty stomach.

While the men below were eating, others dragged mattresses topside and lashed them around the bridge and the gun stations as planned. The 40-mm crew dropped the jackstaff and lifelines forward and the man at the depth charges took down the flagstaff. The 692 had cleared for action. By 0200 all hands had eaten and were back at battle stations.

At exactly that time, the PC 621 moved out of her position abeam of the transport and headed for the line of departure, a string of LCVPs in her wake like ducklings following their mother. The troops jammed into them were the first or Red assault wave, their objective the Yellow and Blue beaches just to the east of Gela. The 621, as primary landing craft control for those beaches, would anchor at the line of departure a mile and a half offshore and send the assault waves in according to schedule. The instant the PC and her brood got under way, a searchlight down the shore to the west stabbed out into the night, swept back and forth across the water, found a big ship that looked to us like a cruiser, stayed on her for a minute or two, and went out. Perhaps the enemy thought her friendly.

At 0215, the SC 691 muttered off into the shoreward darkness, this time with boats astern, the second or Blue wave. Then it was our turn. All hands were now at general quarters, helmets pulled down, life-jacket collars pulled up, tense and silent. Three or four searchlights were now sweeping the coastal waters, appearing to jump over the ships, but there was still no hostile fire, no air attacks, nothing.

The SC 692 circled back to the starboard beam of the *Barnett* and again I announced by megaphone, "This is the third or Yellow wave for the Blue and Yellow beaches. Fall in astern."

Three LCVPs that had been idling in a circle off the *Barnett's* starboard side straightened out and came over. One lost soul came alongside to ask if this were the Blue wave. We told him he had missed that one but to join up since our destination was the same. At 0228, Sadler, between the depth charges all the way aft, began to blink his blue light and I yelled to the packed LCVPs gathering back there in the darkness, "Two minutes to go."

At 0230, with only four boats astern, Sadler held his blue light steady, and remembering that we had been ten minutes early at the rehearsal, we waited three extra minutes to accommodate any stragglers. It was 0233 when the last announcement sounded over the muttering of LCVP diesels, "Under way." We accelerated slowly to 8 knots, the maximum speed of the loaded boats, and headed in, radar firmly locked on the 621 at the line of departure. It was only a four-mile, thirty-minute trip, but to a small shipful of young men in their first action, it could have been Magellan's Pacific crossing.

With two miles to go, the action began. A searchlight snapped on to port of the PC, found her, and held her like a bug on a pin. Then there was a flash off to starboard, a slamming report, and a column of white water rose close to the PC's starboard side. Another flash, another report, and another splash, this one several hundred yards to port. Whoever the enemy gunners were, they needed more practice, because another round fell well short and ricocheted away. With the 692 and her Yellow wave still a mile to seaward of the PC, another light came on to port and immediately picked us up. It felt something like suddenly finding yourself buck naked at high noon in Times Square. And there was nothing we could do. Our single 40-mm main battery lacked the range to reach the light. We could neither maneuver nor increase speed or we would lose the landing craft that were dependent on us to place them where they belonged. So at 8 knots we crawled straight forward to the bull's-eye at the center of the target where the PC 621 was now slamming away at the light with her 3-inch/50, lighting up the night with regular yellow flashes that reflected from the sea.

On the bridge I was having a minor problem. My mouth was dry and my knee caps had come alive independent of my will and were jumping up and down several times a second. The knee caps were only bothersome and could not be seen under my long khaki trousers, but the dry mouth threatened to affect my voice and I could not let that happen. It was absolutely essential for the fighting effectiveness of the ship that the tall figure at the forward rail of the bridge, visible even in the dark to all hands topside, display nothing but calm and confidence. With some effort I moistened my mouth with my tongue as best I could before I gave any order and tried to hold those utterances to the necessary minimum.

As the 692 closed in on the PC, we waited for the splashes to fall around us too, but they never did, and after about five minutes the light went out. At the same time, the PC must have been getting close with his 3-inch because that light went out too and the firing stopped.

At 0300 we pulled up to the PC and delivered our landing craft, circling back along their little column and instructing them by megaphone to join the other boats in the vicinity and to take their orders from the 621. Fifteen minutes later we headed back for the *Barnett*. We had not gone five hundred yards before the same searchlight picked us up again. But not for long. There was a flash to seaward, a thudding of big guns, and a pair of white projectiles moving very fast rose in a flattened arc and curved down toward the light. An eye-blink before they arrived, the light went out, but the two projectiles detonated in white, sparkling bursts right where it had been. A crash echoed across the water (or so it seemed) and that light never came on again.

But down the coast toward Scoglitti a single heavy gun began to fire on the Blue and Yellow beaches. After three or four rounds there was a burst of flame well to seaward as the HMS *Abercrombie* opened up in reply with her 15-inch guns. Three salvos and the enemy gun went silent.

At the other end of the assault sector, as we groped in the dark for the *Barnett* (she had changed position), the *Savannah* was working over another enemy gun position. We could see the flashes as her 6-inch turrets fired in succession and we watched the three swift white birds in close formation rise after each flash, sail shoreward in a flat but graceful arc, and burst in a shower of white sparks on the target, each set of three striking a few yards farther inland. When she had disposed of that emplacement, she went to work on the remaining searchlights. Within five minutes the coastline was once more comfortably dark.

At 0445 when we found the *Barnett*, the first traces of light were beginning to show to the eastward in the direction of Scoglitti. We came alongside to port and reported in. Down from her high, dark bridge came the response, "Standby to take in another wave." We eased out to some three hundred yards off her port bow and lay to. We had been there less than five minutes, with coffee being passed to the gun crews and topside stations, when he heard a sound like a fast-approaching siren rapidly rising to a sort of basso scream and ending abruptly. A great dirty mushroom of water erupted between the SC and the *Barnett*. The ship shuddered violently with the water hammer of the explosion, and the deck jumped under our feet, but a quick check showed no damage.

We moved out to five hundred yards and had just killed our headway, our nerves beginning to return to something approaching normal when they were dealt another blow: a bright, tremendous yellow flash just to seaward followed by a rising mushroom of heavy orange smoke. Several seconds later a deep, sustained report, like a long clap of distant thunder, shook the little ship. Charlie thought a big enemy plane had been shot down. I didn't think they had an aircraft big enough, even loaded with bombs, to create a flash that size. We found out later that what we had seen and heard a few seconds before 0500 that D-day morning was the instantaneous death of the U.S. destroyer *Maddox* and 210 of the 284 men aboard. A lone Stuka dive bomber, never seen or fired on, had put a single bomb into her magazine.

With the coming of daylight, the boat officers in the LCVPs were apparently able to find their own way to the line of departure, because the 692 was not called upon again as a guide. Instead, at 0700 orders came to set up a close-in antisub screen for the transports. We joined with the 691, 693, 676, PC 621, and several other PCs and SCs to patrol back and forth outboard of the long line of big anchored ships. Along the horizon to seaward half a dozen destroyers steamed back and forth, guarding against enemy reaction by sea. Inside the line of transports were more destroyers and cruisers. The *Savannah* and *Boise* lay close in to the beach, their guns thudding away at targets we could not see. Between the transports and the shore, swarms of landing craft shuttled back and forth throwing water and drawing long white wakes. Through our binoculars the town of Gela on its little coastal hill looked dusty, dry, and hot. No sign of human life was visible. Along the beach to the east of town, LSTs were lined up in a way that reminded me of the seawall at Algiers, bows to shore and stern anchors out. In front of the town and all along the coast LCIs and LCTs were also beached, with others standing by offshore. Around 0900 the transports pulled up their anchors and moved closer into shore and the patrol of SCs and PCs moved in with them.

In the 692 we kept waiting for something to happen. This was D-day, the invasion, the landing assault we had been anticipating for so long, and it seemed too easy. In fact most of D-day was so uneventful that we secured from general quarters and went to Condition II to provide a little rest to men who had been up most of the night.

The relative inactivity provided a moment or two for reflection, and what was left in the head after the action was a memory, despite all the mental preparation, of startled anger when the guns began to flash ashore and the splashes to appear in the sea: "Hey! That crazy bastard is trying to kill me! The only way to stop him is to open fire and kill him first!" What was also left was an irrational determination to add more guns, the better to keep from being killed by getting the other guy first.

Toward evening things warmed up a bit. A single enemy plane, a fighter, came in very low from the west, flying straight and fast down the long beach crowded with men and ships, released a bomb, pulled up in a climbing turn and vanished inland. For a moment, at our distance, we thought he had missed, but in a few seconds a column of black smoke and flame began to rise from one of the LSTs and she continued to burn for a long time. A few minutes later a pair of single-engine aircraft suddenly appeared high overhead and the 692's main battery opened up for the first time, slamming out sixteen rounds of 40-mm at maximum range before a division of P-38s charged in from the south and chased the enemy planes away.

As dusk closed down, signal lights began to flash on the SCs and PCs and a string of LCIs broke out of the welter of assorted craft along the shore and fell into cruising formation. The 692 took screening station on the starboard bow and at 2030 took departure for Pantelleria and Tunis. Before the light faded we noticed with interest that, as they had been on the approach, the decks of the LCIs were crowded with soldiers. As the little convoy pulled away into the darkness of that historic sea, we could see tracers soaring up astern as the beachhead came under attack again.

Pantelleria was in sight to the south at 0800 the next morning, resembling a huge beehive, with friendly fighters swarming at the lower, flatter end and clouds of brown dust rising from the dirt runway there. All the way back to Africa, Kidwell and Guszak tried in vain to tune in a news broadcast so we could find out how the operation was going, why the opposition had been so light, what casualties had been suffered, why the LCIs were returning full of troops. The radio was afflicted with chronic static on all frequencies, possibly enemy jamming, and we could learn nothing.

At 2030 on the eleventh the SC nosed back into wreck-littered La Goulette and tied up to the starboard side of an LCI, the 189. Right away our questions about the troops in the LCIs were answered. They were troops all right, but they were soldiers without weapons for whom the war was ending as ours was beginning. They were Italian prisoners of war.

The next morning some of the SC crew watched the POWs being unloaded. As could be expected under the circumstances, they were a scruffy lot, bearded, dirty, rumpled, in bits and pieces of uniforms. Bill Hawn had the poor taste to laugh at one particularly disreputable-looking individual—and got the shock of his life. The man turned from only a few feet away and looked Hawn straight in the eye.

"What are *you* laughin' at, Jack?" he demanded in flawless, colloquial American English. "I'm goin' back to the States. Where're you goin'?" It was not hard to figure out that the man was one of the many men of dual citizenship (born in the United States of Italian parents or vice versa) who had been caught in Italy at the outbreak of hostilities and drafted into her armed forces.

The men of the 692 finally got caught up on the news that day, mostly by way of LCDR Lowther, with whom I spent a couple of evening hours aboard his PC 624. It was Lowther who explained the thunderous explosion and orange flash off Gela as the death of the *Maddox*. He also reported the loss of the *Sentinel* (AM 113) off Licata about the same time and under the same circumstances—air attack at first light when ships are visible and planes are not. The *Sentinel* had been hit in her after engine room by a dive bomber at 0510 and attacked several more times before going down an hour later. The SC 530 and PC 550 had taken off the survivors, but the big sweeper had lost ten killed and fifty wounded out of a crew of a hundred. The *Sentinel* had been part of the screen from Gibraltar to Nemours. It was like learning of the death of a close acquaintance.

But there was good news too. In the ten minutes after witnessing the sinking of the *Maddox,* Silver Silverstein's PC 543, escorting the British beacon sub *Safari* back toward Malta at 19 knots, had shot down two enemy aircraft. The PC sailors had sighted the first, a twin-engine bomber, low and close on the port beam in the predawn twilight, opened up with the forty and two twenties as the plane crossed the bow, and watched the enemy crew bail out and the bomber crash to starboard. Six minutes later, with the 543 zigzagging radically four hundred yards ahead of the submarine, the same deadly scenario was played again, this time with a single-engine fighter-bomber as the target. Again the plane was first spotted to port and fired on with forties, twenties, and the 3-inch/50 as it crossed ahead. Off the starboard bow the enemy first smoked, then flamed, a chute blossomed briefly as the pilot hit the silk, and the plane quenched its fire in the sea. All of Silver's men and all of us who heard about the action hoped that one of the bombers shot down was the one that got the *Maddox.*

It seemed the 692 had left Gela just in time. The next day, the eleventh, as we were steaming more or less peacefully back across the Strait of Sicily, the *Barnett* had taken a near miss that killed seven soldiers and started fires aboard. That same day the *Savannah, Boise, Glennon,* and a couple of other destroyers had driven back an attack by Italian tanks and German Panzers that had seriously threatened to overrun the Gela beachhead and thus turn back a major part of the invasion force. Now that the landing force was ashore and the enemy knew where to find it (and its supporting ships), air attacks were increasing in strength and frequency.

At 0845 on the thirteenth the 692 got under way to return to Gela, screening a convoy of LCIs. It was a small convoy, fifteen LCIs in three columns of five each, but important. Each LCI was jammed with two hundred troops, three thousand fighting men to reinforce the beachhead. Lowther in the PC 624 was in the lead as OTC, with PCs 627 and 624 to his port and starboard. We screened the port flank, the SC 691 the starboard.

The sea was full of floating mines. At 1730 we pulled out and sank one with the aft 20-mm after peppering it unsuccessfully with rifles, machine guns, and even tommy guns. The aft twenty, we found, worked best because it was higher and could fire down at a better angle on either side. But even with the use of incendiary ammo, the

Silver Silverstein's PC 543, which shot down two enemy bombers
in six minutes off the landing beaches of Gela, Sicily, 10 July 1943.
(National Archives)

mine did not blow up; it just sputtered stubbornly out of sight, smoking from several jagged holes. Later the PC 627 fell back, circled, and
dropped some charges on what must have been a sonar contact.

In the unlimited visibility of that bright afternoon we could see
Pantelleria fifty miles away and four long convoys on a reciprocal
course, one of LSTs, one of LCIs, and two of transports, a total of
some sixty ships not including their escorts, of which fifteen were new
U.S. destroyers. The sight of all those warships, the mines, and the
sub contact gave the men of the SC a feeling of being part of a decisive
operation, members of a team engaged in making history.

The night when it came was calm and windless under a moon so
bright there was a good chance of seeing and avoiding the mines. At
2200 the order came to slow frcm 12 to 10 knots to assure arrival after
daylight. And just after daylight, with the coast of Sicily looming
through a light fog dead ahead, the lethal black blobs of two floating
mines came in sight off the port bow.

On closer inspection they turned out to be the floats of "friendly"
mines that had broken loose from their anchors. But the mines were
there all right, suspended a few feet below the floats. After the previous day's practice we quickly put them down with 20-mm fire, the
heavy explosive slugs making bright detonations on impact and the
brass cascading across the SC's deck.

The little convoy strung out and approached the smoking island through a swept channel off Licata, then turned eastward close to shore, well inside the mine fields. The shallow Gulf of Gela was busy under the warming sun and the shredding fog. We counted two dozen high, vulnerable-looking merchantmen, eight destroyers, four U.S. and one British light cruiser, and scattered between the larger ships, dozens of small ones like ourselves—AMs, PCs, YMSs, SCs, and tugs large and small. Even smaller craft plied back and forth from ships to beach, LCTs, LCMs, LCVPs, and the awkward-looking but highly useful amphibious trucks, DUKWs, called simply "ducks." It seemed strange to see them drive along the shore as though on a highway, then turn to seaward, plunge into the surf, and churn three or four miles out to sea to pick up another cargo.

But the beach and the bay held an aura of increasing danger. The burned-out, torn-up hulk of the LST 313, which we had seen bombed on D-day, crouched at the water's edge. Offshore a nest of eight wounded LCVPs lay moored to a single buoy, listing in different directions, scorched and broken. A few miles out in the transport area a tangle of twisted metal poked up out of the sea, barely recognizable as the stern of an ammunition ship, which we learned had burned and exploded on the evening of the eleventh after an attack by a wave of Ju 88s.

At Gela our LCIs moved in close to shore, formed a line just off the beach, and then in pairs or threes ran in as far as they could go, their eight diesels smoking and their propellers churning the shallow water at their sterns. They seemed to ground about ten yards out, lowered their narrow twin ramps, and the troops went splashing ashore, thigh or waist deep, in long single files.

By 1630 it looked as though the LCIs had finished their job and were ready to head back to Africa for another load. On the 692 we assumed we would be screening them as before, but that assumption was incorrect. About 1640 the signal light on an AVD, a destroyer converted to an aircraft tender and now being used as a command ship, began to flash with our call letters. When LaFlamme answered up with a clattering of our own light, orders came to make the side of the AVD, which turned out to be the *Biscayne*. That began a busy thirty-odd hours that threatened to end with the destruction of the 692.

As the 692 approached the *Biscayne*, her gig was departing, all shiny gray paint and varnish, her crew in immaculate whites. She was flying a red flag with three stars. We learned later that her passenger was General George Patton.

Once alongside we were first ordered to get shirts on all officers and men, then to make the LCI group and instruct the senior officer to anchor his ship near the *Biscayne*. It took about twenty minutes to locate the LCI 17 with a captain aboard and give him the word. Back along the starboard side of the AVD it looked as though we were in for a tour as duty messenger vessel.

A Lieutenant Carswell came aboard with orders to put him aboard an LST, the 389, beached at Scoglitti, fifteen miles to the eastward. He joined us for supper on the ninety-minute run along the shore, a tall, pale, pleasant gentleman who seemed to enjoy the ride.

The LST 389 was in sight, unloading over a pontoon bridge with prisoners, soldiers, and sailors all working together, and we were nosing in toward her when a more urgent job came up. Just astern of an AM off to starboard, a motor whaleboat had capsized and its three-man crew was thrashing around in the water. The AM turned out to be our old friend of Nemours and Beni Saf, the *Seer*, Commander Block. We rigged the Jacob's ladder to starboard, picked up the whaleboat crew, got a line on the boat itself, towed it over to the *Seer*, and put her men aboard.

The LST was just beginning to retract from the beach as we arrived, but the SC came in slowly and gently in the clear, shallow water, nuzzled her port bow against the 389's starboard quarter and Lieutenant Carswell climbed up a cargo net to her deck. As we backed off and turned to seaward, another LST off to port was taking aboard what looked like several hundred prisoners from an LCT alongside.

It was dark when the 692 hailed the *Biscayne* to report our passenger delivered. We were told to "patrol around in the vicinity but stay in sight and stand by for orders." It was a pointless patrol, well inside of everything, with other patrols offshore, and at midnight we hailed the *Biscayne* again and asked permission to anchor. The OOD seemed surprised and quickly granted permission. "I think the sons-ofbitches just forgot about us," Charlie said, and I agreed.

No orders came and nothing happened until 1030 the next morning, 15 July; then the *Biscayne*'s light began to flash. Make the *Nicholson* (DD 442), it said, and report to a Captain Reed.

The SC was alongside the destroyer by 1100. I climbed aboard, saluted the colors, and a sailor on gangway watch took me forward to the captain's cabin. Captain Reed, not tall but husky, unsmiling and businesslike, was seated at a gray metal pull-down desk. With him, in a straight-back aluminum chair, was a Marine lieutenant colonel. Not a moment was wasted. The captain handed me a single sheet of white lined paper. On it was written in pencil longhand "Embark Col.

Brower, USMC, and take orders from him while he arranges for two LCMs. When this has been done, return him to this ship and deliver the two LCMs to Commander Messmer in the USS *Staff* at Empedocle. Guard 2150 enroute. Return and report to DD 442."

It seemed straightforward enough. I had only the roughest idea of the location of Empedocle, somewhere along the coast to the west, but it was on the chart and we could find it. It was obvious that this was no social call and the captain was a busy man. I said my "Aye, Ayes" and returned to the ship. The Marine officer followed in about two minutes.

We took him in to Blue Beach and flagged down an LCM, which put him ashore to arrange with the beachmaster for his boats. He was back in an hour in one LCM with another following, and we returned him to the *Nicholson,* passed sandwiches, milk, and water to the three-man LCM crews, and at 1330 shoved off on what turned out to be the hairiest mission in the short combat career of the USS SC 692.

A look at the chart confirmed that Porto Empedocle, in millennia past the port for the Greek city of Agrigento in the hills just inland, was in fact forty-five miles west of Gela. Since the best speed of the LCMs was 8 knots, the voyage would take about five and a half hours. ETA was 1900. The return run alone at 12 knots would get us back to the Gela anchorage by 2300. It looked like a milk run, no convoy to worry about, just the two landing craft trailing docilely along in the wake, no flashing light to send or receive, only three minor course changes to clear a couple of capes before the run in to destination. The sea was calm, the sky clear, visibility unlimited, and the enemy appeared to be lying low, licking his wounds after the thwarted counterattacks of the past days.

We laid off the track line on the chart, set Condition III, and settled in for a pleasure cruise along the high coast of Sicily. At 1500 I left word with Charlie to call me when we made the final turn for the breakwater at Empedocle and went below for a nap.

At 1700 the whistle sounded at the head of my bunk and André's voice from the pilothouse announced, "Mr. Coffey would like you to come to the bridge, Captain." From there Empedocle was in sight off the starboard bow, a distant, dusty cluster of masonry at the water's edge and a barely visible breakwater just offshore. Although we checked thoroughly with the binoculars, we could see no sign of an AM or any other ship in the little harbor.

But that was not why Charlie had called me. Hull down to seaward, broad on the port bow, what looked like a cruiser and a destroyer were firing. Their targets appeared to be in the vicinity of Empedocle. We could see the yellow flash of their guns and several seconds later puffs of dust and dirt rising from the shore to the west of the town. The dull booms of the firing and the crisper reports of exploding shells came clearly across the afternoon sea.

Obviously there was still enemy resistance west of Empedocle. But that was not our business. Our orders were to deliver the LCMs to the *Staff* at Empedocle. Presumably, although the busy captain had not mentioned it, the AM was supposed to meet us there. If so she should be in sight, and to seaward, except for the two ships conducting shore bombardment, the horizon was unbroken from west through south to east.

We checked along the coast. In the hills above Empedocle we could see the white buildings of Agrigento looking much as they must have looked to the watch on the Carthaginian galleys standing in from Africa to capture the town two thousand years before, but nothing was stirring anywhere along the shore.

At 1725 we came right to 325 degrees true. Empedocle was now six miles dead ahead. For thirteen minutes we watched the destroyer and cruiser hammering the brown hills west of Empedocle, searched the harbor ahead for any vestige of a minesweeper or any U.S. warship, and swept the nearing coastline and the beaches for signs of human activity. On the last two counts, nothing.

But there was human activity over there all right. At exactly 1738 a flat whistle close overhead made us involuntarily duck; then a slap sounded aft, and a tall, thin, dirty brown tower of water rose from the sea about two hundred yards outboard of the LCMs.

Even while the SC's men raced to their battle stations, two or three more rounds came in, sending up more splashes in the same vicinity but slightly closer to the two landing craft. The LCM coxswains reacted instantly, normally, and, as it happened, correctly. They went to full power, separated, and headed back out to sea.

The 692 also went to full speed, zigzagging radically and keeping between the landing craft and the shore from which we assumed the fire was coming. "Assumed" because, search as we would, we could find no clue along the coastal hills as to the origin of the incoming rounds. It was even conceivable, we thought, that the friendly ships to seaward had mistaken us for hostiles and taken us under fire. Or perhaps they were not friendly ships at all but units of the Italian fleet firing at friendly positions ashore and were now attacking us as well.

All we knew for sure was that someone, somewhere, had us in their sights and were trying to wipe out what must have appeared as a mini–amphibious attack group. The splashes, although higher than the SC's stubby mast, did not seem big enough for the 5-inch or better guns it would take to reach us from those distant ships. And the probability of major enemy warships firing in a leisurely, uncontested manner at friendly forces within a few miles of the busy Gela beachhead was pretty remote. So the hostile artillery had to be ashore.

Desperately we searched the hills again, and over a cemetery just east of town, we made out a light blue veil of smoke, which we figured might well be coming from the muzzles of heavy weapons. I gave the target to Washer down on the 40-mm, the long barrel swung out, and the little ship began to jar with the recoil as the rounds pumped out, one each second, and the brass clattered across the deck.

The effect on the crew was miraculous. Now they were fighting back, not just taking it—running—hoping not to be hit. The graveyard was at or beyond the maximum effective range of the forty and the enemy battery might or might not be there. It didn't make any difference. In an instant the SC sailors had changed from passivity to activity, from the attacked to the attackers, from the defense to the offense. That twenty rounds of armor-piercing 40-mm, even if it only turned over some turf in a Sicilian cemetery, was exactly what was needed to transform a couple of dozen frightened young men into the mean and angry fighting crew of an American warship.

But the SC's return fire had no noticeable effect on the enemy gunners, wherever they were, and it was time to take care of our charges, the LCMs. We circled to seaward, caught up with them, and told them to head back for the shelter of the high cape we had rounded before changing course for Empedocle. The SC maintained a protective position to shoreward of the two boats as they churned off at their best speed, smoking and splashing and leaving broad foaming wakes. Since we had passed close in to Punta Blanca and drawn no fire, it was reasonable to assume it was unoccupied or in friendly hands. And east of the cape we would be masked from the guns near Empedocle.

But the turn of all three craft to seaward created an uncomfortable change in the action. With the three ships inbound, an observer ashore, say the gun captain of a coastal battery or a unit of field artillery, could not tell what was in the LCMs. Their high, toaster-grill bow ramps obscured their cargo holds from forward. If he were a good soldier, this observer would have to assume a combat load of some kind—a couple of light tanks, selfpropelled guns, or a couple of platoons of Rangers. So the LCMs would have been his priority targets.

But when the LCMs turned away, presenting their relatively low sterns to the shore, our observer could immediately see that they were empty. Empty landing craft would be no threat, nor especially valuable, not worth firing at. But a small warship of more than one hundred feet with several guns showing and a radar antenna would be a worthwhile target, especially since its small-caliber guns probably did not have the range to reply.

In any case, as soon as course was reversed, the SC 692 became the target. And two more guns, bigger ones, opened up. Now most splashes came in pairs and they were taller and louder. And closer. We estimated a battery of two German 88-mm dual-purpose guns.

A few minutes after the turn the SC took a straddle, one round about twenty yards to port, another about thirty to starboard. Buckets of cordite-smelling water fell on deck. There were buzzing and chunking sounds, shrapnel. With the guns now useless as we increased the range from shore, I ordered all hands topside flat down on the deck, and no order was ever obeyed more quickly. But it is a rule of thumb that unless drastic action is taken, a straddle is an immediate preliminary to a hit.

The SC 692 turned to port with full rudder, toward the shore, a direction we hoped the enemy gunners would not expect. She was already at maximum speed, the twin diesels roaring at the 1420 RPM to which their governors had been advanced in anticipation of just such a need. The SC was no PT boat; she was not built for speed, and now, all out, she was making just over 15 knots. As she turned hard to port, she heeled ten or fifteen degrees to starboard. The twenty rounds of 40-mm brass rolled across the foredeck and brought up against the starboard cap rail. A few pieces tumbled overboard. From the port exhaust outlets black smoke puffed up and trailed out just above the wake.

The next salvo of eighty-eights landed one hundred yards to seaward. The turn had worked. It might work again. Reverse the turn. Right full rudder. Open the range. A spotter ashore would see that his rounds had been over and correct by lowering his sights, decreasing his range. Now the right engine was smoking black. But sure enough, the next two splashes were to port and slightly astern but only fifty yards away. A swarm of shrapnel hornets buzzed across the deck, pinged off a lifeline stanchion aft, and popped through the canvas weather cloth around the bridge, leaving jagged holes of assorted sizes.

Left full rudder. Let's keep this game going as long as it works. I remembered now. I had read about this tactic somewhere in training—chasing splashes. I hoped that Kraut gun captain ashore had not read about it too.

Right full rudder. Rudder amidships to let the speed build back up. Left full rudder toward the latest splash. Rudder amidships. How close would the next salvo be? Once, right after a turn, a double splash tore into the sea ten yards off the port quarter, directly on the extension of the SC's wake, exactly where she would have been had she not turned hard to starboard twenty seconds before.

But all the time the three ships were drawing closer to Punta Blanca and farther away from the enemy guns. And as the range opened the heavy salvos became less frequent, as though with their target approaching the limit of their range, the gunners were taking time to aim and spot more carefully but were less accurate nevertheless because of the greater distance.

As the tempo of the action eased, a full realization of the situation surged into my consciousness for the first time. I found myself the only man standing erect topside. I was all the way forward on the bridge, the knuckles of my left hand white on the top rail above the weather cloth, my right hand clutching the vacuum-cleaner voice tube to the helm and engines, my pelvis pressed against the forward rail. All around me and down on the main deck fore and aft the men I knew so well sprawled flat in life jackets and helmets. No one spoke except occasionally in a low voice to a man nearby. All eyes, all attention were focused on the man at the forward edge of the bridge. And in a terrible flash of sudden knowledge I knew why. Because, with other voices stilled, on the words that one voice spoke their lives depended.

With that knowledge and the lessening of the danger, my knee caps began to dance again. But by bracing my legs back they could be stilled. And my mouth was not as dry as at Gela. As we approached the relative safety of Punta Blanca, I realized that what I was experiencing was the ultimate expression of the responsibility of command. Suddenly it came to me, as it probably should have long before, that being in command meant a hell of a lot more than being called captain, sleeping in the best bunk, and making routine daily decisions. What it ultimately meant was the *actual, direct, personal* responsibility for the lives of twenty-nine other human beings. Only in a small ship under fire, with all hands except two engineers in easy mutual visual contact, could that awesome fact have been demonstrated with such clarity.

It was about 1815 when the little task unit finally put the solid rocks of Punta Blanca between it and the enemy battery at Empedocle. With the shooting over, a lot of questions needed to be answered and some decisions made. The LCMs were ordered to idle back and forth close inshore while the SC lay to to seaward. That put all three craft well inside the protection of the cape and out of sight of the hostiles to the west. And whether the ships offshore were friendlies who had mistaken our identity or enemies who had not, it made us hard targets to find, either visually or by radar.

The logical first step was to report back to Captain Reed at Gela and request instructions. For the next thirty minutes Kidwell and Guszak tried to make radio contact, voice and CW (continuous wave—Morse), on the frequency we had been given and two others. Nothing. Next they tried to raise the *Staff* to determine her location and desires. No response.

The 692's officers met on the bridge for a council of war. The question before the council was simplicity itself—what do we do now? But the answer depended on a major unknown—who owned Empedocle? If it were the enemy, we obviously could not accomplish our mission and the logical course would be to return with our charges to Gela, reporting the circumstances and questioning the intelligence or lack of it that had resulted in ordering us, unwarned, into an enemy-held port. But if Empedocle were in friendly hands, perhaps they needed the LCMs. In which case our job would be to get them there even if we had to fight our way in, possibly under cover of darkness.

The council was still in session and the radiomen were still vainly attempting to get someone to talk to them, when a lookout reported several ships on the horizon, on an easterly course. After a few tense minutes we identified them as friendlies, a pair of AMs and some YMSs, apparently on a minesweeping mission. By about 2015 they were close enough in the gathering dusk for visual signaling, and we quickly determined that one of the AMs was the *Staff*. That greatly simplified our problem.

WE HAVE TWO LCMS FOR YOU, we told her. WHAT SHALL WE DO WITH THEM?

But the disposition of the two landing craft did not hold top priority aboard the sweeper. Our light was still clattering with the final groups of the message when a tower of white water several times higher than their masts sprang up between the two minesweepers. At the same instant, the *Staff*'s signal light, which had been holding steady on us to indicate he was reading each word as it was transmitted, went dark.

After the experiences of the afternoon, the first impression in the 692 was that the sweeper had been hit by shore fire. But on further consideration, given that single huge splash with no preliminaries and the nature of the sweeper's operation, we concluded that she had hit a mine.

Then came conflicting orders from the sweeper group. At 2029: COME OUT TO STAFF AND ASSIST HIM PICKING UP SURVIVORS.

Then, six minutes later, as we were instructing the LCMs to stand by where they were until we returned: DO NOT COME OUT HERE X THESE WATERS ARE MINED.

That was the first anyone in the 692 had heard of a mine field off Empedocle. Why had we not received routing instructions?

In another five minutes we could see that the *Staff*, although down by the bow, was under way again, and we asked her the big question: IS EMPEDOCLE IN ENEMY HANDS?

The response came back in two minutes: YES WE BELIEVE IT IS.

There would be no night battle to force our way in, and our course of action was evident, but we wanted it in writing. One more message flashed out across the darkening sea: WE ARE TAKING THE LCMS BACK TO GELA X DOES THIS MEET WITH YOUR APPROVAL?

And, finally, the welcome one-word answer: YES.

There were some relieved grins on the SC. But the three-man LCM crews greeted the news with unrestrained elation, leaping into the air, pounding each other on the back and yelping with glee. Nor could anyone blame them; they would have been prime targets in their vulnerable, uncomfortable landing craft, with no protection except what we could provide from a distance.

At 2040 the task unit headed back for Gela over a dark, calm sea and under a full canopy of stars. In all three small vessels the young men were innocently confident that a most dangerous day was finally over. At 2200 one of the engines in one of the LCMs coughed, belched black smoke, and quit. Since the landing craft was unacceptably slow and hard to handle on one engine, Boats and his men, working in the dark, rigged a bridle and we took the crippled boat in tow.

As the little force passed off Licata, a big fleet salvage tug came charging out of the harbor, a huge bone in her teeth, and turned back the way we had come, presumably to assist the wounded *Staff*.

By 0010 on the sixteenth, the clustered dark shapes of the ships anchored off Gela were in sight. All that remained was to check in aboard the *Nicholson*, arrange for the disposition of the LCMs, and drop the hook. In the 692 there was no officer or man who was not relishing the prospect of a few hours of oblivion in the cozy comfort of his bunk.

But first the gods of war had one more surprise. Close overhead from astern came the sudden roar of an aircraft engine screaming in high pitch and full throttle. On the SC's bridge every man instinctively crouched and looked up at a rush of dark wings and a blue flicker of exhaust just above the mast. There was no time even to straighten up before the sound and the sight were repeated as another plane followed close on the tail of the first. But this time, above the deafening crescendo of the straining engines came a heavy, sustained rattle of machine-gun fire and two streams of glowing red tracers stabbed out, converging in the darkness ahead. In another second a bright yellow ball of flame blossomed low in the sky at the point of tracer convergence, a little off the port bow. As we watched, mouths open with the suddenness and violence of sound and sight, the yellow ball plunged downward and impacted the surface perhaps half a mile to port. A pool of red flame flared, spread briefly, and died out as it passed down the side. Silence and darkness returned to the Gulf of Gela.

When our minds began to function again we realized we had been reluctantly close witnesses to the shoot-down of a low-flying enemy aircraft by a night fighter, probably a twin-engine Beaufighter.

It was 0045 when the SC 692 tied up once more to the port side of the *Nicholson* where the Empedocle adventure had begun only eleven hours before. She was there exactly ten minutes, which was the time it took to make an oral report to her officer of the deck and turn over custody of the two landing craft and their crews. At 0105 the Danforth dug itself into the sandy bottom of the Gulf of Gela three and a half fathoms down, and ten minutes later only Roy Washer as OOD and Tony Curato as gangway watch were left awake.

But we had not heard the last of Porto Empedocle. Just after 0800 the next morning a peremptory message came in from the *Nicholson:* "Commanding officer report aboard." By 0820 the 692 was once again alongside the destroyer, and her CO, whose twenty-fifth birthday it was, was standing at attention before an obviously displeased Captain Reed. The first thing he asked for was the handwritten single sheet of orders he had written the previous day. With that safely in his pocket, he administered what amounted to a royal chewing out. The LCMs should not have been returned to Gela, he said. They should have been left "up there" with "the next senior man." It did no good to point out that the port "up there" was in enemy hands, or that "the next senior man," in a damaged ship in an enemy mine field at sunset, had approved the return of the boats.

The lack of logic displayed by so senior an officer was disillusioning and the gratuitous and undeserved scolding offensive. At the anchorage to which we were ordered to await instructions I prepared an official and comprehensive account of the action and personally delivered it the same afternoon. Later Charlie and I agreed that so unquestioning was our trust in higher authority and in the validity of our orders, that had the enemy not fired on us, we would have steamed straight into the harbor at Empedocle with the two LCMs and tied up, providing a gift to the enemy of a fully manned and armed United States warship complete with all classified publications, codes, and ciphers. Or, alternatively, we would have recognized the enemy presence too late and lost the ship with heavy casualties just offshore.

In spite of the official opinion of the incident, the 692 had learned something about the ship's capabilities in the tight maneuvering to avoid enemy shore fire. The action off Empedocle had been the first time we had used the full power of the 692's big GM 268A diesels, at the same time applying full rudder. The result had been a lot of heavy, black smoke from the inboard engine on each turn, making the ship even more conspicuous and obscuring the view of the gunners on that side. The morning after the action, Chief Morton educated me as to the cause and the means of prevention. He explained that the black smoke was the result of an overload on the inboard engine and that it could be avoided by reducing RPM on that engine by about one hundred turns just before giving the rudder order. Good advice that became standard procedure after that.

That same afternoon the 692 joined up with the 651 to escort a little convoy of cripples back to Bizerte. Our charges were two damaged LSTs and two LCIs, also damaged but loaded with prisoners nevertheless. Towing on a long hawser astern of one of the LSTs was the SC 1030, with an ugly plywood patch in her side where she had reportedly been rammed by a PC. Convoy speed was ridiculously slow to ease the wounded ships, but the sea was calm with a light breeze to cool the air and visibility unlimited: except for the ever present danger from drifting mines, a pleasure cruise.

After a restfully uneventful night, Pantelleria was in sight at dawn, and all day fighters from the field there were overhead, covering two big convoys of troop-laden LSTs and merchantmen with escorts of destroyers and PCs bound for Sicily.

As slow as we were, a convoy of LCTs ahead, escorted by three subchasers, was slower, and when we finally caught up with it in late afternoon we found that the SC on the port quarter was our old friend the 535, also bound for Bizerte. At 2300, when the convoy slowed still more in order to make port at 0800 as ordered, we shut down an engine for routine maintenance and were still off the Bizerte breakwater an hour early.

The harbor at Bizerte was like that at Tunis but worse, full of sunken ships, some on an even keel with rusted decks awash, others listing at radical and awkward angles, all with jagged open wounds from bombs and shellfire. We picked our way carefully between the wrecks, down a narrow channel with shattered buildings on both sides, past a holed and grounded ferryboat and some perforated grain elevators, to a little fuel pier where we made fast to the port side of the 535 and rigged hoses to take on fuel and water.

Thus began a full month of operations out of Bizerte with its narrow, wreck-strewn entrance washed by surging tidal currents and its tight little channel leading to a spacious lakelike anchorage big enough for several fleets. It was an enemy attack on the lake at Bizerte that had provided the subchaser's crew with the first air raid they had ever seen, safely witnessed from anchor off La Goulette at Tunis two weeks before. It was hot in Bizerte but there was nearly always a cooling breeze out in the lake where the SCs, PCs, and YMSs anchored almost every night, often joined by several boats from PT Squadron 15 when they were not out on harassing missions along the coast of Sicily. Since we were based at one port for more than a few days, the blessed mail was able to catch up, the paymaster found us, and spare parts for the engines became available once again. There was even liberty for the crew in nearby Ferryville from 1400 to 2000 each day, although tightly regulated and controlled with a responsible petty officer in charge of each party.

Of equal importance to the crews of all the small warships that shared the quiet lake anchorage—the piers and fuel docks and movies and convoys and patrols—the warm and mutually beneficial companionship that had begun back in Nemours and Beni Saf and flowered at La Goulette resumed and grew. In many a late evening bull session over a mug or two of contraband and inferior vin rouge, experiences were shared, views exchanged, and solutions to a myriad of common problems proposed and discussed. And working in ways no one could ever list, social relationships were established that smoothed out operations at sea, increased efficiency and survivability, and worked significantly to the detriment of the enemy.

On that first day at Bizerte we learned at first hand from her saddened and subdued skipper, Chuck Highfield, the details of the damage to the SC 1030. According to Chuck, she had been on night patrol off Scoglitti, Sicily, when the PC 591, apparently also on patrol but on a track at 90 degrees to that of the 1030, crossed her bow from port to starboard some five hundred yards ahead in poor visibility, and then unexpectedly turned hard to starboard 180 degrees and came straight at the SC. Chuck, making a patrol speed of 8 knots, backed down emergency full at the last minute but the steel bow of

The port of Bizerte, Tunisia, summer 1943. The LSTs and LCTs along the docks are taking on combat loads, and a dozen subchasers are moored at the French pier at upper right. (National Archives)

the PC hit his ship dead amidships penetrating to within four feet of the subchaser's keel, wrecking the starboard engine and flooding the engine room. Fortunately the steel bulkheads at both ends of the engine room, designed for just such an emergency, held and prevented the flooding and sinking of the entire ship. The one man on watch in the engine room was agile (and no doubt scared) enough to escape without injury.

The PC skipper is reported to have claimed he was making only 4 knots, a claim difficult to defend in view of the extent of the damage. It was the considered, entirely unofficial, and uncorroborated view of the 692's officers, remembering the ramming of the SC 1470 off Alligator Reef and our own experience astern of the Bermuda-to-Gibraltar convoy, that the PC mistook the 1030 in the limited visibility at night for a surfaced sub and maneuvered deliberately to ram, discovering his error too late to avoid collision. There were unconfirmed rumors that the 1030 would be decommissioned and cannibalized for weapons and spare parts.

Hearing that a PT squadron was also based at Bizerte triggered a memory that my friend George Steele had said this was his destination, and I found him at the PT base on the edge of the otherwise unused air base near the docks. He left orders for his boat, the 215, to follow us out to the lake and moor alongside for the night, came aboard, helped us through the tricky little channel to the anchorage and spent the evening.

George had also been having some adventures. His squadron had been in on the invasion that captured Pantelleria and had been dive-bombed off and on for an hour and a half without damage or casualties. (A PT boat maneuvering at 40 knots would be a tough target for a dive-bomber.) He had also been off Gela on the night of the landings, patrolling against an attempt by enemy E-boats to interfere, but had seen no action, and no wonder in view of the weather on that night. Before Gela his squadron's mission was to make the enemy think the landings would take place at the western end of the island by reconnoitering the beaches and harbors there and shooting up targets of opportunity. By coincidence, even as he was telling us about that mission, there was a news report about a captured Italian general who said the attack in the east was a surprise and that most of the opposing forces had been ready in the west. Now he was running up to Sicily nearly every night, picking up and putting ashore agents and conducting general harassment to keep the enemy off balance.

George had one particularly good yarn about a reconnaissance of the harbor at Palermo, the capital of Sicily. He had moved right in close to the breakwater when he was picked up by a searchlight. Before his gunners could open up on the light, another one came on at the opposite side of the entrance and both then obligingly focused on the inlet to help him through, apparently mistaking him for a friendly E-boat. The PT 215 then ungratefully moved straight into the inlet and thoroughly shot up both lights and adjacent gun positions with its port and starboard twin .50 calibers.

The final item on the news that first day in Bizerte noted that American Rangers had captured Porto Empedocle on Saturday, the sixteenth, the day after our abortive attempt to enter the harbor. It appeared that Captain Reed's SC/LCM operation had been okay in concept. His timing was just a little off.

Early the next morning Kapfer and Hawn traded an old pair of dungarees and a few cigarettes to some Arabs in a bumboat for forty-two fresh eggs, which Rees combined with corned beef hash and toast for a truly memorable breakfast. George Steele, who had spent a refreshing night under the stars on a cot on the bridge, remarked with awe about the luxuries of "these big ships."

But our first stay at our new base turned out to be a short one. At 1045 on the nineteenth, the SC 692 stood out the channel and joined up as part of the screen for two empty LCIs and a yard tug bound for Licata. The only other escort was the SC 666, whose skipper had been a student of mine at midshipman's school. He was nevertheless the screen commander and we did not argue the matter, having been substituted at the last moment for another ship that couldn't make it. That turned out to be a questionable decision since landfall the next day was twenty miles off and we had to tactfully suggest a revision of the ordered course to keep clear of the mine field off Gela.

The only excitement of the passage was an unproductive search for the pilot of a fighter seen to crash several miles back on the port quarter of the force the first afternoon, and a turtle, which Washer shot and Hoffner cleaned but which Rees rightfully declined to serve to the crew because "it just don't look good."

On arrival at Licata about 1730, the 692 took up an all-night patrol offshore and the next morning received orders from the destroyer *Buck* (it seemed anyone could issue orders to an SC) to change to a new patrol line closer inshore and just off the beaches where the initial landings had taken place. Her new beat was two and a half miles long, extending from the port itself eastward to where three big Liberty ships were being arduously unloaded by DUKWs and LCTs. Parallel to the patrol line was the coastal highway, now as heavily congested with traffic of all descriptions as a stateside urban thruway. Trucks of all sizes, half-tracks, jeeps, staff cars, and commandeered civilian Fiats roared back and forth continually, each with its own private feather of dust. On the beach itself, about halfway down the line, was a wrecked P-40 fighter, its gear up and one wing broken off but the engine and cockpit apparently intact. A couple of soldiers, stripped to the waist and deeply tanned, were climbing over and under it, presumably checking for anything salvageable.

Around noon that day we found an excuse to visit the harbor of Licata. A small, heavily built rowboat drifted by, holed and awash and dangerous to navigation. We quickly took it in tow, reported our find, and were directed to deliver it to "Boat Repair" inside the breakwater. Apparently Licata also had facilities for ship repair as well, because there we found the *Staff*, still down by the bow, a PC down by the stern, and an assortment of damaged landing craft. There were also several LSTs unloading over their bow ramps and a Polish freighter.

The town appeared to have been built on the side of a coastal hill topped by the still recognizable ruins of a large castle. At the bottom of the hill were the four tall chimneys of some sort of processing plant, and the white tower of a small lighthouse stood at the water's edge. Although we could not see it, there was obviously an airfield back behind the hill because steady streams of aircraft were letting down and disappearing there while still others were climbing out from the other side. Most of the planes were twin-engine transports, but we watched while one flight of nearly one hundred B-25s circled down to land.

By 1930 that day, after an hour or more of crossed signals and changed decisions about the makeup of the screen, the 692 was bound back to Bizerte with two other SCs, the 695 and the 978, two LCIs and an LST. We had the starboard flank, with the 978 to port and the 695 ahead. Convoy speed was 9 knots. The escorts patrolled back and forth in their assigned sectors at 10. When the last of the daylight had faded and before the moon came up there were so many stars in sight it was hard to see the sky between them. And under that dome of slowly swinging constellations the ancient sea was busy with the comings and goings of many ships. The radar scope in the SC's pilothouse showed a geometric pattern of ordered white blobs ahead, which we knew was a big convoy of LSTs also bound for Africa. About ten miles to starboard were three fast-moving targets, destroyers that had passed close aboard just at sunset. And between the LST group and the destroyers, too far away at twenty-four miles to distinguish individual units, was another big force, probably fast merchantmen or transports because it was drawing rapidly out of radar range.

About an hour into the first watch, the 692 was called upon to pull out to starboard and provide the coordinates of the swept channel into Bizerte to a British hospital ship, the *Oxfordshire,* which was paralleling the convoy course, a dazzling spectacle on the night sea in her floodlighted white paint and red crosses.

At daylight the familiar bulk of Pantelleria was in sight ahead, and by the time it had faded into the haze astern, Cape Bon was visible on the port bow. Late in the afternoon the starboard lookout reported another expended aircraft drop tank ahead, and we changed course to sink it with rifle fire, a task that always livened up a dull watch because when hit with an incendiary round, the residual gasoline vapors exploded in a most satisfactory way. But this time it was no fun at all. With the rifle at the ready and the round chambered, the tank turned out to be the bloated belly of a naked corpse. We slowed and came close alongside to see if there were any clues as to nationality. The man's facial features had long since been obliterated, there was no dog tag, and the life belt that was holding him afloat was foreign and un-familiar. The task of getting the body aboard and the effect thereafter on the morale of the crew were both unacceptable, and we left him to the sea.

At 1830, still somewhat chastened by that harsh reminder of our own mortality and the dicey nature of the waters in which we were operating, the signal came to "Proceed independently," and once more the 692 stood in between the breakwaters of Bizerte, through the wreck-strewn outer harbor, and down the long channel to the lake, assuring the signal station on the way that we had "No damage, no casualties."

The big lake was full of anchored, heavily laden ships, mostly merchantmen, but we found a spot off a shallow cove near the PT base and set the hook in two and a quarter fathoms at 1854. It was good to be in port. Bizerte was already beginning to feel like home. The stiff, warm breeze that had followed us in little cat's paws down the channel died out quickly and the evening settled in clear and calm. Half a dozen of the SC sailors rowed ashore in the pram and explored along the beach. A like number of British soldiers swam out and climbed aboard for coffee and conversation with the crew. At dusk in the lake at Bizerte, in the idyllic North African summer weather, the war for a while did not seem so bad.

But the war was there all right. That very afternoon General George Patton's Seventh Army, which had landed across the beaches of Gela only twelve days before, marched unopposed into Palermo, the capital of Sicily, a port city long to be remembered by the men of the 692. And just before the SC's arrival, four PTs of George Steele's squadron had roared off for that same city to be the first naval units there. But on the northeast side of Sicily the British and Canadians had been stopped at Mount Etna and the Germans were reinforcing. Although the issue in Sicily was still in doubt, the word at Bizerte was that Palermo would be strongly held as the major supply port for Al-lied forces on the island, and that the SCs and PCs now anchored in the lake or moored at the French pier would be there to help out with the holding.

How soon we would be leaving no one seemed to know, so every-one tried to make the best use of the remaining time in port. The next morning we received permission to take down the starboard engine to clean injector tips, and across the pier we could see by the array of parts spread out on the dock that Prent Horne's engineers were doing the same thing for the 535. At the same time the deck force, not to be outdone, turned to to paint ship and by evening had completed the entire starboard side and about a third of the port. While all this was going on, Roy Washer found a ride over to Tunis and returned the same evening with a bulging sack of mail that sent crew morale soaring. He also exercised his own commendable initiative and brought back with the mail six quarts of above average vin rouge for the 692's little wardroom and its entertainment fund.

That evening, nested at the French pier with the 535, 538, 508, 978, 979, and a YMS, an informal gathering of the combined wardrooms pretty much took care of the vino in the course of exchanging actual and questionable experiences, ideas, and outright rumors. Under all the tall tales, the wild conjectures, and the wishful thinking was a solid undercurrent of concern about what would happen next, what it would be like at Palermo close to enemy air and naval bases with Panzers engaging the British just across the mountains, what the next operation after that would be, where, when, and what part would be played by these little warships and their young crews. It was a subject that was never far from the mind of any man there. While that convivial meeting was in progress, like a symbol of coming events, nine of the eighteen boats of MTBron 15 filed down the channel past the nested ships, their big engines rumbling and bubbling at idle, and headed across the strait to begin operations from Palermo.

Almost as though it were a continuation of the theme of the previous evening, the next morning at the operations office ashore I ran into a former student from the Officers' Indoctrination School in Newport, now the skipper of the LST 315, who volunteered that his ship would be here until the twenty-ninth and then was to start training "for the next one." And the very next day Boats returned from one of his usual foraging missions with the news that the engineering officer of the base was tearing his hair because of orders he had received to have 125 "small craft" ready in all respects to participate in "another invasion" on the twenty-ninth.

Late on the evening of the twenty-fifth, the captains of the SCs 535 and 692 were finishing up a bull session on the same general subject at the port 20-mm ready ammunition locker of the latter, now gleaming in her new paint, when Charlie Coffey popped up out of the wardroom hatch with the news just reported on the radio that Benito Mussolini had resigned. It seemed to the three of us that night that the next logical step, since Mussolini had been the unquestioned, absolute ruler of Italy since we were children and had personally brought his country into the war, would be the cessation, in one way or another, of further hostilities by the Italians, whose hearts had obviously not been in it from the start.

The following morning it looked as though we were right. The radio reported Italy under martial law: a dusk-to-dawn curfew in

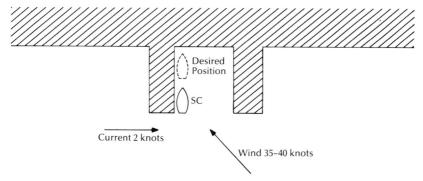

Shiphandling Problem, Bizerte, 26 July 1943

effect, gatherings of more than three people prohibited, troops authorized to use firearms to enforce the emergency regulations.

But there was not much opportunity to conjecture about events across the narrow sea, as interesting and relevant as they were. At a convoy conference ashore at 1100 we learned that the 692 would be sailing that very afternoon as part of the screen of a convoy consisting of four LSTs and three LCIs loaded with troops and vehicles to reinforce Patton in Sicily: destination Palermo. My former student, the captain of the LST 315, would be SOPA (senior officer present afloat) and the other escorts would be the SCs 638 and 978 and the PC 546.

The 692 was under way early to accomplish the chore of unloading a fifty-five-gallon drum of used lube oil onto the salvage dock before sailing, a project complicated by the location of the dock, a grit-laden wind of over thirty knots, and a two-knot ebb current at about a forty-five-degree angle to the wind. Somehow we got in, off-loaded the drum, and got out again. But when we regained the channel, we were surprised to see the LSTs and LCIs of our convoy heading back toward the lake and away from the sea. After some twenty minutes of signaling back and forth and of intercepting visual signals not intended for us, we learned that the wind was so strong and from such a direction that the unwieldy LSTs with their acres of sail area were unable to make it out between the derelicts in the harbor.

Back at anchor in the lake we were treated to a dinner of fresh chicken for which one of the crew had traded a mattress cover. Country boy Rebel Posey had expertly wrung the birds' necks and readied them for the pot.

The next morning nothing happened until 1230, when a flag hoist went up on the LST 315 ordering departure two hours later. As the SC made her way out the channel, the crew was witness to a little drama. At the same time, a large group of LSTs and LCIs, most of them loaded with prisoners, was entering the narrow passage. One of the LSTs was empty, riding high, and when she attempted to turn to port from between the last two wrecks into the channel, the wind, which had freshened again almost to the previous day's velocity, caught her bow and would not let her turn. We could see the water frothing under her broad stern as she backed down hard, but she had too much way on to stop in time, and we watched as she scraped along the bank, knocking down small trees and bushes and sending empty fuel drums rolling, until she brought up with a crunch against the unfortunate ferryboat now under repair. Three French workmen who had been aboard the ferry saw what was happening and abandoned ship with great alacrity, so that happily there were no injuries. As the SC passed, the signal station was shouting over their bullhorn that tugs were on the way.

Outside the breakwater there was a lot of activity. A couple of dozen ships were anchored there: merchantmen, transports, hospital ships, British minesweepers, and the usual assortment of landing craft. Out on the horizon we could make out the silhouettes of a sizable British task force, including a carrier, two battleships, two cruisers, and at least five destroyers. Then as our own charges were finally coming out and forming up, a big force of British merchant ships came in, escorted by destroyers and corvettes who passed close aboard and waved in such a warm and hearty way it left us all in good spirits.

PALERMO

As the convoy took departure and headed off for Sicily, the weather showed some tricks we had not yet experienced in this landlocked sea. Visibility was about four miles in haze with the wind gusting up to fifty knots, then dying down to nearly nothing before shifting 180 degrees and increasing to forty or fifty again. To add to the strangeness of the evening, some large warship was apparently shelling the coastal hills to the east. We could hear the heavy booms of the firing, the rumble of big projectiles; and we could see the bursts ashore but never the firing ship.

After sunset the wind settled down to blow steadily and hard from the southeast. Since the convoy course was northeast, that put it squarely on the beam and the 692 squarely in the trough. When you add in the repeated squalls of nearly horizontal rain, the sum equals a miserable night, dark, wet, rough, and rolling. After the days in port, most of the SC sailors spent a lot of their time at the lee rail. To add to the eerie nature of the night, as a preliminary to each of the passing squalls, a kind of luminous mist appeared in the air, which clung, shining softly, to the hair on the backs of the hands, to the eyebrows and eyelashes and the radio antennas, and disappeared, washed away, when the rain arrived.

But in the light of a cloudily prosaic dawn all returned to normal. At daylight the island of Marettimo was twenty miles abeam to starboard and the convoy turned east along the north shore of Sicily. By early afternoon, approaching destination, the capricious wind that had provided such an uncomfortable night was down to zero, and as the force turned south for Palermo through mirror-calm seas, a strange little formation of three LCTs, surrounded by an escort of no fewer than five SCs, passed by on an opposite course. In the 692 conjecture was intense about the nature of a cargo in the LCTs that would require that much protection.

On the first dog watch a destroyer came in sight ahead, on offshore patrol for Palermo, and in another hour a familiar little ship, the SC 693, captain John Hinkley, volunteered to guide us into port. By 1800 we had our first view of the ancient city that we would come to know so well, its clustered buildings rising in a crescent from the sea to the inland hills topped by the majestic old cathedral at Monreale, the vertical cliffs of Monte Pelligrino like a sentinel at the water's edge to starboard.

It was exactly 1858 when we moored port side to the 693 at a large pier that was noteworthy for the two medium-sized cargo ships that were not at it but *on* it, high and dry and canted on opposite directions. Apparently they had been blown up there by the near misses of very heavy bombs. And those two awkwardly positioned ships seemed more fortunate than a score of others in the harbor. In a sense they were dry-docked, and there they could be patched up with relative ease and refloated. The others, alongside the various piers, were firmly on the bottom and would have to be sealed, pumped out, and then docked to complete repairs. The double effect of Allied bombing and thorough German demolition had made a mess of the once extensive port facilities. At one dock, a third of the length of a badly battered submarine lay across the cargo hatches of a sunken freighter.

Nor was there a single intact structure along the waterfront adjacent to the docks. There, damage ran from mere piles of masonry and plaster, which presumably not long before had been houses, to recognizable homes with at least the roof and one entire wall missing, exposing all the pathetic domestic arrangements within to the weather and public view. Family portraits still hung slanting from the single remaining wall of someone's living room. A feather duster hung neatly beside the wash basin of a second floor bathroom whose door, swinging back and forth in the wind, opened only onto space. A chandelier, which in other days had lighted a cozy bedroom, now dangled above two stories of dusty rubble and the public street. At the seaward foot of each street, blocking it, were the remains of barricades made from the wreckage, indicating that the departed defenders had anticipated the arrival of a hostile landing force.

From the reports we picked up in the first few hours in port, the city's suffering was not over. At a pier near the SC's berth lay the destroyer *Mayrant*, leaking badly and without power, whose damage was the result of an attack by three Ju 88s while on patrol offshore. Moored to her port side, providing pumps and power, was the minesweeper *Strive*, whose softball team had fallen to Ray's invincible pitching back in Nemours, and which had been part of the sweeper force off Empedocle the day the *Staff* was mined. There was every indication that the Luftwaffe, familiar with every detail of the Palermo area, would be giving it considerable attention as it came to be a major port for the reinforcement and supply of Allied armies in Sicily.

In the long Sicilian summer evening, with all the chores of arrival completed and the watch on both ships set, John Hinkley of the 693, his exec, Bernie Tygraeber, and I buckled on our .45s and went ashore to see the town.

The damage to the city appeared limited to the area around the port. A few blocks inland only an occasional crater in the street or a wall chipped or holed by shrapnel was evidence of the continuing hostilities. Beyond that the streets became wide and pleasant with gracious homes, sidewalks, and shade trees. In some yards were lemon trees and the smell of the fruit was in the air. But no one was there. Palermo was not a ghost town but a ghost city. The shops were there, their plate-glass windows intact, and the homes, and streetcars, still and silent on their tracks, but there were no people, except for perhaps a pair of carabinieri on lonely patrol in creaky boots, or once in a while a skinny, ragged little boy running up out of a side street to ask for "Cigarette—Papa?" or "Caramella?" Our voices echoed from the empty buildings we passed, and once a distant, loudening hum turned out to be a jeep-load of GIs, which, after it passed, could be heard for five more minutes before distance brought the silence back.

It was dark when we got back to the harbor and the nest of familiar little ships, thoughtful, stimulated, and deeply impressed by what we had seen ashore. Aboard the 693, over a Spartan supper of K-rations and ice water and joined by Ben Partridge of the 978 and his XO, Bob Belknap, an NROTC graduate from Yale, we stayed up talking until after midnight. From Ben we learned for the first time of the tragedy at Gela on the night following the landings when a flight of more than one hundred C-47s loaded with paratroops had come in low over the anchorage during an enemy air raid and twenty-three were shot down. According to Ben no one had even discovered the error until the drifting bodies of the friendly troopers were recognized the next morning.

But there was something in addition to the experience of the evening that was keeping the skipper of the 692 awake and talkative. According to the latest information I had received, this was the day, back in Vermont, in that distant, half-forgotten world of peace and beloved people beyond Gibraltar and the Atlantic, my first child was to be born. I had learned long ago to control my thoughts and feelings about what was going on back home in order to be able to do the job here, limiting those thoughts to the privacy of my bunk and the moments before sleep. I could neither prevent nor overcome the separation so intolerable at such a time, nor communicate more rapidly than the week to ten days it took a V-mail letter to make the trip one-way.

But now, when to the best of my knowledge the time had come, the discipline I had imposed on my thoughts was breaking down. There was still nothing I could do, but that did not keep my mind from exploring and conjecturing, to the detriment of my concentration on matters that urgently required it and of my peace of mind. I was painfully aware that the inexorably accelerating biological process that had been merely idling in that beloved body on my departure back in March had now revved up to full power and had taken over to accomplish its primal reproductive purpose. What was it like for her? Would she be all right? Would the people around her be both kind and competent? Would she be able to handle the inevitable pain without the support, however naive and unknowing, of him who, however lovingly and long ago, had most assuredly caused it?

Was there now, at this moment, a new person in the world, a son, a daughter, of my own flesh with whom all the remaining years of my life would be inextricably enmeshed in love, in joy, anxiety, concern, pride, and awesome responsibility? A person who would one day marry and give life to others who would not exist, with whatever contributions they might make to mankind, had not this particular subchaser captain once missed a train out of Penn Station and found a beautiful Irish girl on the next one?

With a world war and three thousand miles between Sicily and Vermont, all I could do, whatever my feelings, was wait and watch the mail.

At daylight the next morning, sirens howled ashore and the radio announced, "Condition Red," but no planes appeared and "Condition White" resumed in ten minutes. Perhaps, we thought optimistically, the army air forces have fighters based around here somewhere and we won't have to worry about the Luftwaffe.

Since the convoy with which the 692 had arrived was only the second group of ships to enter Palermo since its change of hands and had entered only one day after the harbor had been opened to shipping, there were as yet no arrangements for or regulations governing crew liberty in the city. But the young subchaser sailors were understandably eager to explore, as their officers had been and still were, and there had been little enough recreation of any kind to compensate for the long days and hours of hard work, discomfort, and danger they had been through. So the SC 692 made her own arrangements and regulations for liberty.

The uniform would be army coverall fatigues with brown helmet liners and the high-topped field shoes liberated from the dock at Nemours—in order that it would not be immediately apparent to a casual observer that these were man-of-warsmen. Each man would be scrupulously logged out and back aboard. Liberty would be for two hours only. And before they left the ship, the crew received an earnest and emphatic lecture as to the conduct expected of them. They were not under any circumstances to enter a private home, damaged or intact. They were to treat the people they encountered with the same respect they would expect from visitors to their own hometowns and cities in the States.

They were reminded that the people of Palermo, apart from language and location, were no different from their own friends and neighbors, and that they deserved special consideration because of the troubles they had recently been through, with many of their homes and possessions destroyed, relatives killed or wounded, and years of repression and abuse by first their own Fascist bullies and then their German "allies." What might seem to a sailor like the casual collection of a souvenir might appear to the local populace as looting, they were told, a crime punishable by shooting on sight, and one which, in any case, would result in the immediate cancellation of any further liberty from the SC 692. The liberty party left the ship at 0900, uncharacteristically serious and thoughtful, and returned, clean and sober, at or before 1100.

The part of that little talk about these people being much like the SC sailors themselves was literally true in the case of Gunner's

Mate Second Tony Curato. Although Tony had been born and raised in Brooklyn, New York, his parents had been born, brought up, and had met in Palermo. Not Italian, not even Sicilian, but pure Palerman was the language Tony had learned to speak as a child and the one he now spoke to the astonished and delighted inhabitants of this city of his ancestors. (Nor was Tony the only man aboard with a second language. Charlie Nader, of Syrian parents, spoke Arabic; Archie La-Flamme and Frank Hagan had French; radioman Guszak was fluent in Polish; and Arnold Kapfer could at least understand German.)

That same evening I asked Tony to come ashore with me as interpreter, and we talked to a lot of the people who were now streaming back into town from their refuges with relatives in the nearby hills. It was wonderful to watch the expressions on those Palerman faces when out of the mouth of this good-looking young American sailor came the syllables of their very streets and neighborhoods. Most, when they had recovered from their initial surprise, told about relatives in New York, whom they insisted Tony must know. A few had been to the States at least once and wanted to go again. But all told the same bitter story of mistreatment by the Germans, of being treated not like allies but like a conquered and occupied people. Their most common complaint was that the prisoners being shipped out to Africa were only the little guys who had been forced into the army, whereas the Fascist big shots were still at large.

On the way back to the ship, we passed a group of about one hundred of those little guys on their way to embarkation. If they were bitter or resistant to their fate, it was certainly not apparent. The entire block-long, straggling column was in the custody of a single American sergeant who ambled along at its head, a tommy gun slung by its strap over one shoulder and taking only occasional glances back to see whether his charges were still with him. We heard later that it was common for a detail of such prisoners under similar circumstances to arrive at its destination with more men than when it had started.

In the last days of July more of these docile prisoners were pouring into the Sicilian capital as the U.S. Seventh Army pushed eastward along the north coast toward Messina, and the port of Palermo was increasingly busy as engineers cleared the piers for scores of ships bringing supplies and reinforcements in and taking prisoners out. Every inbound and outbound vessel was part of a convoy, and every convoy had its escorts.

The USS SC 692 got under way at 0600 on the thirtieth as part of the screen for the same little group of landing craft with which she had arrived only thirty-six hours before—less one LST and the PC

546. This time the LSTs would be carrying wounded men, and the LCIs prisoners. And this time the 692 had additional responsibilities. By special order of the convoy commodore in LST 315, we were assigned the ahead position and charged with leading the force. But, anticlimactically, any leading had to wait a solid hour until a harbor tug finally got the word and arrived to open the antisub net at the entrance.

Nor were we the only ones inconvenienced and delayed by the net's late opening. While we lay to on one side of it, half a dozen PTs came dipping and swooping in from night operations to the westward, throwing sheets of white water at 30 knots, only to slow and settle ignominiously and drift around, waiting outside. One of the PTs was George Steele's boat, the 215, and we conversed briefly by semaphore, promising to get together on our return.

Then, as we led the little column of landing craft in single file out the swept channel, we were treated to the impressive sight of the cruisers *Philadelphia* and *Savannah* and three destroyers entering, long, lean, and mean-looking, bristling with the guns they knew so well how to use as we had witnessed off Gela. One of the destroyers was the *Nelson,* and we wondered whether the chief who had so valiantly attempted to repair our sonar in the mid-Atlantic was still aboard.

In deep water off Cape Gallo the convoy finally formed up, with the SC 3,500 yards ahead, Ben Partridge's 978 the same distance on the port flank, the 630 on the starboard, and the landing craft arranged in two columns of one LST and two LCIs each.

In welcome contrast to the trip up, the sea was calm with only a long and gentle swell, and visibility unrestricted. By 1700 the purple hills of the island of Marettimo were abeam to port, and that night, with no moon but clear under a billion stars, the ships full of wounded Americans and their conquered former enemies crossed the Strait of Sicily, as so many others with similar cargoes had done down the millennia. A course change was scheduled for 0345 the next day, when the force would be off the island of Zembra in the Bay of Tunis, and I had left word to be called at 0300. But the call came half an hour early when Roy Washer determined that we would arrive at the turning point earlier than planned.

At 0240 radar showed the island just ten miles due south, and with hooded light we signaled that news back to the convoy commodore in the LST 315 so that he could reschedule the turn. But then things got busy. Radar also showed a group of targets six miles off to starboard and the 692 was ordered out to investigate. We approached fast with all guns manned and trained out on the radar bearing. But at two miles a flashing light from the target spelled out the proper coded two-letter challenge for that day and hour. We replied with the correct response and turned back to rejoin, but before we could get back in position, another challenge came flashing out of the dark, this time from a speedy formation, somehow overlooked by Rebel Posey on the radar, which turned out to be a force of fast merchantmen with an escort of British destroyers. A few minutes later it passed with a rush, close enough to starboard to be visually identified. That couple of hours demonstrated with dramatic clarity the value of having the correct challenge and reply instantly at hand. Royal Navy destroyer captains are not known for their patience, particularly when on night escort duty in disputed waters.

The familiar Bizerte breakwater was in sight by 0700, but it was 0840 before all the ships were safely in port and the 692 tied up at the Naval Operating Base for fuel and water. Unexpectedly, and unknown to her crew from day to day, the SC 692 was in Bizerte a solid week as the SCs and PCs gathered there to assure the delivery of men and supplies to the forces fighting in Sicily.

Prent Horne's SC 535 was right where we had last seen her, securely moored to the French pier with eight other subchasers, and her skipper was most unhappy. It seems a rather dramatic mission had been planned, with the flag in the *Biscayne,* four destroyers, six YMSs, one other subchaser, and the big British monitor backing them up with her 15-inch rifles while they ran in to force the capitulation of the Egadi Islands off the northwest corner of Sicily (Marettimo, which we had just passed coming south, was one of them). Prent's job would have been to sail into each of the islands' little harbors and announce the terms of surrender over specially fitted loudspeakers manned by a POW assigned to his ship for the purpose. The force was to have sailed this very morning, but last night the inhabitants, isolated and hungry, had spoiled the whole operation by announcing their unconditional surrender to the world at large on several different radio frequencies.

The hottest pieces of news in the humming nests of subchasers were first that the LCIs were allegedly being trained "for street fighting in Venice" (the Lord forbid such a fate for that lovely and unique old city), and second, and far more authentic, that there would be a single Italian plane over Bizerte in the next day or two that was not to be fired upon. We also learned that the heavily escorted group of LCTs we had noted off Cape Gallo was carrying an Italian general, and that in one of the LCIs of our own convoy had been both a general and an admiral.

A study in small ship leadership, these are the men who ran the SC 535 as she operated with the 692 from Miami to Italy. From left to right: Chief Signalman M. E. Thornton; Lt. (jg) Prent Horne, skipper; Ensign Don Byers, the executive officer; and Chief Motor Machinist's Mate J. W. Leemon. (Prentice C. Horne)

On the following day, Sunday, and as far as we knew the only day we would have in port before heading back to Palermo, since we could see the LSTs and LCIs being loaded at their docks, at the suggestion of Chief Ham Morton, naval precedent was broken on the 692. The crew, except for the watch on deck, were permitted to sleep in as late as they liked. Breakfast was made available until 0930: if a man slept in after that he would have to wait for lunch. In practice, the last man was up at 0830, youthful hunger having won out in every case over the warm comfort of the bunk. But what was important for morale was that it had been possible to sleep in until noon had that been necessary or desired.

An added benefit of this arrangement was the omission of Boats's effective but raucous reveille, which had never varied since his first day aboard. "Reveille! Reveille! Reveille!" it went. "Leggo your cocks and grab your socks! All out, sailors! Chop Chop! Ding How!"

On that first sleep-in Sunday and each day thereafter, the gangway watch kept an eye on the dock for the messenger from operations who would be bringing sailing orders, and when day after day no such orders came, the priceless in-port time thus made available was put to good use. For nearly three hours on Sunday afternoon, the SC 692 steamed back and forth in the lake east of the anchorage as a very congenial and highly competent Lieutenant Williams, late of somewhere in Kentucky and recently out of a special school at the Naval Observatory in Washington, D.C., compensated her magnetic compass. It was well that he did since considerable errors were found on some headings and corrected.

With the hull and superstructure recently painted and in good shape, there was now time to do the interior as well. André turned to on the pilothouse and Chief Murphy's deck force hauled everything movable out of the forward crew's quarters and soon had it gleaming in fresh white like an operating room. In the engine room, electrician Bennie Braverman with some help from Casey and Christman broke down and overhauled one generator at a time.

Some duties were smaller but collectively important. There was a chance to get caught up on personal laundry, done on deck in a bucket with bar soap and a lot of knuckle-skinning rubbing and hung on the lifelines to dry with amazing rapidity in the hot, dry African wind.

On one of his routine scavenging expeditions, Boats somehow acquired a twin mount of Lewis .30-caliber machine guns, which in accordance with his usual practice in such situations, he immediately welded into place and painted gray so that it appeared to be an original and permanent installation, in this case back on the fantail where it could be brought to bear through nearly three hundred degrees. Similarly, a large and most welcome supply of fresh meat—roasts, steaks, and other good cuts of beef—turned up in the ship's reefer and were enjoyed by all hands. Since in the first instance the ship's defensive capabilities were obviously improved, and in the second morale was just as obviously served, it was judged best not to inquire too closely into the technical niceties of the acquisition process.

One acquisition of unquestioned legality was a double hot plate rescued from Chuck Highfield's severely damaged SC 1030 before she departed under tow for Algiers. It was installed in the engine room, and from it Charlie Casey periodically produced generous and tasty hamburgers for early evening or late night snacks.

By a stroke of luck that warmed the hearts of witnesses on both ships, the SC 977 pulled in and moored alongside the 692 late one evening with the last of the light. Aboard was Cleveland Ray's own brother, and their tearful, enthusiastic reunion under these circumstances was something to be remembered.

By the evening of 2 August there were no fewer than fourteen SCs at the French pier in Bizerte, a nest of seven on each side. They composed, in effect, a small community of young Americans trans-

Cleveland H. Ray, assigned to the 692 as a mess attendant but in practice a man of all work, the ship's best lookout, whose phenomenal pitching kept her softball team permanently undefeated. Here he goes on liberty in style in Palermo in the fall of '43. (H. Braverman)

planted to this former pirates' lair in their country's cause, and they had in common not only the nearly identical little warships on which they lived and fought but a sense of adventure, a certain amount of anxiety concerning the immediate future, a pride in their own competence, a lot of hopeful dreams and plans for the postwar world, a kind of exuberant camaraderie, and an unspoken but pervading homesickness. As in any such close-knit community, there was much visiting back and forth and swapping of news, ideas, and conjectures.

Two pieces of recent news were of special relevance and interest, and both were firsthand. The first involved Lieutenant Commander Lowther's PC 624. On the mid watch of 30 July she had been one of only two escorts for a small landing craft convoy from Bizerte to Licata. Off Pantelleria about 0230 she picked up a single radar contact at eight thousand yards and ran over to check it out. At three thousand, when the target failed to respond to a challenge, Lowther illuminated it with a star shell, and in the pale light of the lowering flare, there, unmistakably, was a surfaced submarine. Before the gun crew could load an armor-piercing round, the star went out and the target vanished from the scope.

But sonar immediately made contact and the PC charged in for a depth-charge attack. She had barely begun her run when a torpedo passed close enough down her side to be plainly visible from the bridge and highly audible on the sound gear. Nevertheless, the 624 delivered a full pattern of charges on a good sonar solution and lost contact in the resultant roiling of the waters. Since the convoy that was her responsibility had been left with only one escort, Lowther could not hang around to confirm a kill or prosecute additional attacks, and he resumed his station. Officially and conservatively, and since he had not brought back "the skipper's pants" (reputed to be required to confirm a sinking), he reported only "possible damage." Unofficially he and his officers were pretty sure they had killed the sub.

The sub story continued. Three days later, the destroyer *Buck*, screening another convoy from Licata to Oran, had almost the same experience in almost exactly the same place. Like the PC, she was one of two escorts, but since both were destroyers, presumably much more effective alone, the *Buck* stayed around for two hours after the sub submerged and evaded two torpedoes, finally depth-charged the enemy to the surface, shot him up, rammed, sank the sub, and captured all but three of the Italian crew, including the skipper (and his pants). Whether that was Lowther's sub, which had survived, or another hunting in the same spot was anyone's guess.

The second news item concerned the really savage German air raid on the ships and the port at Palermo on the night of 31 July–1 August, the day after the 692 had departed. The report came from Lieutenant (jg) Hellfer of the PC 627, whose ship had been moored outboard of the *Strive*, still providing electrical power to the damaged *Mayrant*. Forty or fifty enemy planes had apparently approached from behind the hills around the city, avoiding the newly installed warning radars, and attacked with heavy bombs by the light of flares dropped by the leaders. One of the first ones detonated some fifty yards off the PC's bow, killing one man, seriously wounding two more, and perforating the steel ship with shrapnel.

The raid lasted for more than an hour, the enemy aircraft returning again and again until all bombs were expended. After the first few minutes, flares were no longer necessary since the burning fuel depot lighted the scene with a red glare like the fires of hell. A train at dockside loaded with hundreds of tons of ammunition caught fire and exploded for three hours after the raiders had flown home, showering the anchored and moored ships with shell fragments and jagged chunks of assorted debris. The crippled *Mayrant* was damaged again and suffered more casualties. Five SCs were present but two were safely out on patrol, and the three, including the 693, moored in the inner harbor suffered no damage except that caused by a 5-inch projectile, which landed on one ship still in its steel container and was promptly jettisoned.

The 692 had missed the action at Palermo on 1 August, but the Luftwaffe was not content with a single raid, as effective as they no doubt knew it had been. Long-range, four-engine aircraft from Italian bases could reach down to Africa to disrupt the resupply and reinforcement shuttle at its source. Early on the morning of 7 August, they hit Bizerte.

In the beginning minutes of the first watch, the gangway petty officer reported flares overhead, and there they were, drifting down slowly, hard and bright and an ugly yellow, just as they had appeared over Sicily as the invasion fleet approached, and over the beaches of Gela a few nights later. The general alarm brought the 692's men tumbling up out of the hatches to their guns, and the ship was fully manned and ready when the first five-inch bursts from the destroyers outside the breakwater began to sparkle overhead, searching under radar control for the incoming raiders.

To port and starboard and throughout the double nest of subchasers it was the same. On the foredecks, the long barrels of the forties swung in unison as the gun captains responded to orders to track the nearest enemy. Aft on all the ships, the twenties stood silent, but loaded and ready if a target came in range. Fire-control discipline was firm; not one gunner, understandably jittery and angry, lost control and opened up on these planes so far out of his effective range. The forties fired only when the range was right, and then only on orders from the bridge. It occurred to me, observing in the dew-wet chill atop the SC's pilothouse, that these officers and men were now veterans, seasoned by the landings, the raids, and the convoys of the past weeks. They had matured quickly, grown up fast under the pressures and threats of the summer. A scene of such calm control would have been unthinkable as recently as June.

There was not much opportunity to fire. In the hour the planes were overhead, the 692 expended only twenty rounds of 40-mm. Mostly they seemed to be working over the anchorage in the lake. Time after time the searchlights would fix on a plane, holding it at the apex and intersection of several beams like the poles of a tepee. Then as the target dived and banked and slipped to escape the lights, the tracers would go streaming up to find it, the forties bright red and widely spaced, the twenties not so bright and closer together in long, wavering, searching strings. From a British destroyer in the lake, double salvos of pom-pom projectiles soared skyward in neat white pairs, and back on our starboard quarter, the 3-inch/50s on the sterns of the LSTs flashed and the rounds made a sharp cracking sound as they passed overhead.

Through the binoculars, the white crosses on the big black planes were clearly visible. Once a single searchlight transfixed a single plane directly over the nested SCs and in the next instant, while the long row of 40-mm barrels was elevating to get on, lost it. For a long, tense minute, four hundred officers and men waited in the flashing, staccato darkness for that bomb to fall, and then one-by-one they began to breathe again. Another time, while the searchlights were busy out over the lake, there came the sudden sound of an unseen aircraft at full throttle close overhead, and again the SC crews drew in their collective breath for a bomb that never came.

Indeed, for all the fireworks, only half a dozen bombs could be counted from the ships at the French pier, flashing blue-white down behind the anchored ships or the buildings ashore. Nor were any planes seen for certain to go down, although several dropped precipitously out of the intersecting shafts of light while under heavy fire. Later, in the returning sanity of the new day, we heard that a freighter outside the breakwater had been damaged by a bomb hit forward, and as far as we knew that was the total result of the night's action.

The next evening, appropriately a Saturday, many of the SC sailors had the special treat of a first-run movie in an actual movie theater. The theater in downtown Bizerte was, like the city itself and many of its citizens, a war casualty but ambulatory and carrying on. Its masonry and plaster walls were patched here and there with laths and canvas, and the air-conditioning system was kaput. But the seats were intact, the projection booth and associated systems fully operational, and, making all such minor problems irrelevant, the feature was *Ziegfeld Girl,* starring Lana Turner and Hedy Lamarr, a duo of such entrancing and provocative beauty that the war-torn theater's shattered walls and crumbling ceiling rang almost continually with the male shouts and groans of the most appreciative audience in recent history.

Back aboard, after the movie, I had a revealing conversation with Gunner Walter, whose lusty and indiscriminate appreciation of women had been the cause of a whole series of disciplinary and medical problems in the SC and previous ships. In the course of a recent lecture to the crew on the prevention of VD, I had strongly, and I thought quite reasonably, urged them to steer clear of any woman known or thought to be infected. Apparently that was on Walter's mind.

"Captain," he asked, looking me straight in the face for any sign of doubt or indecision, "do you mean to say that if you thought that Lana Turner had the clap, you wouldn't have anything to do with her?"

"That's right, Guns," I told him out of entirely honest conviction but reassured by the extreme unlikelihood that the occasion would arise, "I wouldn't touch her with that boat hook there."

Walter was evidently convinced of my sincerity but in total disagreement. Shaking his blond head in wonderment, he stated his case in eight words: "Captain, if she's got it, I *want* it!"

But on Sunday, after a second luxurious sleep-in (filled in all probability with lusty and lurid dreams of Lana and Hedy) and a late breakfast of ham and eggs, it was time for the 692 to go back to the war. The convoy was a big one, but scheduled to split up off Cape Bon, with part going to Licata and part to Palermo as men and equipment continued to pour into both the south and north coasts of Sicily. With the hearty although unneeded approval of her crew, the SC 692 would screen the Palermo group.

It was rough and blowing outside the breakwater and it took a while for the twenty LSTs, heavily laden with trucks and half-tracks topside and no doubt tanks below; the eight LCIs full of troops; and the six Liberty ships, deep in the water, to form up. When they were finally organized and on course they were well protected, with our old boss Commander Block in the *Seer* as OTC, two PCs, and no fewer than eight SCs as escorts. For the second time in recent weeks, the 692 was out ahead in sector A with the *Seer* astern and close in to the leading LSTs, a PC (the 543) to port, and an SC to starboard. The remaining subchasers completed a defensive ring around the loaded ships.

As the land faded into the haze astern, the wind and sea increased. The LSTs, with those heavy vehicles topside, rolled worse than we had ever seen, the LCIs did very little better, and the little SCs and PCs were tossed with inspired malevolence. As if to demonstrate for any doubters the blustery violence of which this landlocked sea is capable, the Mediterranean treated the convoy to the sight of a British cruiser with a single destroyer screening ahead, bound for Algiers or Oran, making 20 knots straight into the wind and sea. The cruiser plowed strongly ahead, occasionally burying her bow and throwing a lot of water. But the destroyer was literally invisible. All that could be made out in the screening position where a destroyer should be was a pulsing tower of white water. Only when she came directly abeam could she be glimpsed for a second or two now and then between the solid sheets of spray that hid even her highest truck and yardarms.

It was a dramatic, dashing sight, somehow representative of the professional flair and verve of the Royal Navy, but on the tossing, soaking bridge of the 692 we could not help wondering what good she was doing the cruiser. At that speed her sonar (Asdic) had to be useless, and with that much water coming aboard, her lookouts could not have spotted a B-17 fifty feet above their heads nor a periscope or a mine at fifty yards.

In late afternoon off Cape Bon, three of the Liberty ships and one LST split off and headed for Licata in the charge of a PC and three SCs, one of which was Prent Horne's 535, and the 692 dropped back to the starboard quarter.

When it was time for the scheduled turn at Marettimo the weather was still rough and nasty, and the island appeared on the scope late and passed abeam at two miles instead of the planned nine. Either Commander Block had revised the routing instructions or his navigation was less than precise. Fortunately the Egadi Islands were now in friendly hands and there was deep water right up to the beaches.

As so often seemed to happen, the dawn broke over a calm sea, and at noon, off Cape Gallo, the force reformed to enter port. But with so many ships, and with the reasonable requirement that the escorts patrol against submarines until the last ship is safely behind the breakwater and the nets, it was 1600 before the SC 692 got over her mooring lines.

This time those lines went up to the high main deck of the cruiser *Philadelphia,* because there was a sick man to transfer for treatment. Leading radioman Kidwell was showing all the symptoms of either food poisoning or an intestinal inflammation, had been unable to hold down anything or stand a watch since leaving Bizerte, and was as pale and weak as a ghost. Charlie Coffey turned him over to the cruiser's medical officer, who diagnosed the problem as gastroenteritis and agreed to keep Kidwell under observation until either they or we got under way.

Never a man to let an opportunity pass that might benefit his ship and shipmates, Charlie Casey boarded the *Philadelphia* right behind Coffey and Kidwell and in a matter of minutes was at the rail calling for a working party. In the ensuing quarter hour the SC's larder was increased by five armfuls of freshly baked bread and five gallons of chocolate ice cream, the latter such a welcome treat that it was divided and consumed on the spot by officers and men alike. An hour or so of conversation and trading between the cruiser and SC sailors followed, the former incredulous that people actually went to sea in a craft whose radar antenna reached only to their own ship's main deck, the latter trading off the souvenirs (mostly captured enemy weapons and equipment) they had picked up here and there for many times their cost of acquisition.

At 1830 the SC pulled away from the cruiser's side and anchored just offshore east of the city in three fathoms of water so clear it looked more like three feet. In another rather creative liberty arrangement, a dozen men were allowed ashore via the pram and the rubber raft until 2200, and again all came back on time and in good shape.

In the little more than a week since we had left, Palermo had turned into a busy port. As darkness fell we counted two cruisers; eight destroyers; four big sweepers like the *Seer;* at least a dozen LCIs; a like number of Liberty ships; and dozens of SCs, PCs, and YMSs. It was a cool and peaceful night with a half-moon, a gentle, cooling, westerly breeze, the mountains huge and black against the starlit sky, and all around us the darkened shapes of the anchored ships.

Bright and early next morning the bustling business of the war began again. At a conference in the LST 336, convoy dispositions and sailing directions were issued, and shortly after noon the SC 692 was on her way back to Bizerte with more columns of LSTs, LCIs, and merchantmen screened by the usual SCs and PCs plus the *Speed*. Missing from his usual station was radioman Kidwell, who had been transferred from the *Philadelphia* to the British hospital ship *Oxfordshire*, also bound for Bizerte, where we were assured we could pick him up. In deference to an aged and decrepit freighter, convoy speed was a creeping 7 knots, but that allowed time to share and digest all the news acquired in the course of conversations at the conference of the morning.

Jack O'Meara of the PC 546 was the source of most of that news. From him we learned what all those warships based in Palermo had been up to while the 692 had been running the Bizerte-Palermo shuttle. Covered by the big guns of the cruisers and destroyers, and closer in by the not-so-big guns of the PCs and SCs, the landing craft had been putting army units ashore behind enemy lines to cut communications and supply lines as the Germans were pushed along the north shore of the island toward the Strait of Messina.

As expected, the Luftwaffe had resisted those amphibious operations, and some brisk actions had ensued. In one off San Stefano, the American ships had been attacked by Focke-Wulf 190 fighter-bombers, an LST hit, and Jack's ship near-missed close enough to punch a fair-sized hole in one side and inflict minor wounds on a couple of his men. Of special interest was the fact that in the same action the SC 530 had beaten off two attacks by a particularly persistent Fw 190 that nevertheless broke off its runs at two thousand yards in the face of the subchaser's 20-mm fire. The PC 546 was with the slow group to Bizerte but would go on from there to Tunis for repairs.

More serious, and carrying an obvious moral, was news that a fleet tug, the *Brant*, had been badly smashed up and ten of her men killed and another twenty injured by 5-inch hits when she had failed to respond to a challenge by one of our own destroyers.

Except for the necessity of sinking a couple of floating mines, the voyage to Bizerte was uneventful, but back at the French pier we heard another fascinating story. Reportedly the SC 530, around 6 August, was assigned the routine chore of escorting a freshwater barge from Palermo out to the dry little island of Ustica, about thirty miles north. The barge was sufficiently slow at 4 knots that the 530 and her charge ended up off Ustica in the middle of the night.

Some time in the early part of the mid watch she picked up a couple of big radar contacts approaching at high speed. Since it was a clear night, she identified the two targets at about half a mile as cruisers. To make her own identity certain (and avoid the fate of the *Brant*) she challenged the lead cruiser by flashing light. What came back was not the expected reply but a flash and a salvo of heavy projectiles, which fortunately—probably because of the close range—landed well over.

When he had recovered from his shock and surprise, the SC skipper rechecked his challenge-and-reply publication and tried again, with the same disconcerting result. There was another way to establish his friendly status and he turned on the coded recognition lights for that day and hour. When that drew fire from both ships, he doused the recognition lights and in desperation illuminated first his own ship and then the cruisers with his 12-inch signal light. That did it. The two cruisers ceased firing, reversed course, and sped off into the night.

The next morning, back in Palermo, the 530's skipper stormed into operations and complained bitterly about being fired on by his own ships when he had been doing all the right things to establish his identity. But he became very calm and quiet when the duty officer informed him that the ships he had encountered were not friendly but Italian cruisers, probably bound for Palermo to shoot up the harbor. Apparently his illumination had spoiled their intended surprise and they had returned to base.

By this time, the PC and SC skippers in the Med had done enough escort-of-convoy work to know how it should and should not be done, despite their youth and nearly total lack of seniority. And this particular convoy, in the charge of none other than the redoubtable Commander A. F. Block, now commander escort sweeper force, provided them with textbook examples of the latter.

Item. Because of one merchantman in the convoy that was unable to make more than 7 knots, it was impossible to make Bizerte during daylight of the second day, thus exposing the entire force to another night at sea and the very real possibility of submarine attack. The signal lights on the little ships halfway out to the horizon around the convoy columns wondered in flashing Morse why the one slow ship was not detached with a single escort and the remaining thirty or so permitted to increase speed and reach port and safety.

Item. At 0700 on 11 August, an exceptionally ugly and lethal-looking mine was sighted from the SC 692 on the starboard bow of the convoy. A report went immediately to the *Seer* with the suggestion that one of the escort LCIs without sonar be detailed to destroy it. The short, impatient order came back at once. "YOU SINK IT." Obediently we peeled off and did so. But simultaneously, the SC 506, also on the convoy's starboard beam, found a mine and was also peremptorily ordered to destroy it. Thus, for almost a full hour, the entire starboard flank of the force was wide open to sub attack, protected only by a single landing craft with a couple of extra antiaircraft guns.

But the enemy fortunately failed to take advantage of either error. Off Cape Bon, three LCIs and the PCs were detached and turned southwest for Tunis while the other LCIs cranked on 13 knots and went churning off straight ahead for Bizerte like dray horses suddenly released and smelling the barn. But it was midnight before the slow merchantmen and LSTs came to anchor off the Bizerte breakwater in calm seas and under a bright moon. Three SCs patrolled the perimeter of the anchorage and were not challenged.

The SC 692 was in familiar Bizerte for only forty-eight hours, spending the days at the French pier and the nights in the cool, dark safety of the lake. There was some mail (but no birth announcements), a movie ashore, some fresh provisions, and the usual resupply of fuel and water, and then she was off again for Palermo with another batch of landing craft and merchant ships, presumably of greater than usual importance since the escort consisted of four destroyers (one the well-remembered *Nicholson*) and two SCs.

This convoy did not dawdle, and it took the direct route across the strait from Cape Farina to Marettimo, so that by 1300 on the fifteenth, all ships were safely in port and the SC securely moored to the south breakwater at Palermo. Later in the afternoon she made a run around the harbor for fresh water, showers for the crew, some grape-juice extract from a friendly LCT, and then out to a night anchorage in Palermo Bay. And while she lay peacefully at anchor there, her captain went to war.

The south breakwater was adjacent to the newly established PT base, and as soon as the 692 had tied up there George Steele came aboard with an invitation for me to go with him for "a speedboat ride" that night. I was not at all hard to get. The only problems were what commitments the ship might have during my absence, and the little matter of permission. We had been told to report to Commander Messmer in the *Strive,* and my plan was to ask his permission on reporting. But when the subchaser approached the big sweeper we were told in effect to go away, that the commander was asleep, and to anchor for the night. That last order took care of the matter of prospective commitments, and since my sleeping senior could not be aroused to consider the question of permission, I assumed that responsibility myself and granted it. It took about ten minutes to make a temporary turnover to Charlie, who was abreast of everything anyway and had been certified as qualified for command, and about 1750, PT 215 came alongside the 692 at her anchorage.

Despite George's assurances of a peaceful speedboat ride, I took along my helmet, life jacket, .45, and a tommy gun with a loaded drum. The SC's crew were all on deck as the PT backed away. "Bring him back in one piece," Hawn yelled over; and with reference to my heavy personal armament, Tony Curato told the PT crew, "You guys are safe now!" Finally, almost out of earshot, John Roughan thoughtfully advised, "It isn't too late to change your mind, Sir."

There was never the slightest question of a change of mind. After the relatively heavy and plodding gait of the subchaser, the PT at cruising speed was an exuberant revelation. She swooped and dipped with easy grace from swell to swell, banking into the turns like an aircraft, all swift, fluid, eager motion. It was like flying while still in a kind of tenuous, reluctant contact with the sea's surface. In an instant this fleet little warship was making three times the very best speed the 692 had ever done, and she was not even at full throttle.

In seconds we were outside the harbor and had formed a V with two other boats of MTBron 15, PTs 205 and 216. With George's boat in the port position, we flew eastward along the coast over a calm sea, standard speed 25 knots. The PTs generated broad, white, foaming ribbons of wake and high, arching "rooster tails" right at their sterns. As we left Palermo, the *Philadelphia, Savannah,* and two destroyers were also leaving, also heading eastward, and later six more destroyers came out and joined up. It looked like a major action in the making, and when we had settled down on course, George called his crew together and over the roar of the engines and the whistle of the wind, with his sandy hair blowing and his blue eyes fixing each man in turn, he explained what it was.

The cruisers and destroyers of Task Force 88 would be covering a landing well out on the northeast tip of Sicily just across the mountains from Messina. At the same time paratroopers would be attacking

The PT 216, which took part with the 205 and George Steele's 215 in the running battle with German E-boats off the Lipari Islands in mid-August 1943, here takes Lt. Gen. Mark Clark to his advance command post at the Anzio beachhead, 2 February 1944. (U.S. Army)

the coastal town of Barcellona, a few miles to the west. Our three PTs would set up a patrol from the Lipari Islands east to the instep of the Italian boot to prevent reinforcement, evacuation, or interference from that area. Three other boats would be operating closer in and just north of the Strait of Messina. Since our patrol line would be no closer than twenty-five to thirty miles from the landings, and there had been little or no seaborne resistance to these operations in the past, it looked like a routine night, a speedboat ride.

As the three PTs approached the Lipari Islands, the red sun was sinking into the sea back on the port quarter and the full moon was rising from behind the hazy mountains of Sicily on the starboard bow. But there was something eerie about that moon. There was a nick out of its left upper edge as though someone had almost missed it with a cookie cutter. George sent his quartermaster below to verify that the moon was supposed to be full this night. It was. But the nick stayed and grew larger, biting a real chunk out of the golden disk. The quartermaster ducked below again and reappeared in about five minutes to report what we had already figured out to be the case; we were watching a lunar eclipse. The growing nick was the round shadow of the earth on the moon's face.

We passed close between the high volcanic islands with clusters of white houses on their lower slopes in the deepening dusk, with that strangely mutilated moon hanging low in the eastern sky, then took

PALERMO • 169

cruising disposition in column, five hundred yards between boats, and headed across toward Italy.

Having settled into the PT's routine and with nothing but sea, sky, moon, and the two other boats ahead to look at, I found myself worrying about what I could contribute in the event of action with the enemy. It was uncomfortable being purely a passenger: I needed a battle station and told George so. He showed me how to operate the torpedo-firing controls just forward of the helm in case we made contact with a major surface target and assigned me to a .30-caliber machine gun mounted on the starboard torpedo tube as a normal general quarters station. By midnight the earth's shadow had completed its passage across the lunar disk and the moon was full once again. Somehow we all seemed to feel better.

It was early on the mid watch when I discovered that I could contribute more to this little operation than I had thought. Apparently all those hours of searching the horizon through binoculars from the SC's bridge had given me some expertise as a lookout. At 0035 radar reported a small target at 030 relative and I made out two objects immediately. George took a quick look and identified them as friendly destroyers. "Cans," he said and settled back. But they didn't look like destroyers to me. "Cans, hell," I told him. "They're PTs or something similar. I can see rooster tails."

That was the magic phrase. Every pair of binoculars on the boat went up and in a minute from all around came the identification, "Goddam E-boats," the German equivalent of the PT. George was picking up the mike to report to the OTC in the lead boat when she turned hard to starboard, increased speed, and the little column of PTs went to battle stations and roared in to engage.

"Increased speed" in this case is a misleading understatement. What George (and the other skippers) did was to jam his three throttles as far forward as they would go, and then, not content, continue to pound them against the stops with the heel of his hand. The PT 215 came suddenly alive. The already loud engine sound doubled and she leaped forward, her bow lifting a little as though to see the enemy, her deck trembling slightly underfoot as if in anticipation of action.

At first sighting, the two E-boats had been on a roughly parallel but opposite course to the PTs, but as we turned to starboard, they had turned away to port, and a pursuit developed, with the racing PTs slowly gaining on the enemy. The feeling that pervaded the 215 was pure combative aggressiveness, best expressed by what I heard one sailor mutter as he climbed into one of the twin fifty mounts and charged the guns—"Let's get the bastards!" Surprisingly, shorn now of the responsibility of command, I found myself feeling the same way, with none of the kneecap-jumping anxiety of Gela or Empedocle, and I watched with excited fascination as George's frequent boast that his boat was the fastest in the squadron was most convincingly proved true.

Instead of staying in the wakes of the two other boats, the 215 pulled out to port and slowly, inexorably, passed first the second and then the lead boat. I expected at any moment to hear the radio crackle with orders to get back in line, but apparently that was not in the PT tradition of hell-for-leather individual aggressiveness in the face of the enemy. In a matter of minutes the engagement had turned into single combat between the PT 215 and the two E-boats, with the 216 and the 205 somewhere back astern. Ahead, the enemy was plainly visible to the naked eye as two speeding, ominous dark shapes on the silvery surface of the sea, and the gunners in the twin mounts to port and starboard swung their guns down and looked inquiringly at George for the order to open fire. But he knew his business as well as his boat. He needed to close the range to be sure of making hits, and he was not about to waste ammo in an action that could last another hour.

But the enemy was not going to let himself be overhauled and shot up without trying a few tricks. A big puff of white smoke blossomed on the sea ahead and in an instant the two black shapes had disappeared behind it. As George banked around to port to avoid the smoke, a high, thin splash erupted close to the PT's bow—a 40-mm apparently fired under radar control through the smoke screen. In half a minute we rounded the patch of smoke and the two dark shapes were back in sight, larger now and closer.

"Okay," George yelled over the wind and engine noises, calm and steady, "Keep 'em down. Take your time. Commence firing."

The noise of the four fifties firing together was an angry hammering that would have shattered the ear drums if cotton had not been passed around shortly after GQ was called. The four streams of tracers lanced out across the moonlit sea, red and very fast, converging on the speeding shapes ahead. Some landed short and ricocheted at crazy angles. Some seemed to sail over. With one tracer belted for every three rounds, some must have been going home.

Seconds after the fifties opened up, the twenties aft joined in, firing at a sharp angle along the PT's side at the targets now broad on the bow. They looked and sounded familiar, a slower, heavier hammering, the bigger balls of red sailing out, slower. Thus far, the single round of 40-mm had been the enemy's sole response, but now, as though the twenties had stung him into action, those two racing shadows threw handfuls of white tracers that flew swiftly and beautifully three or four feet over our heads. They looked lighter and less lethal than our fifties and twenties, which meant we were now in .30-caliber range and I could man my battle station.

The thirty was belted and ready and it just took a second to pull back the action and let it slam forward to load the first round. Keep it down. Take your time. Try for the lead target; it's probably the command boat. The Browning was smoother and steadier than I remembered from training, and it was easy to tell its paler, smaller tracers from the other streams going in the same direction. The flights of white pellets squirting toward us from the target helped to keep it just over the front sight, and the thirty pounded away in a most satisfactory manner in bursts of forty to fifty rounds with time to line up and resight between.

I don't know how long the action lasted. Maybe twenty minutes. For one long minute we were tearing along at full throttle, the enemy boats almost abeam, the other two PTs now in company, every gun on the 215 spitting out its tracers in angry red streams, and no response at all from the targets. I saw three 20-mm tracers impact on the lead E-boat with bright, sparkling bursts. That meant about nine solid hits. Then, at the end of that minute, came the showers of white bullets, no longer all overhead, some ripping the water close aboard, some singing off in ricochets, some whacking into the plywood somewhere nearby.

At some point my target vanished, and when I rose for a better look I saw only a tattered cloud of smoke out there low on the water. Instead of charging straight through, the OTC led our three boats to port along its edge and when we rounded the corner there was only the empty sea. George thought the division commander was trying some new tactical trick, but it turned out his radar had failed and he had simply not seen which way the E-boats had gone.

Radar search turned up a faint blip in the distance near the Italian coast down toward Messina, and once we caught just a shadowy glimpse of something in that direction and gave chase, but it was no use. The enemy boats had given us the slip. During the action, Admiral Davidson, Commander Task Force 88, had been kept advised, and we were now told that the destroyers north of the strait would take over and to resume patrol.

With the three boats back in column at cruising speed, it was time to assess damage and casualties. We had been lucky. Almost a casualty was the gunner in the starboard fifty mount who had been heard to mutter "Let's get the bastards!" as he took his station at the beginning of the action. The bastards had very nearly gotten him. A bullet had torn off the sole of his right shoe and shredded the sock so that his bare foot was in contact with the deck but had not drawn a drop of blood. Another round had passed between the two fifteen-hundred-gallon tanks of one-hundred-octane gasoline to smash the instrument panel in the engine room, and still another had severed a control cable between the bridge and engine room so that control of one engine was now by shouted command only. Other bullets had passed harmlessly through lockers, bunks, and mattresses below, and in some mysterious way 3 or 4 knots of speed had been lost.

Both the other boats had also taken hits, and on the 216 four men had been wounded, none seriously. With all the lead that had been flying back and forth, that amount of damage and casualties seemed acceptable. We hoped the enemy had not gotten off as lightly.

There was a respite of about an hour before the PTs went back to battle stations. This time it was a single large surface target to the north that got their attention. The target's size and location made it a possible enemy cruiser on a raid against the landing forces, and the word was passed, "Set the fish."

The three boats spread out in line abreast, accelerated again to flank speed and headed in, torpedoes armed and set, all guns manned. Range was about ten miles. Something about the look of the target on the scope, its position and apparent easterly movement made me uneasy. If there had been a possibility of major enemy surface ships at sea, it seemed the PTs would have been warned.

"George," I asked, "Don't you have IFF in this thing?"

"Sure we do."

"Do you know the code setting for today?"

"Jesus no. No idea. We hardly ever use the thing. But I see what you're thinking. Wouldn't hurt to turn it on. It's only got six positions. We could switch through them all, just in case."

"Where is it?"

"All the way forward, high on the bulkhead."

I grabbed a flashlight and dived down below. While the 215 roared in toward whatever was out there, I rotated the pointer on the little black box up forward through each of the six numbers on the dial, one of which would indicate on the cruiser's radar scope, if she was friendly, that we were too, holding it on each one while the sweep second hand on my watch made one full revolution. Then, while the boat trembled, rising and falling as it flew from swell to swell, I turned it back, one minute on each number again. It was a long twelve minutes.

It was a relief to get back topside in the fresh air and blowing night wind. The men on the bridge were tense and silent. The target was plainly in sight dead ahead, a big warship, broadside, black on the moonlit sea, steaming slowly port to starboard, range about three miles. George's left hand was on the wheel, his right on the torpedo release. Off to starboard the other two boats were right abeam about five hundred yards apart, their bows clear of the surface, white water flying aft in sheets from amidships, rooster tails arching high at their sterns. On all three PTs every man waited, dry-mouthed, for the flashes of flame that would come at any second from that dark and silent silhouette ahead.

Suddenly the radio speaker on the bridge crackled loudly, breaking the tension.

"Break off to port!" it ordered. "I say again, break off to port! She's a limey!"

Simultaneously the PTs banked to port, forming an instant column with the 215 in the lead, and the British cruiser faded quickly back on the starboard quarter. All around the bridge you could hear the exhaled breaths. "Jesus," George said with a relieved little grin, "that was close."

It was beginning to get light and we were back at the Lipari end of the patrol with the brown plume of volcanic smoke from Stromboli ahead when we sighted a small sailboat, its single sail drooping in the windless calm, but full of people. The PTs were taking no chances and approached it warily, guns manned and sighted in.

"Don't fire unless they do," George ordered, "but if there's one shot, let 'em have it."

There were six men in the boat and they were harmless but highly vocal, a natural enough reaction to the heavy machine-gun muzzles they were looking into. At first they all shouted at once in Italian with violent, emphatic gestures. Since most of the pointing was straight down and we could catch a frequent use of the word *profundo,* we gathered that their ship had been sunk. After a man from the 205 who could speak the language had talked to them, that proved to be the case. They were merchant sailors whose ship had been lost (how, we never knew) and they had been making their way through the islands back to the mainland. One man, who had been glumly silent, turned out to be a Luftwaffe fighter pilot who had been shot down by a Spitfire and had an injured foot.

The OTC, Lieutenant Ed DuBose, decided to take the whole bunch back to Palermo, and most of them, along with suitcases and rolled-up blankets, ended up on the 215. The Italians seemed docile and grateful and were billeted under guard in the crew's quarters up forward. The fighter pilot was a cocky and arrogant kid of about nineteen with a wristwatch the size of a chronometer, and George ordered him held under the muzzle of a cocked carbine, back on the fantail.

Whenever anyone attempted to talk to him, he would come as close as he could get to attention, raise a stiff right arm and yell, "Heil Hitler!" That went over very poorly with George, who gritted his teeth and told me, "If he does that one more time, I'm going to throw the son-of-a-bitch overboard." Perhaps the kid understood a little English, or read the threat in George's face, because there were no more "Heil Hitlers." In one of the minor wastes of war, the little sailboat, intact and seaworthy, was simply abandoned and left to drift.

At 0915, in the bright, hot sunlight of the new day, the captain of the SC 692 stepped back aboard his ship, to the silent awe of the crew who could only gape and shake their heads at the dozen or so splintery bullet holes in the PT's hull. Charlie looked at the shot-up 215 and then at me and remarked in his quiet, lawyer's manner, "That must have been one hell of a speedboat ride."

On 17 August the 692 took on a new task—inner harbor patrol. The orders came from Commander Messmer in the *Strive*. We were to run back and forth through the eastern half of the anchorage at idle speed, keeping the small bumboats away from the anchored ships, and all the local fishing boats ashore. Roger Robinson in the 694 had the western half. At night we would both move out and patrol to seaward. Robinson would also drop small antiswimmer depth charges around the harbor entrance at irregular intervals.

It was a thankless and meaningless job. We took Tony Curato off the watch bill and kept him on the bridge to yell at the locals in their own language to get ashore and stay there or we would have to fire on them. The trouble was they didn't believe that anyone who spoke Palerman would actually shoot at them. They would obligingly row ashore while we watched, and then row back out to fish some more when we had gone by. It was hard to be stern with them since it was obvious they were only trying to feed themselves and their families, but we had to try.

To be more convincing, big, burly, and hairy Charlie Nader, bearded and fierce-looking, stripped to the waist and stood threateningly out on the bow, brandishing a rifle with fixed bayonet, while Tony crouched out of sight in the hatch behind him and swore at the fishermen in highly colloquial Sicilian. It was not much of a job for a warship, and we were relieved when orders came to escort a fleet tug around the corner of the island and back down to Licata.

The tug turned out to be the *Nauset*, and the reason we got the job was that Prent Horne's SC 535, which was supposed to go, had broken a shaft and was scheduled for dry-docking back in Bizerte. The *Nauset*'s skipper was a mustang lieutenant who *always* wore an Afrika Korps sun helmet. In over a week I never saw him without it.

Charlie commented that it must be uncomfortable in bed. We got under way at 1715 on the eighteenth, two thousand yards ahead of the tug, speed 12 knots on this routine run, which almost immediately developed a mystery yet to be solved.

Off the now familiar Cape Gallo, the sonar gear, in addition to its usual reverberating pings, suddenly began to give off the dots and dashes of Morse code characters. Guszak dashed up from the radio shack and copied two messages addressed to Radio Algiers, one of thirty-five groups and one of eighty. They were classified and encoded in a system we did not hold, so we typed them up and passed them to the tug by heaving line for decryption. The whole idea of receiving radio messages of whatever kind on sonar was downright surrealistic and not explained to this day.

Around 0100 on a clear, calm, and beautiful mid watch, right after a scheduled course change, Ray, on lookout, spotted a dim white light off the starboard bow, flickering on and off at random. Radar showed no target there, which meant whatever it was had to be very small and low in the water. We had just changed course and increased speed to investigate when orders came from the tug to do so. It could well have been a trap, a decoy to set us up for a torpedo shot. As we approached, when sonar got an echo on about that bearing, the SC went to battle stations. We passed the object very close aboard, dead slow, and it turned out to be a small, floating white light like those attached to life jackets. We circled warily around and checked out the sonar echo. It was large, stationary, and nonmetallic, a ledge or a lump on the bottom. This mission was starting out anything but routine, but it was better than harassing friendly fishermen.

Off Licata in early afternoon, the SC was released by the tug with thanks for a job well done and told to report for duty to the CO of the destroyer *Woolsey* (DD 437). For the next two days we ran errands for the destroyer, delivering orders to ships under way and taking people to shore or moored and anchored ships. In between jobs we patrolled off the harbor entrance. From one of the ships to which we passed orders we learned that the troops crowding her decks were combat engineers being withdrawn from the Gela area to pick up new equipment and prepare for another major landing somewhere in Italy itself. Then, at 1315 on 21 August, we headed back for Palermo, again with the *Nauset,* which was now towing a long and heavy pontoon bridge she had dragged off the old assault beach at Gela. Speed with the heavy tow was supposed to be 7 knots, but the tug skipper (still in his Afrika Korps helmet) said he thought he could make 8 and actually did nearly 10 all the way.

The run northwesterly past Agrigento and Empedocle, then north through the Egadi Islands, and finally east across the broad Gulf of Castellammare to Cape Gallo and into Palermo was 240 miles, so that at about 10 knots it took just one day. Thus, by shortly after noon on the twenty-third, the SC 692 was moored port side to the 771 in a nest of four subchasers at the shore end of a spacious slip in the inner harbor of the Sicilian capital. Inboard of the 771 was the 696, and port side to the pier itself Roger Robinson's 694, looking very colorful airing bunting, all her signal flags crowding her halyards and flapping brightly in the summer sun. On the other side of the pier, across from the nest of subchasers, was the big fleet salvage tug *Narragansett,* with whom we had crossed the Atlantic and with whom we had also relocated and rejoined the convoy on that lonely morning when the sun had risen over an empty sea.

There had been some changes in the few days the 692 had been down at Licata. Over at the Naval Operating Base (NOB) we learned first that we could expect to remain at Palermo at least until the next major operation, doing harbor patrol, short escort runs and various odd jobs (good news since it meant the mail and payroll would have a chance to catch up); second that liberty was now formally authorized for the crews from 1300 to 1800, uniform whites; and third that the order requiring all small escorts to anchor out every night had been rescinded and they could remain in port at the CO's discretion.

That afternoon half the crew took advantage of the new liberty arrangements, and Charlie and I found a little shop with a concrete floor, wire chairs and tables, and huge hogsheads of marsala in the back, where we enjoyed a water glass apiece of the cool, amber wine at the price of a nickel each in the new occupation currency.

At 1800, when liberty expired, neither Hoffner nor Gunner Walter were back aboard. Hoffner returned at 1830, but it was 1940 before Walter climbed unsteadily across the other SCs and apologetically reported in. Both men were put on report and scheduled for mast in the morning. But now it was decision time. Stay in port, or get under way and anchor out.

It was of course a lot easier just to stay. No action was required, a simple absence of action would make the decision. In the soft Mediterranean evening the sky was clear, the sea calm, visibility unlimited, and later the moon would be in its final quarter. On the other nested ships sailors lounged on deck, smoking, talking, reading, drinking coffee, enjoying the cool of approaching dusk after the ninety-degree heat and blowing dust of the day. On none of the three was there any sign of preparations for getting under way.

But the very conditions that made it so tempting to stay, made it seem advisable to go. When the moon rose, the sleeping city in the clear of the night would lie naked and vulnerable to air attack, and the piers and docks of the inner harbor would be priority targets. At the French pier in Bizerte we had experienced an air raid from a nest of firing ships that themselves had constituted a tempting objective for an enemy pilot, and it was a lesson that needed no repetition.

At 1950 the last of our lines snaked back aboard from the 771, and twenty minutes later Nader lowered the big Danforth into four fathoms of warm, translucent water in the Gulf of Palermo, half a mile outside the breakwater and a couple of hundred yards outboard of another SC, the 649. On the way out we passed the two YMSs, 62 and 69, in whose company we had departed Miami and Hampton Roads in what seemed like another age. By now the three ships' crews were old friends and there was a lot of waving and shouting back and forth.

It was cool, quiet, and pleasant in the anchorage. Except for the watch on deck, the SC's officers and men relaxed each in his own way and turned in early. In the crew's quarters it was dark, except for the red battle lights, by routine order at 2200. The light at the head of my bunk was the last in our little wardroom to go out as I finished another chapter of Phillip Gibbs's *The Cross of Peace*.

It seemed only minutes after I had closed the book and doused the light that the flexible tube in its clamp above my head sounded its always pregnant little whistle. When I picked it up Charlie Nader's voice reached me from the pilothouse. "Two flares, Captain" was all he said, but it was enough to get me to the bridge in coveralls, tennis shoes, and helmet in about ten seconds. It was 0410. The pair of harshly glaring yellow lights was drifting slowly down above the harbor, adding to the illumination of a half moon high and bright almost directly overhead. At about eight or ten thousand feet there was a deck of thin broken clouds with large gaps through which the moon shone in bright splotches on sea and land. To starboard, beyond the close familiar silhouette of the 649, the city stretched up into its crescent of low hills, the rows of buildings a dim silver in the moonlight.

With only the two flares, it could have been just a scouting flight to check for future targets and cause some loss of sleep. So we waited hopefully, the heavy dew glistening on the SC's decks and on the barrels of the guns under the lights of flares and moon. But when a string of four more yellow lights snapped on to seaward and the two destroyers on offshore patrol began to blast their white 5-inch tracers up across the sky, the loud, discordant buzzer of the general alarm brought the 692's sailors scrambling to their guns.

They were still settling into place, shrugging on life jackets and ducking into helmets, when searchlights began to spring up around the harbor and swing back and forth, searching the sky. Then dead astern about a quarter of a mile, a huge antiaircraft gun opened up, firing right over our heads. It must have been a 90-mm. First came a bright yellow flash, then a thunderous report and a shock wave that actually jarred the flesh. There must have been a whole battery of those big guns, because in another minute we could see more of the yellow flashes all around the broad arc of the harbor and feel the heavy thuds of their firing. One at a time, as each found a target, the ships in the anchorage and inside the breakwater opened up with 5-inch and 3-inch forties and twenties, until the sky was laced with tracers of every size and pocked by the greasy little black puffs of bursting shells.

For a while we saw no planes at all; the destroyers and the guns ashore must have been in radar control, and the searchlights were often thwarted by the deck of clouds, which looked thin but stopped the bright beams like a white ceiling and gave good protection to the attackers. When the lights did pick up a target, the volume of fire trebled and quadrupled until the whole harbor seemed to erupt in fire like a volcano. Through the glasses we could get glimpses of black twin-engine planes with white crosses, Ju 88s, diving, banking, and jinking to slip the grip of the grasping beams.

It quickly became apparent that for every Ju 88 caught in the lights and getting the concentrated attention of the defensive guns, half a dozen others were busy making their bombing runs. They seemed to slant down along the contours of the hills around the city, come in low and fast across the port and harbor to release, and escape at full power into the darkness to seaward. The sound of aircraft engines screaming at emergency power periodically overcame even the insistent hammering of the guns. Once a black shape came hurtling out from the fires now burning red in the inner harbor and swept at masthead height between us and the 649. There was no warning. Sight and sound came at the same instant. Only Hoffner on the starboard twenty was able to slam a few rounds into it before it vanished into the night, but they looked like good hits and we hoped angrily it had vanished for good into the sea.

Twice more after that the twin-engine raiders came roaring out from the direction of the harbor, followed both times by screens and streams of tracers that whipped close overhead with staccato snapping sounds that made us duck even while our own tracers lanced out to meet them. We could see from the heavy flashes and lingering red flames in that direction that the port was taking a savage beating, and it was brutally evident we had made the right decision in getting out of there when we did.

After the raid had been in progress ten or twelve minutes, about 0420, the wisdom of that decision was dramatically confirmed by a sudden, sustained, roaring blast that overwhelmed all other sounds, punished the eardrums, and lighted the whole inner harbor with a brilliant, livid, pulsing flash lasting several seconds.

Within ten minutes after the big explosion, the AA fire grew sporadic and died out, the searchlights went off, and except for flames that continued to lick upward and redden the sky at the site, and an ominous pall of smoke, the Palermo region returned to normal. But just at 0500, as the SC's men were leaving their battle stations to go back to bed, another thundering explosion from the same vicinity rocked the harbor as though to put a period to the lethal activities of the night. Then all was once again quiet.

At 0845 the anchor came up and the SC 692 headed into the harbor for fuel. Mercifully, news of the night's catastrophe came to her crew in bits and pieces. As the 692 entered at the breakwater, the 1029 was coming out and slowed to hail us. They wanted to know if we would take their place as standby patrol ship while they tried to untangle a fishnet from the port propeller. The reason they had the standby, they explained, was that the SC that was supposed to have it "was sunk last night."

Shocked and startled, we asked which SC.

"The 694."

The 694! Skinny, blond Roger Robinson, who had been with us at Algiers, Tunis, Gela, and Bizerte; with whom we had shared the inner harbor patrol just the other day; who had been airing bunting in the sunny breeze yesterday; and with whom we had been nested only twelve hours ago! Suddenly, with that casually imparted news, the whole war seemed to change. The adventure, the drama, the excitement, the sense of history seemed to fade, blotted out by the actuality of friends killed and ships wrecked. In an instant the bombs and the tracers of the night and other nights became more lethal and more real, not the stirring fireworks they had seemed before, despite the intellectual awareness of their reality.

As we motored down the harbor toward the wrecked tanker that was the fuel depot and passed the end of the slip where we had been moored with the other SCs last evening, the adventure of the war turned to something close to nausea. Where three subchasers had been nested there was now only the charred and blackened bow of one, canted against the head of the slip, listing horribly to port, washed by oily harbor water full of wreckage and debris.

Fueling completed, we tied up in the adjacent slip and walked over to find out what had happened to our friends. It was twice as bad as we had thought. The burned and broken bow poking up out of the harbor slime was painted pathetically with the numbers "694." But down there under that scum, with nothing showing above the surface, was all that was left of the SC 696 as well. For a couple of bad minutes we thought the 771 might be down there too, but then someone saw her safely tied up across the pier. The outboard ship in the nest, she had backed clear and made it out into the gulf when those first two flares appeared.

The scene at the head of the slip where the two SCs had died was one of chaos and carnage. Two truckloads of bodies and parts of bodies had already been hauled away, but the concrete pier was stained dark with blood that seemed impervious to the streams of water a detail of soldiers was directing at it. The debris we had seen in the slip as we passed on the way to fuel consisted in part of torn and slashed life jackets, a few vegetables, half a life raft, parts of an SC helm, and a dirty white hat. Part of a burned blanket dangling from the twisted mousetraps on the bow of the 694 showed that some of the crew had been sleeping on deck before the bombers came. A hundred yards away, clear across the waterfront street, was a twisted chunk of metal that was recognizable with some difficulty as most of a 20-mm gun. It had been blown onto the concrete sidewalk with such force that the barrel appeared to have been poured full of concrete that had been left to harden. We tried not to think of what must have happened to the gun crew. Across the pier, forward of the 771, the big tug *Narragansett* was scorched and blackened, with open gashes in her hull and superstructure and blood on her decks where still more men had died.

No one at the scene knew definitely about the casualties, but back at NOB we learned that twenty-four men on the two SCs had died and twenty-three more had been badly wounded. In the 696 all three officers were dead. In the 694 all were alive but hospitalized in serious condition. Roger Robinson was said to have a lower back full of shrapnel but was expected to be okay eventually.

As nearly as could be determined, a 550-pound bomb had made a direct hit on the pilothouse of the 696, penetrating to her forward fuel tanks before exploding and sending burning diesel oil cascading across the nest and the dock, setting fire to the nearby *Narragansett* and a British merchantman, the SS *Speedfast*. That must have been the first big detonation we heard and saw at 0420. Before those fires could be controlled they reached the magazine of the 696 and the resultant blast at 0500 had instantly sunk both the 696 and 694. Given the force of the detonations we had seen, heard, and felt from more than a mile away, it seemed a miracle that anyone had survived.

A sober, chastened, and thoughtful crew took the SC 692 back out on patrol that night.

The big raid, by what we later learned had been twenty Ju 88s, of which four had been shot down, came in the early days of a solid month of patrol and odd jobs at Palermo. The SC 692, along with the 649, 771, 978, and 1029, was now assigned full-time to the operational control of Commander, Naval Operating Base (COMNOB), Palermo. And what COMNOB wanted of his five little ships was continuous, round-the-clock patrol of the harbor entrance and occasional short escort missions to nearby ports. The broad mouth of the gulf required a coordinated two-ship patrol, one to the east and one to the west. At first that meant for each SC two days at sea and two in port. But as the buildup for the invasion of Italy gained momentum and more escort jobs were required, that changed to two out and one in.

As it turned out, harbor patrol at Palermo in late summer was not a bad way to fight a war. By then the city was busily back to normal. Mornings in the anchorage outside the breakwater we could see the commuter trains rumbling in from the countryside, loaded not only to capacity but with people jammed together on the roofs of the cars and clinging in clusters to the sides.

Although there were still Palermans waiting outside the waterfront gate in donkey carts who were eager to trade the hospitality of their homes, and presumably their daughters, for a few cans of C-rations (*"Signorina, marsala, spaghet?"*), the city's economy seemed to be reviving. A barber shop ("salone") had reopened close to the docks, and the barbers were very intense and skillful, working with elbows high and great snipping and snapping of scissors between actual cuts. Although they offered shaves and shampoos as well as haircuts, it was difficult to bring oneself to expose the bare jugular to a straight razor in the hand of a man who could very well have been bombed out of house and home by one's countrymen in the very recent past.

Mail now arrived with reasonable regularity; the payroll had finally caught up to us. An officers' club with a bar, a nickelodeon, and a Ping-Pong table was open for business in a gracious old mansion near the port. And from some unknown source had come a most welcome supply of good books with which a man could improve and enjoy his off-duty hours.

The patrol job itself was relieved of boredom by the comings and goings of a variety of ships of many nations as the port increased in importance to the expanding Allied effort in Sicily and Italy; by the side trips to Termini, Zaffarano, Castellammare, and other pretty little harbors; and by the perfect Mediterranean weather—it was sometimes actually enjoyable for days at a time.

And yet, as had been the case earlier in North Africa, the tension caused by the ever-present preparations for the coming invasion continued to build. Obviously when it came we would be closer still to enemy air and naval bases on the European continent itself. We had been lucky up to now, but could our luck hold? The 694 and the 696 had been lucky too, but suddenly that luck had run out.

A great deal of history was made in August and September of 1943, much of it within a few hundred miles of where the SC 692 was taking her turns at plowing a furrow in the sea across half the mouth of the Gulf of Palermo. But for the captain of that subchaser, a single event eclipsed it all. The news came like this.

The twenty-eighth of August began in routine fashion. The 692 was relieved on patrol at 0700, entered port, tied up at the water dock, and filled her tanks. The crew went down to breakfast, the mail was censored, and the skipper walked over to the NOB, reported in, and then stopped by the post office. Sonarman Senecal, the mail orderly, was already there, with signalman LaFlamme to help him in the happy but improbable event that there was more mail than one man could carry, and Roy Washer, who had arrived out of just plain youthful impatience. The post office was a single, bare little room opening directly on the hot and dusty street. Senecal flopped his bag of outgoing letters on the worn wooden counter, reported it all censored and ready to go, and asked the routine but crucial question, "Anything for SC 692?" The postal clerk's response was just as routine, depressing and maddening, "Don't think so. Haven't had any mail in for a couple of days."

But, seeing in the eyes of the four man-of-warsmen before him the definite possibility that he might be lynched, he shuffled off into an adjoining room to check. Then in a moment there came to our listening ears the inexpressibly welcome sound of a heavy bag dragging across the rough board floor, and in a second or two the man reappeared, smiling, magically transformed in an instant into a prince of good fellows, hauling behind him a misshapen gray sack bulging with mail. "Looks like I was mistaken this time," said this now perfectly lovable man and yielded the bag to three or four pairs of grasping hands.

It didn't seem possible for any man to be more anxious to get at the contents of that gray sack than I, but I was resigned to waiting for it to be sorted and distributed back aboard. But Washer couldn't wait. To my annoyance, but before I could stop him, he extracted a couple of small bundles of letters that happened to be right at the top. In one of the bundles there was a letter for him and a small V-Mail for me. We both ripped them open at once. I don't know what was in Washer's, but what was in mine brought my instant forgiveness for his impatience, and caused a broad, uncontrollable smile to spread across my face and a sudden warmth to flood the area around my heart. The V-Mail was from my mother, written on the fourth of August, and the words that flew off the page were "Your son was born at 7:56 PM yesterday (the 3rd) . . . and both mother and child are doing well."

No combination of words can begin to describe the poignant blending of relief, pride, wonder, and love that flooded over me that day—a young man in a foreign land in the middle of a war—when, abruptly, on a dingy waterfront street in the heat of an ordinary day, I learned I was the father of a son born to the woman I loved. I yearned to leap into the air like an idiot and yell the news to the world (in this case the port of Palermo, Sicily), to bear-hug and pound on the back every brother-in-arms I saw, especially all those suddenly faultless paragons of loyalty and nautical skills in my own crew. In the next moment I wanted to weep with frustration that I was not present when the world changed and had no idea when I would be. And in the next, I was overwhelmed and awed by the unfamiliar weight of personal responsibility for that beloved new person who bore my very blood and name.

With all that happening inside, I felt the need for action, to *do* something. But what?

I floated back to the ship, where I also had responsibility but a kind I was used to, broke out the cigars I had been hoarding for months in anticipation of this day, and since I couldn't seem to settle down to anything anyway, yielded to the temptation to visit all around the harbor, presenting the cigars and announcing the news to old friends, new friends, bare acquaintances, and any strangers who might be in their company.

Then, at 1630 when the workday was over, I rounded up Charlie Coffey from the 692, Ben Partridge from the 978, Prent Horne from the 535, and George Steele from the PT base, dragged them uptown to the little vino shop with the hogsheads of marsala in the back, and, flushed with pride and a powerful kaleidoscope of emotions, bought us all more tumblers of the cool, semisweet wine than we really needed, especially when accompanied by the unfamiliar but obligatory cigars. Whatever other dangers that little celebration might have created, overspending was not one. With three half-pint glasses apiece, the tab came to $1.80 in occupation paper.

Back aboard much later, I was startled to find on the desk beside my bunk a tiny, blue baby dress and combination rattle and teething ring with a little handwritten verse, unsigned but in the easily recognizable hand of Roy Washer. "A gift for little Stafford," it read,

> Long may he wave,
> A chip off the old block,
> Stalwart and brave.
>
> You realize you're a lucky rat,
> My first will be a girl.
> But here's to you and little Chip,
> All the luck in the world.

The assignment of personnel to warships in wartime obviously cannot and does not make any attempt at matching compatible personalities, and although my rapport with Charlie Coffey had been almost instantaneous and had quickly developed into a warm and lasting friendship, relations between Washer and his captain had remained merely cordial and professional. While he had my entire trust and my respect for his ability to get things done, there were aspects of his personality that simply did not mesh with mine and prevented the development of any relationship beyond what was necessary to work and fight the ship and to get along in close quarters from day to day.

Thus I was truly and deeply touched by the totally unexpected gift and verse and felt more than a twinge of guilt that I had not made more of an effort to overcome my little irritations and built a better rapport with this capable young officer.

Although for the CO of the SC 692, the whole world seemed to have changed with the news that he was the father of a son, no alterations were externally apparent. The two-day patrols continued to alternate on a regular basis with the single day in port; the tempo of events leading to the next assault landing continued to accelerate; the short, welcome escort missions broke up the patrol routine; and the ship's work went on in the usual, sometimes unorthodox manner.

Except for the drastic differences that there were no homes or loved people to which to return when they were over and that the possibility of action with the enemy was greatly increased, patrol opera-

Lieutenant (junior grade) Roy J. Washer, who came aboard the SC 692 in Miami as an ensign and third officer and left as her last U.S. captain in Toulon, France, almost two years later. (R. J. Washer)

tions out of NOB, Palermo, were reminiscent of the idyllic days at Key West in what seemed like another world and another time. The most noticeable similarity was the perfect weather. Day after halcyon day, the light blue, cloudless sky met the dark blue, calmly shining sea at a perfectly defined horizon to the north, and the warmth of the sun was tempered by a gentle ocean breeze. To the south, the green coastal hills stood out sharp and clear between sea and sky, and the white buildings of the city climbed the slope of the shallow valley between the hills behind the town. Patrol uniform of the day for all hands was shorts and tennis shoes, and every man in the SC's crew sported a suntan that would have caused heads to turn on the Riviera or the golden sands of Palm Beach or Malibu.

The patrols themselves were run at a leisurely 6 knots on one engine and with one of the two generators on the line. Most of the crew —engineers, gunners, and deckhands alike—rotated every twenty minutes through the stations of helm, radar, sonar, lookout, and depth charges, thus keeping alert and cognizant of the ship's essential sensor and control equipment.

Off watch, there was the blessed new supply of good books to make the time pass as pleasurably as possible aboard a warship at sea in wartime. For the CO, the pleasure of those books was increased in late August, when from some local scrap yard sonarman Senecal brought back the seat from a wrecked fighter of unknown make or nationality and secured it on a couple of planks laid athwartships across the pipe support structure for the radar antenna about 8 feet above the bridge. From that comfortable vantage point, every square foot of the SC's topside was visible, the elevation and lack of obstructions made it an ideal lookout, every order to the helm and engines and every report to the OOD was audible, and the conning station itself instantly accessible. In that chair, in the course of that month of patrols, while remaining fully knowledgeable about every aspect of the ship's missions and operations, I was able to read and enjoy, among others, such worthwhile and unforgettable works as Thomas Wolfe's *Look Homeward, Angel* and *The Web and the Rock*, John Steinbeck's *Grapes of Wrath*, A. J. Cronin's *Citadel*, Cornelia Skinner's *Our Hearts Were Young and Gay*, the play *My Sister Eileen*, and the short stories of Alexander Woollcott.

Every convoy, every task force, in fact every single ship arriving in and departing from Palermo in those busy days before the landings in Italy, passed close by the subchaser patrol at the mouth of the gulf. Since most arrivals and departures occurred during daylight, and since the 692 was out there two-thirds of the time, her crew had a chance to observe most of them. The various landing craft, merchantmen, and the U.S. destroyers and cruisers were familiar and received respectful but routine notice. Of more interest were the warships of the Royal Navy, which now seemed to be appearing in increasing numbers.

There was something about the British ships that made them easily recognizable from a considerable distance and distinctive from their American counterparts. Perhaps it was in the curve and camber in foredeck and hull, whereas the lines of our ships were straighter. Perhaps it was in the way the white spray flew up from their cutwaters, whereas our bows just seemed to slice through. Or the way they seemed to be handled with verve and dash rather than everyday, matter-of-fact efficiency. There was a feeling that the warships under the proud white ensign were more fragile, less heavily armed and armored, perhaps less well equipped than ours, but that those discrepancies, if indeed they really existed, were more than offset by the superb skill and seamanship of their crews. The impression, right or wrong, was that what made our ships formidable was primarily matériel, whereas the Royal Navy's effectiveness depended above all on personnel.

One of the side trips that broke up the patrol routine was as escort to the fleet tug *Brant* to Termini, a few miles around the corner to the east. It was a slow passage, and the return run was even slower since the tug was towing a British LST badly damaged and deeply down by the bow. But the tug herself was not in very much better shape; it was she that had been shot up by a U.S. destroyer when she failed to respond to a challenge, and her own bow was seriously torn up. Later we learned the details of that tragic encounter from no less an authority than the executive officer of the *Benson,* the destroyer that had done the challenging and the shooting.

According to the destroyer's XO, they had challenged the unidentified contact four times, twice with a small shielded light and then twice with an unshielded, 12-inch signal light, and only then, having received no response of any kind and with the target headed straight for the destroyer, did they open fire. Unfortunately, in this case, their shooting was good. The first salvo made hits and the *Benson* went to rapid fire with her 5-inch/38s for a full minute. Finally, by the light of the flames on the target, they made out the unmistakable outlines of a U.S. Navy 26-foot motor whaleboat, recognized the tug as friendly, and ceased firing.

On another occasion we had a chance to talk to one of the *Brant*'s officers, and, not surprisingly, his version was quite different. Their first warning, he said, had been a flash of gunfire followed by the bursting of star shell overhead, and they had immediately made recognition signals and sounded GQ. Ten seconds later there had been another flash and the fountaining of a salvo close by. By the light of the flashes and the star shell, they had made out what appeared to be a surfaced sub about four thousand yards away, but they sent "BRANT" by flashing light in the direction of the other ship just before the first salvo hit, knocking every man on the bridge to the deck. One of the rounds destroyed the radio shack and the captain's cabin, another set the starboard whaleboat afire, and others hit an engine room and det-

In a sad case of mistaken identity, the destroyer *Benson* (above) shot up and seriously damaged the fleet tug *Brant* (below) in the Strait of Sicily on the night of 10 August 1943. Ten of the tug's men were killed and twenty wounded in this tragic battle between friends. With the *Brant* is a yard tug in Placentia Bay, Newfoundland, June 1942. (National Archives)

onated in the rigging, spraying the topsides with shrapnel. Flames from the burning boat leaped instantly higher than the masthead and the tug went to full speed, circling and making smoke. When the tragic action between friends and countrymen was over, the *Benson* had come alongside and put aboard a medical officer and a corpsman.

In the first days of September the little force of patrol craft at Palermo was decreased by one when the 771 somehow ran aground and damaged her bottom sufficiently that she was predicted to be out of commission for a full month. But on the days in port, although some things changed, others went on exactly as before. One of the things that had not changed since Nemours and Beni Saf was the receipt and issue of cigarettes to the ship's company. Periodically, a case of smokes came aboard. In each case were twenty cartons of cigarettes of assorted brands and a few packages of pipe tobacco. Out of the thirty individuals aboard the SC, by coincidence there were twenty smokers. In one of the few exercises of democratic principles in the innately undemocratic community of a man-of-war, the cartons were distributed by lot. Numbered slips from one to twenty were drawn from a white hat and each man took his choice in the order of the number drawn. The most inveterate and appreciative smoker in the ship was her executive officer, but never, in all the months in the Med, despite the odds, which should eventually have turned in his favor, had Charlie drawn a number lower than fifteen. As a result, the aftermath of each drawing became perfectly predictable. Charlie, distastefully clutching his carton of Wings, Marvels, or Kentucky Winners, and a couple of dollar bills, would approach anyone with a recognizable brand, smilingly but insistently urging a swap.

In the category of changes for the better,—in this case under the grim heading of "It's an ill wind . . ."—Boats made friends with one of the divers working on the salvage of the sunken subchasers, and the 692 fell heir to a washing machine from the 696. Casey welded up the shrapnel holes in the tub, Braverman took the motor ashore and got it rewound, and a day or two later it was swishing and spinning away back on the fantail, an immeasurable improvement over the soak-and-scrub-in-a-bucket system to which we had grown accustomed.

Another Murphy coup did not pan out nearly as well—his acquisition, cost free, of fifteen gallons of Italian gray paint, enough to coat the SC's entire topside. On the first full day in port after it came aboard, the chief supervised its application, and although it was not precisely the shade of gray we were used to, it did look pretty good. Through his many tattoos Boats glowed with pride. But the glow of pride turned to a glower of anger at "those goddam Wops" when the next day on patrol a passing thunderstorm washed most of his beautiful new paint away.

The gray paint caper was just about Chief Bosun's Mate Patrick Murphy's last official act as head of the deck force and OOD in the SC 692. Early in September he was transferred to Commander Landing Craft and Bases at Bizerte for further assignment. And it was time for him to go. Although he had been a good bosun's mate and a competent OOD, he had also been, with Gunner Walter, the source of most of our personnel problems since Gibraltar. His fuse was short, his temper flared with irritating frequency, he could not hold his liquor, and most disturbing (and what precipitated his departure), he had allegedly in recent weeks begun to make advances to some of the younger sailors up forward.

Of greater loss to the ship was big, able, good-natured Charlie Nader, who left with Murphy but for a different reason. Orders had come in to transfer a bosun's mate second class back to SCTC for further training and reassignment, and Nader had been longest aboard and was most deserving of going home. Now we would have to develop a more conventional means of coming to anchor. The 692 had long been known among her peers and larger ships for her distinctive anchoring. From the bridge would come the order, "Stand by the anchor," and Nader would pick up the 125-pound Danforth as casually as a school girl picking up a pencil. "Let go!" and Charlie would simply chuck it over.

It had been common knowledge aboard the SC that Chief Murphy was a "junk merchant," a collector of whatever he thought he or the ship might ever in the future conceivably require. Most of his acquisitions were immediately bolted or welded into place and painted gray, so that to anyone other than ship's company they appeared to be original equipment. In all fairness, although he obviously enjoyed the process of procurement and spent much of his time ashore searching, scavenging, and scrounging, with minor exceptions what he came back with benefited the ship and her crew in one way or another, such as the washing machine. But only in the first few days after his departure did we come to realize the extent of his acquisitiveness. Huge coils of manila line turned up; untold gallons of paint in a dozen shades; tools, tar, and oakum in prodigious quantities; and a total of seven extra anchors.

Not long after Boats had left, as though his tradition of accumulation had been too well established to end even in his absence, the

692 came into the possession of two vehicles. Both were Fiats: one a small, cab-over-engine truck with double back wheels and no muffler; the other a little gray sedan about waist high with a tiny, puny engine and a chorus of squeaks and rattles that announced its arrival before its mouse-power engine could be heard. Both vehicles were inherited from the 1029, which was going back to Africa for an indeterminate stay and had acquired them apparently by default immediately after the Germans had left town. Presumably they had been requisitioned by the enemy, abandoned when they pulled out, and turned over more or less officially for the use of the local U.S. Navy.

It was astounding the difference those vehicles made to the men of the 692 on their days in port. No more long, hot, dusty hikes to operations, the post office, or supply; no more hours wasted trying to cadge a truck to haul ammo, provisions, parts, or other heavy gear to the ship. Suddenly all the facilities in the port area and the city were within convenient range. After the first day we wondered how we had survived without those wheels.

Naturally the two Fiats were not used 100 percent for ship's business. One afternoon Charlie and I took the little sedan up the slope behind the city to visit the beautiful old Norman-Byzantine cathedral of Monreale and its catacombs hung with long-dead monks, which I remembered (and could not forget) seeing as a boy of ten. It was a wonderful afternoon—after we made it up the hill in the puny little car. Halfway up, grinding along in the lowest of the four gears, we stopped to pick up a pleasant-looking young couple trudging upward at the roadside. But our kindness was misplaced. With four adults seated inside, the Fiat refused to budge even in low with full power, and, embarrassed, we were forced to off-load our passengers.

Since the ship's first arrival in Palermo, Tony Curato had been requesting enough liberty to allow him to visit an aunt and uncle who, according to Tony, lived in a small town only about twenty miles away. During one period of a forced four days in port while a reduction gear on the starboard engine was being rebuilt, the little sedan was pressed into service to make the trip. Tony rode in back, I drove, and Ben Partridge of the 978 rode shotgun. It was a spectacular drive despite the power limitations of the little car, which needed all four of its forward gears to negotiate the narrow, winding, climbing road with its hairpin turns and sheer drops to the valleys and plains below. The road led through a number of small farming towns with cobbled streets and overhanging buildings and swarming with people who stared curiously at us.

Between the towns we passed long lines of mules pulling brightly painted and fully laden carts with high wooden wheels, also painted, and other mules with huge sheaves of grain on each side. The mules and donkeys we had seen down in Palermo had been small, tired, and moth-eaten, but these rural animals were just the opposite—big and husky with gleaming hides. And there was a similar difference between the children of the city and the country; the latter looked dramatically stronger, better nourished, and more alert. Although the mountains through which the road led were barren and littered with huge white boulders, the plains and valleys between them and the blue sea beyond were lush and dark green with vineyards and olive orchards, vastly different from the parched brown hills and flatlands around Gela and Licata.

Finally, after close to thirty-five miles, the little Fiat chugged around a bend in the road and into the piazza of the town of Alcamo, our destination. Tony disembarked in his liberty whites, and after several long conversations in rapid Sicilian with the somewhat startled local carabinieri, returned to the car with the sad news that his uncle had died a year before and his aunt some six months later. But if elections had been held in Alcamo that noon, the name of the new mayor would have been Curato. A score of families invited him to their homes since his relatives were gone, and when he gently refused, citing his uniform and duty, pressed a variety of gifts upon him, mostly farm products: cheese, grapes, vegetables, sausages, and even, as the gray Fiat got under way again, a couple of live, loudly protesting roosters, which one enthusiastic donor kept trying to push in through an open rear window.

On the return trip, in the outskirts of Alcamo, we picked up a sixty-three-year-old priest in a brown cassock and a broad-brimmed, low-crowned black hat, who was routinely starting out to walk to Palermo, and who, we suspected, after the Fiat with its weak brakes and heavy load had careened around a few steep curves coming down out of the mountains to the city, might well have preferred his original means of transportation.

Toward the end of the first week in September, seaborne activity approximately doubled in the Gulf of Palermo, with literally dozens of ships of all kinds arriving and departing daily. Then, on the eighth of the month, thirty-one PTs and a score of the comparable British MLs filed at high speed out of the harbor and sped off to the northnortheast. In the afternoon came the news that Italy had surrendered unconditionally and that the Anglo-Americans would invade the peninsula early the following morning. Obviously this was one assault landing that would be made without the assistance of the SC 692, and we were tempted to believe she would not be involved in that operation at all, a belief that was soon to be proved most emphatically in error. A few more days of the comfortable patrol routine were left, and the results of the Italian surrender became evident almost at once.

Early on the morning of the tenth, a British crash boat came in from seaward towing a trimotor Italian float plane with its crew sitting, smiling and waving, on its wings. Then a big convoy of merchantmen and tankers entered, all heavily laden, several of their topsides brown with troops. Toward evening a huge, snow-white hospital ship entered the gulf from the north, and simultaneously a message flashed out to us from shore,

EXPECTING ITALIAN HOSPITAL SHIP X ESCORT HER TO ANCHORAGE VICINITY TOWER WELL CLEAR OF OTHER SHIPS.

Alongside, an officer on the bridge far above us spoke English, and we instructed him to follow us in and anchor at our signal. But when we were within a few hundred yards of the intended anchorage, the people at NOB changed their minds and sent a new message.

INSTRUCT TOSCANA CRUISE ON 080T FROM HARBOR ENTRANCE X RETURN AT DAYLIGHT.

Feeling a little foolish, we signaled the *Toscana* to stop, and with Tony close behind to act as interpreter should that be necessary, I jumped across to her lowered accommodation ladder and made my way to the bridge. Neither Tony nor I were feeling very good about this whole thing. I was uncomfortable because the entire Italian crew was in immaculate whites and I was in dungarees sporting a day and a half's beard and issuing conflicting instructions, and Tony because he felt his linguistic ability outclassed by these real Italians from Italy, not Brooklyn. "Jesus, Captain," he muttered to me on the way up, "I don't speak Italian. I speak dago!"

He need not have worried. *Toscana*'s captain spoke precise English that sounded as though he had learned it at Oxford or Cambridge. He was a rather short and intense gentleman with soft but alert brown eyes, and the soul of courtesy and cooperation. I gave him the instructions from NOB and showed him the track on his chart. When I felt obligated to apologize for the informality of my appearance on this rather formal occasion, he shrugged expressively and simply said, "We are working now."

There was a lot of saluting at the head of the accommodation ladder and Tony and I scrambled down and jumped back aboard. A few minutes later the *Toscana* was on her way on the prescribed course, which was a relief since with her bright lights and forty-foot red crosses she would have made the best possible navigational beacon for the incoming bombers of her very recent ally.

The *Toscana* turned out to be the first of very many Italian ships to pass the 692's patrol line and anchor in the broad Gulf of Palermo. On 12 September the parade began with a rusty little coastal submarine, well escorted by four British destroyers and with a Royal Navy officer plainly distinguishable atop her conning tower. She was followed later in the morning by six Italian destroyers, smaller and more lightly armed than their U.S. and British peers, and around noon by another destroyer, three torpedo boats of World War I vintage, and what appeared to be two yachts converted to patrol craft. Then around 1530 in came ten Italian PTs, looking very much like the British MLs we were used to but armed also with torpedoes and with depth charges all along their deck edges. Their crews were lined up smartly on deck in red life jackets, the officers in whites. With the 40-mm manned and trained out just in case, the 692 steamed down their long column flying the international flag signal to anchor outside the harbor, which they promptly did.

That busy day ended around 1930 with the entrance of an entire British task force: one large and four small escort carriers, three cruisers, and ten destroyers, one of which, by her colors, was Polish. By dark the waters outside the breakwater were full of warships—American, British, and Italian—indistinguishable as blacked-out silhouettes on the still night sea.

The end of that stint on patrol was very nearly the end, at least for the present, of the SC's relatively easy and predictable routine under the auspices of NOB, Palermo. In port the talk was exclusively of the landings at Salerno, just around the Sorrento peninsula south of Naples, and the bitter and continuing opposition put up by the Germans, who had moved into the defensive positions vacated by the Italians immediately after the surrender. One young officer, a crash-boat skipper, just returned from there, reported that we had lost three thousand men on one beach to Kraut tanks dug into the sand at the water's edge, and that early in the operation the destroyer *Rowan* had been torpedoed by an E-boat and sunk in less than a minute with the loss of more than two hundred of her crew. He told us the *Savannah* had taken a bomb hit, the *Philadelphia* a damaging near miss, and that air raids on the beachhead and ships offshore were nearly continuous.

A German radio-controlled 660-pound bomb makes a direct hit on the number three six-inch turret of the light cruiser *Savannah* off Salerno as a PT passes by, 11 September 1943. (Collection of Admiral H. Kent Hewitt, Naval Historical Foundation)

What details we could glean of the damage to the *Savannah* were particularly disturbing. It seems she had been hit by a radio-controlled gliding bomb with a warhead of more than six hundred pounds that had made a direct hit on her number three six-inch turret, detonated in the lower handling room with resultant heavy casualties, and blew a big hole in the cruiser's bottom. Only superb damage control had kept her from sinking. She was reported to be en route to Malta for repairs.

Waiting for us ashore was long-lost leading radioman Kidwell, certified ready to return to duty, but looking pale and thin. He said he had been transferred from the *Oxfordshire* to a hospital in Bizerte for treatment of his gastroenteritis, but when he had recuperated and was awaiting transportation back to the ship, he had caught a piece of shrapnel in his knee during an air raid on the city and spent more weeks back in the ward he had just left.

The mid watch of 17 September found the 692 snugly at anchor off the breakwater, but not for long. At 0315 came the familiar but always disquieting whistle and the voice of the gangway watch: "There's an officer here to see you, Captain. Says it's very important."

Even emerging from the depths of slumber, I knew the truth of that last phrase was evident. Three o'clock in the morning a mile offshore was an unlikely occasion for a social call. The officer was Ensign Ayler from NOB Operations, a friend of Charlie's with whom we had chatted over Scotch and water at the club an evening or two before. He was very pleasant and very professional. He handed me a single sheet on which was typed our orders, and when I whistled at their content, he told me earnestly, "This is a matter of the utmost urgency."

I could see that it was. The PTs and MLs operating around Salerno were dangerously short of fuel, there was none available locally, and a gasoline tanker, the *Anticline,* was sailing at once to relieve the situation. The SC 692 would be her escort. The code name of the two-ship convoy would be "Hemingway."

SALERNO

Since Ensign Ayler was going from the 692 to the tanker with similar orders, there was time to plot the points and courses specified in the routing instructions before heading out. Surprisingly, they did not match. The first line of the instructions read, "Proceed on course 080 to point BE," and gave the latitude and longitude of BE. But when those coordinates were plotted, there was no way to arrive there by steering 080. We could either steer the prescribed course or go to the prescribed point. We chose to go to the point since we figured there was less probability of error in the ten digits of the coordinates than in the three of the course.

At 0415 we found the small tanker heading slowly out from the breakwater, deep in the sea with her load of precious fuel, and at their request came alongside within hailing distance. Someone on her darkened bridge shouted over that although they had a good gyro compass, they lacked an accurate speed curve, and if we would check their speed with ours and give them a reading, they would then do the navigating.

While the sky grew lighter in the east and the stars began to fade, subchaser and tanker ran side by side for the ten miles out to point BE, where we closed again and informed her bridge that according to our calculations she was making 11.5 knots. Someone shouted back their thanks and informed us their maximum speed was 12. The SC then moved out a mile ahead where she belonged and set up a patrol across the tanker's bows at 13 knots, sonar pinging away, the forty and the aft twenty manned and ready, and lookouts on full alert. Distressingly on this vital mission the two little scopes of the SF radar were dark, the gear out of commission. Young radarman Myron Wells, made fully aware of the urgency of his task, manual and circuit diagrams spread all over the pilothouse, tore into the set with grim determination and stayed at it all day.

Meanwhile there was plenty for the lookouts to see and report. Visibility was unlimited under a clear sky over a flat, calm sea, and we counted ten big convoys, almost all on a heading reciprocal to ours, returning from the beachhead, empty. With all those ships coming and going in that perfect weather, it looked like a happy hunting ground for subs, and late in the morning a solid echo came banging back into the sonar at the end of one of its long pings. After the accustomed rhythm of echoless pinging, watch after watch and day after day, an echo that breaks that rhythm, although actually no louder in measurable decibels than the outgoing pings themselves, gets your attention like a cannon shot. Acutely aware of the value of our change and our responsibility, we ran to battle stations, signaled the tanker to take evasive action, and charged in to attack.

The range to the contact was only four hundred yards, too close for mousetraps, but the direction of movement was toward the tanker and we were taking no chances. The SC turned hard on her heel to cross ahead and fired a full pattern of Mark 6 charges set for one hundred feet from K-guns and stern racks. It didn't take long for the three-hundred-pound ashcans to reach firing depth, and when they did, the sea roared, rose, and fountained repeatedly under the lash of the detonating torpex charges. Even though she was well out of the damage zone, the subchaser's stern lifted with the force of the explosions, and their water hammers reverberated against the sturdy juniper strakes of her hull.

On the bridge, the CO and XO exchanged glances of satisfaction. If we had not killed the sub, we sure as hell must have inflicted heavy damage, shaken her up, and discouraged her from further attempts on the tanker. With all guns manned and trained out with safeties off, the 692 circled the big patch of roiled white water left by the charges, while sonar probed its edges to regain contact. In accordance with long planning, the four-round clip in the loading slot of the forty and those ready in the hands of the loaders were armor-piercing to puncture the enemy's pressure hull, while the three twenties and the four light machine guns procured and mounted for the purpose were prepared to sweep the sub's decks and prevent the manning of her guns.

Grimly, fingers tense on all the triggers, we waited for whatever might emerge from below that troubled sea, hoping for chunks of wreckage too big to have been fired from a torpedo tube, a gush of diesel oil, or a body or two. In about three minutes the bodies began to come up, dozens, scores, hundreds of them, long and black and quite dead: the bodies of a school of huge fish, three to four feet long, black on top and silvery white on the undersides, killed by the concussion of the charges.

In an aura of anticlimax that was almost palpable, the ship secured from general quarters and set off in pursuit of the *Anticline,* which was already fast approaching the horizon, having somehow, under the motivation of the moment, found a lot more knots in her power plant than the 12 officially admitted.

The 692 had been back on screening station ahead of the tanker only an hour or so when the raucous buzzer of the general alarm sounded once more. This time it was for two twin-engine aircraft winging straight in high and fast from the starboard bow. From the bridge they looked like a pair of Ju 88s on a horizontal bombing run and we turned back hard toward the *Anticline* while all the gun barrels swung to track the incoming planes. But seconds before we would have opened fire, a two-star smoke grenade blossomed below them, the proper air-to-surface recognition signal for the day. A moment later we could make out the colored disks of their RAF markings and identify them as Beaufighters.

As the planes circled overhead, a signal light began to flash from one of them. "R U Hemingway?" it asked in terse Morse. "Yes," we flashed back, having trouble keeping the 12-inch light trained on the circling plane.

"We R escorts," they announced, and began a climb back to about five thousand feet, where they orbited protectively until dark, providing a fine feeling of security but adding to our awareness of the urgency of the mission and the weight of our responsibility. Especially since none of the big convoys we had counted during the day appeared to have merited their own continuous, dedicated air cover.

As the two ships and the two circling planes approached the Italian peninsula in the dying day, it seemed a passage from peace to war. To port the red sun was sinking into the sea and the sky was clear.

Ahead and to starboard the hunched hills of the enemy-held coast were dark and smudged with smoke, and in the dusk just after sunset the sea was suddenly scummed with oil and littered with wreckage. In the sweet stench of the oil, and with the SC's bow wave that had been frothy white now dirty brown and sliding instead of splashing back across the surface, we checked out one piece of the wreckage. To our horror we found ourselves peering down into the shattered, half-swamped, empty lifeboat of a hospital ship, with bright red crosses on its sides and a green band around the gunwales. The Beaufighters slanted down to inspect two other similar objects and signaled briefly, "No life."

With our aerial escort departing, we dropped back to five hundred yards from our charge to better defend against attack from the air, which in this close seemed the greater threat. As we pulled into position, Wells arrived on the bridge with his face wreathed in a smile of vast relief and more than a tinge of pride to report the radar back in operation. Twenty-nine other men in the SC 692 were as relieved as he. Everyone had known what none had said, that the loss of the radar off Salerno could well have been a fatal failure.

As soon as it was fully dark we turned eastward for the bloody beaches of Salerno, and at 2300 a British destroyer loomed out of the gloom ahead and with a dim, red, shielded signal light, assumed responsibility for the valuable little tanker. We were instructed to follow the destroyer and the *Anticline* to the anchorage and there to report to the HMS *Hilary* for further orders, a directive that sounded simple but in the attempted execution became impossible.

At first we tried to stay always to seaward of the tanker since that would give her the best protection against submarines, but within thirty minutes it became necessary to devote full time and attention to taking care of the SC 692. Visibility dropped suddenly to nearly zero in a combination of fog and a pungent white smoke used to conceal the ships in the anchorage from hostile aircraft. Both the tanker and the destroyer appeared on the now repaired radar to be steering erratically, and when the *Anticline* popped up dead ahead one hundred yards away on nearly a collision course, we decided to try to find a less populated piece of ocean in which to lie to and await daylight before reporting in.

But even that was hard to do. As the mid watch began, radar showed no fewer than a dozen rapidly moving ships in dangerous proximity, and the blasts of a variety of fog whistles came out of the cottony darkness on all sides. Charlie stayed at the radar and kept us advised of the range and bearing of our most threatening neighbor and suggested courses to the nearest most vacant area. I stayed at the conn on the bridge peering out into the night and dodging the occasional shadows that loomed past until my eyeballs felt as though they were halfway down the twin barrels of my binoculars and my nerves were coiled like springs.

Then, as though to show that as bad as things were, they could be worse, there came a roaring of engines from overhead and the crump and flash of exploding bombs as an enemy air raid hit the anchorage. Now at battle stations the SC's gunners trained their barrels upward and waited for a target while the ship continued her hairy game of blindman's buff in the crowded fog and smoke. Streams and strings of tracers soared upward from the direction of the land, heavy guns flashed redly through the murk, and enemy engines screamed back and forth above, but not a single plane appeared to the frustrated gun crews of the groping, fogbound subchaser.

The raid lasted about half an hour, but the problem of the fog and the moving ships did not go away with the enemy planes. The anxiety felt by all hands as the small, fragile wooden ship maneuvered to keep clear of destroyers, cruisers, landing craft, and transports many times her size, all easily able to slice her into splinters at the cost of some scraped paintwork, reminded Charlie in a moment of tension-releasing humor of the down-home Tennessee expression, "As nervous as a long-tailed tomcat in a room full of rockin' chairs."

But it was not the least bit humorous when at the end of the watch, despite our best efforts and vigilance, the sharp bow of a British destroyer on a converging course tore through the shreds of smoke about twenty yards to port. We watched her green starboard light pop on well above our heads. On our bridge we could hear her conning officer yelling for hard left rudder even as I was shouting for full right, and for several very long seconds before the two ships passed clear, a man could have jumped from one to the other.

As though now the worst had happened and the crisis had passed, suddenly on the radar scope all the menacing little blobs that had been converging on us seemed to be retreating, and with a few minutes more of Charlie's coaching, we found ourselves out in the clear with the nearest target a comfortable three thousand yards away. In exhausted relief we lay quietly to and drifted on the calm waters of the Gulf of Salerno until dawn.

At 0825 on a bright morning we finally located the HMS *Hilary*, anchored off the northern end of the long Salerno beach, still surrounded by shreds of the odiferous white smoke of the night. She was a big, clumsy-looking attack transport and flagship of Task Force 85,

Scene at sea off the south beaches of Salerno, September 1943. Two PTs of Squadron 15 patrol inboard of LST 404, while a covey of LCIs surround flagship *Ancon* to seaward. (National Archives)

the Northern Attack Force. LaFlamme's shutter had just begun to clatter with the first groups of our message reporting in when he had to break it off and dive for his battle station. From somewhere directly above came the loudening, angry roar of diving aircraft, a rattle of machine-gun fire in the sky, then from nearby the hammering of a couple of alert 20-millimeters, and three or four black, single-engine fighter-bombers flashed low overhead, closely followed by a pair of Spitfires with gray gunsmoke streaming back across their wings. They had come and gone so fast there was only time to hit the buzzer for GQ and make a grab for one of the thirties on the bridge, but that had been time enough for the Focke-Wulfs to release three small bombs. We watched one of them as it entered the water between the SC and the *Hilary*. It was still moving forward with the motion of the fighter, and hit at an angle, making only a small splash and a round slick on the surface before exploding with a heavy crump and a fountain of white water that made the deck jump under our feet but caused no damage that we could see to either ship.

For the next half-hour we waited at general quarters for more attacks while we concluded our business with the flagship. We were told to report to Captain Zimmerlie in LCI 10, the same gentleman who had been convoy commodore from Bermuda to Gibraltar. Alongside the LCI we were given a load of smoke pots to be used on signal from her and told we would stay in the area until the *Anticline* had dispensed her fuel, then escort her back to Palermo.

Now began the longest period of continuous combat operations the 692 had experienced to date. We never saw the *Anticline* again, but we made a lot of use of those smoke pots. And some operating changes were made as a result of the morning's attack. From sunrise to sunset a special sun lookout with shaded binoculars was added to the watch bill, and the forty and the aft twenty were manned around the clock with magazines loaded and rounds chambered. On the bridge and fantail belted ammunition remained at all times in the feed mechanisms of the light machine guns. If there were any warning at all we would be ready.

Most of the ships at Salerno had been there since the initial landings early on the morning of the ninth, and a full-scale warning system had been developed. Ideally, the first announcement would come by radio, "All stations this circuit, Yellow Avalanche north" (the direction from which the attacking planes were coming). Then, usually in a minute or two, "All stations this circuit, Red Avalanche north."

Simultaneously with the first radio warning, the *Hilary* and all the larger ships would run up huge yellow flags. With the second message, red flags would replace the yellow, and the *Hilary* would sound the danger signal of a series of rapid short blasts on her whistle. Ships too far away to hear the whistle could see the jets of white steam from her stack.

But that was the ideal and it only happened that way occasionally in practice. The swift little Fw 190s and Me 109s with the white crosses on their wings attacked several times a day, most often during morning and evening twilight, and nearly always with fighters on their tails. As often as not, as they did that first morning, they would come diving in and drop their bombs before the radio and the red flags could give warning. Sometimes they would arrive as the yellow flags were rising to the yardarms. And sometimes, happily, the radio and the flags would go from yellow to red, all the ships would wait at battle stations, trained out and ready, and no attack would come, the defending Spitfires and P-40s having intercepted and turned it back.

After dark there was seldom any warning. As the 692 patrolled slowly a mile or so offshore that first night, her crew was startled by the flash of a big explosion on the airstrip just inland from the beach, followed by the all-too-familiar sound of aircraft engines at low alti-

Two SCs putting down smoke to protect against air attack off Salerno, September 1943. The large ship at the left is the USS *Ancon*, the flagship of the American southern sector. (National Archives)

tude and high power and a fire at the site of the explosion that burned fiercely until dawn.

That attack gave the SC the first of many opportunities to use her newly acquired smoke pots. In the instant after the first flash and blast, the order came by radio from the LCI 10, "Make smoke," and for the next thirty minutes we steamed back and forth upwind of the anchorage, between ships and shore, an obscuring white cloud billowing and curling up from the stern to smother the anchored Liberties, landing craft, and men-of-war in a smelly but friendly blanket.

It felt good to be doing a job that without doubt in the long run prevented casualties and damage by denying the enemy pilots—and later his gunners—well-defined, identifiable targets. It did not feel as good to be the easiest target around, instantly locatable at the small, upwind end of the smoke cloud by any enemy airman who felt like taking out his frustration at having his objective obscured with a quick strafing run on those who were so obviously doing the obscuring. The most tense and vigilant men aboard were the three 20-mm gunners, who kept their barrels trained up and aft, with safeties off and fingers curled around the triggers to meet any such attack with a concentrated triple stream of explosive rounds.

Despite the enemy's ability to conduct quick, hit-and-run, sneak attacks with fighter-bombers in daylight and to harass the beachhead at night, the blue skies above Salerno were dominated by the friendlies. Several times each day the SC's men would glance anxiously up at the sound of many engines, and turn back to their duties relieved at the sight of wedge after tight wedge of Mitchells or Marauders or, usually higher, formations of Fortresses or Liberators winging northward toward Rome and Naples. And, closer to home, the little airstrip along the beach was busy all day with the comings and goings of the Spits, Seafires, and P-40s that flew cover over sea and shore.

In fact the gravest danger to the 692 and her sisters at Salerno came not from aircraft at all but, as at Gela and Empedocle, from the enemy guns ashore. The high, rugged wooded hills behind the town of Salerno provided the German gunners with emplacements from which they could fire on the ships in the northern anchorage with relative impunity, and they made full use of that terrain advantage, skillfully concealing the flash and smoke of their guns so that it was next to impossible for the ships' crews to discover the source of the incoming rounds. By the time the 692 arrived in the area, most of those guns had been eliminated. But at least one stubborn crew remained, firing, as nearly as could be determined from the sound of the rounds and the size of their splashes, a 6-inch howitzer. The SC, charged with protecting that anchorage with her smoke pots, engaged in a deadly, almost personal contest with that gun crew lasting several days.

With Teutonic punctuality, the howitzer would open fire within a few minutes of 1700 each day, although just to keep us off balance, a few rounds might come in around noon and a few more in the early evening. First would come a dull boom from somewhere up in the hills, then immediately a whistle sliding rapidly down the scale as the projectile passed overhead, and a flat, sharp, harsh "whap" as it struck the water and detonated, sending up a tall, dirty brown splash.

After the first day we learned to position the ship between the hills and the anchorage, and when the first round came in we would get under way while Bennie Braverman, the "Smoke King," lighted off his pots, two at a time. Then it became a contest to see if we could obscure the ships before the enemy gunners could hit one. The SC would charge back and forth between unseen battery and targets, sometimes with the help of a British ML, or a YMS or an LCI, the white smoke billowing from the fantail, and her crew, all topside and in helmets and life jackets, would watch as the fall of shot closed in on a selected ship. First the splashes would orient themselves properly in deflection, on a direct line between gun and target, but short. Then, a couple of hundred yards at a time, they would walk out, reaching toward their goal—a Liberty ship, an LST, a transport. Almost always, before the final rounds could hit, the rising clouds of smoke would have blanketed the bay, and the firing would stop, only to begin again when visibility returned.

But sometimes the howitzer crew got lucky. One afternoon toward the end of the 1700 shoot, the threatening splashes had advanced right up to the edge of the wall of smoke, by then impenetrable to the eye, and on the basis of past experience, it was time for the firing to cease. But this time the German gun captain must have decided to increase the range a few hundred yards and try one more shot in the blind. The round whistled over as usual, but instead of the normal "whap," a loud, sharp report came blasting out of the smoke cloud, and we could see red tongues of flame licking up from where a British LCT had been unloading a small freighter. We learned later that the howitzer shell had made a direct hit on the little conning station at the stern of the landing craft, killing the skipper, the exec, and four "ratings," and wounding four other men engaged in handling cargo.

Electrician's Mate Harold (Bennie) Braverman, the SC's "Smoke King," whose pots and smoke generators protected the anchorage and the ship herself from constant air attacks at Salerno and later at Anzio. His informal attire was the uniform of the day during the endless summer patrols in the Gulf of Palermo. (C. D. Casey)

But the enemy battery or batteries did not go unchallenged. Each day the big British monitor *Abercrombie,* mined on D-day but repaired and back in action, would stand off Salerno, elevate her ponderous 15-inchers, and hammer away for an hour or two. When she had finished, the cruisers would move in and open up with their 6- and 5-inch guns, the yellow cordite smoke blowing downwind across their decks. And at night the army 155s ashore would blanket the hills with barrage fire. One night they put on an incredible effort. There must have been hundreds of guns concealed along the shore and in the low hills to the south of the town, and they fired steadily for two full hours. So steadily that the white muzzle flashes were literally continuous and the sound of the firing a sustained, deep-throated rumbling. It didn't seem that anything could have survived that bombardment, and we were confident we would have no more contests with that howitzer.

The following day all was quiet in the anchorage off Salerno, and in the late afternoon the 692 moved in close to the high, green hills of Sorrento and dropped the hook while her men, including her captain, enjoyed a refreshing swim in the cool, clear water. I was floating lazily astern, thinking that this was not such a tough war after all, when the first dirty brown splash erupted forward and to port, dangerously close to the nearest of the anchored ships. It took the swimming party only a minute or so to get back aboard, and in another minute the anchor was up and the smoke going while a mostly naked crew struggled into their clothes at their battle stations. Conditions were ideal for making smoke, with just enough breeze from seaward to take it down over the ships but not enough to blow it away, so that before the howitzer could fire again, it was completely shut off from its targets.

In the SC there was utter amazement that the enemy gun crew had survived the fire of the ships and the barrage we had witnessed the night before. (Chief Ham Morton was convinced that the enemy gun crew wheeled their howitzer back into some deep cave each night and took off down the other side of the mountains to "pitch a liberty with the senoritas and the good vino in Naples" and returned at their leisure late in the morning to resume operations.) But there was also a certain amount of pride that we had thwarted them once again so quickly and thoroughly even though taken by surprise. Then we made our second and nearly fatal mistake.

As we had done on occasion before, when the wind was right, instead of steaming back and forth to put down our smoke, we just lay to, to windward of the ships, and let the breeze blow it down across them. Apparently that was too much for the enemy artillerymen, who despite Morton's theory had probably been shaken up by all the fire directed at them and then frustrated once again by our smoke. Because as the SC lay dead in the water, engines idling and the smoke pouring from her stern, another round came in. But the whistle this time did not slide down the scale. Instead the pitch rose to a screech, ending abruptly in a report so loud and close that both Charlie and I whipped around to see if the stern of the ship was still there. It was, but a tower of dirty water was falling back into the sea not fifteen yards from the port quarter, and the air was filled with the same nasty whirrings and buzzings last heard off Empedocle. One sizable chunk of shrapnel ripped through the canvas on the port side of the bridge a few inches aft of us, another twanged off a pipe stop for the port 20-mm, and others stuck up out of the tough juniper strakes of the SC's side or bounced off some structure or other and fell hot and jagged on her decks.

The final drops of that splash had not yet settled back into the Gulf of Salerno before there was a boiling of water under the subchaser's stern as she got under way with a surge to continue her smoke-making on irregular courses and at varying speeds. A quick check showed that the luck of the little ship still held, and of the two dozen officers and men fully exposed at their guns and stations topside not one had suffered as much as a nick or a glancing blow.

Most of SC 692's duties at Salerno were at the northern end of the gulf, where the long, white crescent of beach joined the Sorrento peninsula at the town itself. This was known as the Northern Attack Force Tactical Area, or NAFTA. It was here that the British forces had gone ashore and it was still primarily a British show, whereas down south at SAFTA, most of the ships and units ashore were American.

One evening the SC received orders to pick up the British commander of a flotilla of LCTs and take further orders from him. He turned out to be a Lieutenant Commander Ritchie, and we took him from the LST 585, at anchor off NAFTA, to the little fishing village of Maiori, about ten miles west of Salerno, where most of his LCTs were working. In a case of the exception that proves the rule, Maiori had been taken in the first hours of the original landings by three battalions of U.S. Rangers, and Commander Ritchie's landing craft were engaged in bringing in British commandos and ammunition and supplies in support.

The gravel beach was narrow, with steep hills on both sides and a deep, V-shaped valley opening into the mountains behind. A few hundred feet above the village and the sea, a highway had somehow been carved out of the mountainsides running east and west along the southern shore of the cape. It reminded us of the Storm King highway along the Hudson, and under other circumstances, we thought, must be one of the most beautiful roads in the world. We learned later that we had been looking at the world-famed Amalfi Drive, but on this particular visit the only motorists able to enjoy the grandeur of its scenery were the crews of a long column of British light and medium tanks that clanked and rattled along toward Salerno with their many engines sounding like a squadron of aircraft.

The steepness of the beach gradient was like nothing we had ever seen. Commander Ritchie insisted that we could put him aboard one of his LCTs even though its bow was high and dry well up on the beach. And he was right. The 692 nosed warily in and brought her port bow along the starboard quarter of the landing craft to let him step across, and there were three fathoms of water under the bullnose.

The steep beach at Maiori was covered with hundreds of buck-naked Tommies bathing and sunning themselves with no apparent thought of the main street of the town fifty yards away or of the heavy shells that rumbled overhead from a cruiser just offshore shelling enemy positions deep inland. Each time the cruiser fired, the thunder of her 6-inch guns echoed and reverberated between the hills for a full minute, and a mile or two back at the head of the valley, an echelon of Mustangs was dive-bombing the ship's targets, circling and then plummeting suddenly, down out of sight, at incredible speed.

After half an hour, a light flashed from the LCT and we eased back in, this time with more confidence, and took the commander back aboard. On the way back to NAFTA, despite a few rounds from ashore that sent the crew to battle stations, there was a chance to get better acquainted. With the two American officers and two lookouts on the SC's bridge in helmets and life jackets and a little tense under the occasional incoming rounds, Commander Ritchie lounged amiably in one corner, considerately staying out of the way, bareheaded and in shorts and a short-sleeved shirt with the two-and-a-half stripes of his rank on its shoulders. He had the bluest eyes imaginable, which showed not the slightest concern for the action taking place around him.

We discussed the progress of the war in general and the Salerno operation in particular. He was particularly proud of the fact that the heavy enemy counter-attack in the days after the landings, which had driven the Allies back and had threatened for a while to break through to the beaches themselves, had not so much as dented the lines held by the Rangers and British commandos well up into the hills and passes behind Maiori. He had a wife and children back in Britain and was most anxious to get back there. But not primarily, it turned out, to be with his family. What really worried him was that he might not get home in time to make the inevitable Allied invasion of the continent across the English Channel.

One of the less important subjects touched upon as the subchaser made her way between the anchored ships and the long beach was the regrettable lack of acceptable, civilized alcoholic beverages in the area. When we had said our goodbyes and he had stepped from the SC's bow back aboard his LST flagship, Commander Ritchie held up a hand and asked us to wait "just one moment." He ducked below and appeared almost at once with a package that he passed across with a wave and a smile. To the joy of the 692's little wardroom mess, it contained a priceless fifth of White Horse Scotch. Seldom have Anglo-American relations undergone such an instantaneous improvement, even though in this case they were already at a high level of mutual understanding and appreciation. The White Horse was relegated immediately to the CO's safe from which it was doled out, a shot at a time, only on occasions agreed to be very special and to very special guests.

As the days went by with no word from or about the *Anticline* except that she had gone out to the PT and ML base at Capri off the tip of Sorrento, the 692's operations fell into something approaching a routine. Part of that routine was governed by the meteorology of the Italian peninsula, where daytime heating of the land caused the breeze to blow in from the sea and nighttime cooling below the temperature of the coastal waters created a wind that blew in the opposite direction. Thus, during the day the SC lay to with her smoke pots ready, upwind to seaward of the NAFTA anchorage, and at night she moved in with the land breeze to take station between ships and shore. Usually she just drifted, engines quiet but on instant standby. Sometimes, if wind or current caused unwanted movement, she put down an anchor. But always, as a minimum, a crew stood ready on the forty and the aft twenty, and helm and engine controls were manned.

Almost every morning and most evenings the black fighter-bombers with the white crosses came darting down out of nowhere to scream across the anchorage at masthead level, with Spits or P-40s close behind, to drop their single bombs and race away low over the land. And every day until the very last of the SC's stay, that stubborn howitzer in the hills took its turn at harassing the ships and the unloading operations ashore.

With the hit-and-run air raids, the shelling from the shore, and the repeated orders at all hours to "Make smoke!," sleep, and even just rest, soon became the most urgent need of every man aboard. For one period of more than thirty-six hours I was unable to leave the bridge for more than a reluctant one-minute trip to the head, and when I finally felt justified in getting a few minutes of rest, if only to bring my efficiency back up to a useful level, it was to stretch out fully clothed, including an inflatable life belt, with a strip of canvas over the foot of the bunk to prevent soiling by my shoes. Meals were mostly sandwiches and coffee or hot soup served at battle stations. Beards sprouted, clothing became soiled and wrinkled, and below decks the odor of unwashed bodies was reminiscent of the lion house at the zoo.

All day and all night the voice radio was busy with its scratchy, staccato calls, acknowledgments, and conversations between stations with call signs like Catcall, Lipstick, Shoeshine, and Jazzband. Chief Morton was now standing OOD watches in place of the departed Murphy and, surprisingly, since he was actually an engineer, doing a better job and exercising better judgment—providing calm, rational, and effective leadership.

Fresh water for the small ships off Salerno came from a big anchored tanker named the *Aletta,* flying the ensign of the Netherlands and with Dutch officers but with a Chinese crew and a British armed guard to man the single heavy gun at her stern. Her cargo was six million gallons of fresh soft water from Bombay and it provided the best drinking and the best showers, when there was time to grab one, that the SC's crew had yet enjoyed.

Once on a quick mission down to SAFTA we found not only the *Biscayne* and the *Nicholson* from Gela days; but three or four PCs and half a dozen SCs from Tunis, Bizerte, and Palermo, including the 690 and the 691; and even the two familiar YMSs, the 62 and 69, astern of which we had sortied through the nets at Norfolk in the spring.

Except for fuel and water, logistics during those days—at least for the 692—were informal, haphazard, and catch-as-catch-can. If there were any plans to keep the little ship in such essentials as fresh food, soap, sugar, flour, and toilet paper, or in important nonessentials like mail and cigarettes, there was no evidence of them. We were reduced to bumming, between raids, shellings, and smoke-making, from any likely source, including the DUKWs and LCTs shuttling between the ships and the shore. Poor Charlie Coffey, with his two- or three-pack-a-day cigarette habit, was reduced to rolling his own from little bags of Bull Durham, an effort at which he was persistent but notably unskilled.

When the 692 had been at Salerno for ten days, there came an evening so busy that for a few hours even Charlie forgot all about his smokes. The ship was anchored in her nighttime smoke position to windward and shoreward of the ships at NAFTA, with forty fathoms of four-inch manila rode to the 125-pound Danforth in six fathoms of water with a sand and mud bottom that provided good holding. Around 1600 the barometer began to fall so rapidly it seemed the mercury would break through the bottom of the glass. By 1800 it had dropped eight points, and a nasty little squall blew up out of the northwest, driving wide sheets of rain downwind that rattled like hail against the pilothouse and drew the anchor rode as straight and rigid as an iron bar. The engines were lighted off and we steamed at just above idle to the anchor, taking the strain off the rode.

The squall blew by in about twenty minutes, but the glass continued to fall, and the blackness to the northwest darkened and spread to cover the entire sky. By 1900 the barometer was down another four points and lightning was flashing all around the horizon, becoming confused over the land with the flashes of guns firing behind the hills.

We rigged the anchor for letting go, with a buoy secured to the rode forward of the bullnose, so that if we had to slip the anchor, we could come back later and retrieve it. With engines idling in neutral and radar in operation, we waited to see what was coming. The sky continued to darken and the atmospheric pressure dropped so that the still, heavy air seemed hard to breathe. Then at just about 2000 it hit.

It came suddenly as though the fan had been switched on in some great cosmic wind tunnel; a few short warm-up gusts at first, as the fan built up to speed, and then the full-blown force of the most violent electrical storm conceivable. The wind howled and screamed around the mast and rigging and the covered, lashed-down guns and the whole structure of the ship. It tore at the sea around her with a terrifying, seemingly personal animosity, while the lightning flashed and the thunder crashed so continuously there was more light than dark, and the booming of the thunder overpowered and alternated with the screeching of the wind. In the lightning flashes the gulf was dark green and streaked heavily with long lines of foam that twisted and writhed under the lash of the wind.

We engaged the engines and again steamed to the anchor, but through the streaming windows of the pilothouse, it was impossible to see which way to steer to take the strain off the rode. On the bridge it was nearly as bad. The wind drove the rain into our faces like tiny, stinging pebbles, and only with a hand over the mouth and sou'wester pulled down over the forehead could we manage an occasional glimpse. For a while in that way, we were able to use helm and engines to hold position, and when the rain let up a little, Kapfer was able to haul himself against the tearing wind out on the bow and play a flashlight on the rode so we could see which way it was tending.

But then, as though not to be defeated, the wind seemed suddenly to double in velocity. It caught the bow and slammed it downwind against the straining rode, and the stout manila gave way. By the lightning flashes we could see Kapfer gesturing wildly, and even above the howling of the storm we could hear him yell, "She's parted! She's parted!"

By lightning and radar we picked our way between the scattering of merchantmen and landing craft in the anchorage and out into the open gulf where there was sea room, and there we set up a kind of north-south patrol at a comfortable speed and waited for the storm to blow itself out. By 2215 relative calm had returned to the Salerno area and we were back on station, using the standby seventy-five-pound old-fashioned anchor. The heavy Danforth, which had served us so well and so long, was gone and remains today on the bottom of the Gulf of Salerno. The rode had parted outboard and forward of the bright red anchor buoy that was left dangling uselessly from the bullnose.

Daylight the next morning showed that the SC had not been alone in her difficulties with the sudden storm. The long beach was strewn with broached and grounded LSTs, LCIs, LCTs, and little LCVPs, the surf slapping at their sides and leaping upward in sheets of spray. We counted several dozen, but we learned later that the total came to more than eighty, and that the winds of the previous evening had been measured in gusts to eighty knots.

The twenty-ninth of September turned out to be a good day for the SC 692. Before noon we spoke to an old friend, the LCI 17, just up from Palermo, and from her acquired a badly needed sack of flour, twenty pounds of sugar, and three cartons of Chesterfields. Then, as we were moving into night smoke station off the beach, the radio came alive with a message from Catcall, LCI 10, Captain Zimmerlie. It was short but welcome: "Come alongside ready for sea."

It took a while to single out the 10 from the dozens of LCIs anchored, beached, or milling around offshore, but the search was well rewarded. As the SC eased up alongside, a commander appeared on deck and called over, "You're off for Palermo, Skipper." Sailing orders and recognition signals were handed across and signed for, and at exactly 1900, the SC 692 took departure on the Salerno breakwater and stood out, fast and alone, on the first leg back to Sicily.

Well out into the gulf we were challenged by the PC 591 on offshore patrol, and just before dark a convoy of LSTs passed on an opposite course, inbound to Salerno with an escort of British destroyers. Then the SC was unaccustomedly but most pleasantly alone, dipping and splashing along over a long, smooth ground swell under a bright blanket of stars, another combat tour astern, another bit part successfully performed in the great global drama of the war at sea.

At 0445 the powerful light on Ustica was in sight, and by daybreak that low, dry island was well back on the starboard quarter as the 692 picked up the final course.

It was 0935 on the last day of September when the little ship steamed in through the breakwater with Chief Morton at the conn and moored in her familiar berth across the end of Pier Two, Palermo. It was in a way like coming home. Ben Partridge was there in his 978, just in from patrol. George Steele showed up later in the day sporting a long cigarette holder, sunglasses, canvas shorts, and rope sandals, all of which he insisted are practically requirements at Capri, from which he had just returned. And the welcome mail was waiting for us, several sacks of it, including a telegram from my mother-in-law announcing the birth of my son. Apparently the wire had been sent electrically as far as the fleet post office in New York and then by slow freight from there, arriving eight weeks after the event.

George Steele was full of news. He was on his way, at a leisurely pace and traveling only by day, back to Bizerte for some serious repairs to his PT 215, but for the last few days he had been taking Secretary of the Navy Frank Knox for sight-seeing and inspection tours around Capri and the Bay of Naples. We wondered whether he had been wearing his Capri uniform on those occasions.

George also reported that naval intelligence had learned that the enemy had suffered fourteen casualties in their running battle with the PTs off the Liparis on the night of our speedboat ride, including the German E-boat operations officer for the Mediterranean, who had been killed. Lieutenant DuBose, the OTC that busy night, had been recommended for the Silver Star. Two days after that action, on 17 August, George's 215, with the 216 and 217, had landed unopposed at Stromboli, accepted the surrender of all the Lipari Islands, and taken off a couple of dozen Italian sailors and airmen as prisoners.

Even as life began to settle back into the patrol routine at Palermo, and with the beachhead at Salerno still busy, rumors of another landing farther north started the tension building again on all the little ships nested together at Pier Two. For the men of the 692, the necessary details of daily life helped erase a lot of that tension. A new beer ration went into effect, providing each man with six cans a week. Washer would take all the ration cards ashore and draw the week's supply, which would be stored in the wardroom and a case a day issued to the galley, where Charlie Casey kept accounts. A man could draw up to two cans a day until his ration was gone, or he could take up to all six ashore on liberty.

Ever-willing, many-talented, and unfailingly good-natured Casey now ruled the galley, having volunteered to take over when Ship's Cook Rees was transferred for treatment of a long-standing and frequently incapacitating neurological disorder that had not been helped by the ordeal and the near misses at Salerno. And although he had no

This photo is the only close-up known to exist of the USS SC 692. It shows her at one moment of all the days and hours she spent on patrol in the Gulf of Palermo, Sicily. The 40-mm and number three 20-mm are trained fore and aft, the watch can be seen on the bridge and fantail, and the captain's chair is visible above the bridge. (C. S. Coffey)

formal training, navy or otherwise, Casey, the first class motor machinist's mate, was able to turn out consistently better meals than the rated cook.

His zeal redoubled by recent experiences, Wash was able to procure from somewhere a .50-caliber machine gun, and work began on a suitable mount and the location of a source of ammo for this non-standard SC weapon.

Sometimes, on the radio there were rebroadcasts of the Fred Allen show. And one evening most of the small-craft crew walked up town to a naval barracks in a big hotel to see a new movie, Jimmy Cagney in *Yankee Doodle Dandy*.

On 8 October the SC 508 came haltingly and slowly into port between two small tugs, a victim of one of those fighter-bomber attacks while she was laying down smoke at night off Salerno. The Focke-Wulf had come in so low and so fast that the SC crew had neither seen nor heard it until the bomb was in the water. It hit just astern and slanted down beneath the keel before exploding, springing her wooden hull in several places, shattering the interior of the aft berthing compartment and galley, destroying her supply of engine spare parts, and so plugging up her bilge pumps that she was nearly lost.

She had limped back to Bizerte for dry-docking and patching up, but no one had checked her shaft alignments and clearances. As a result, fifty miles west of Palermo one of her shafts broke and pulled out, taking with it the propeller and a rudder. Her skipper said he thought the fighter had homed in on the smoke and on the little red flame with which each smoke pot burned. I didn't have the heart to tell him about the garbage-can lid we had rigged over our pots to hide that flame.

Then, with the Salerno operation just about over, came the news that the destroyer *Buck,* patrolling well to seaward of the gulf, had been torpedoed and sunk with the loss of nearly all her officers and two-thirds of her crew. Whatever tendency might have existed for any of the SC sailors in Palermo to forget even for a moment, while laughing at the verbal antics of Fred Allen or watching the athletic choreography of Jimmy Cagney, that the war was out there, close at hand and as lethal as ever, vanished with the arrival of the crippled 508 and the news of the loss of the *Buck.*

On the tenth of October, the end of Pier Two was beginning to look like Craig Docks far away in Key West. Nested there, at the terminus of a double set of railroad tracks, between a sunken freighter and an LST on one side, and a pair of LCTs on the other, were six SCs. The 692 was inboard, port side to the dock, and outboard in order were the 508, 978, 1029, 771, and 1044.

Ben Partridge was still aboard the 978, but most of the other skippers who had brought their ships out from Norfolk had been relieved and gone to other duty, most to the destroyer escort program now in full swing. And time was winding down for the CO of the 692 as well. Charlie Coffey had long been fully qualified for command and Roy Washer for exec, and we had recently received some official mail for a certain Ensign William S. Nielson, USNR; with only three bunks in officers' quarters, that seemed a pretty clear indication of things to come.

And then on Wednesday, the thirteenth, they came.

Charlie and I were sitting in the wardroom doing the usual ship's paperwork and talking, when the skipper of the 771 stuck his head down the hatch to say he had seen a dispatch over at NOB with my name on it, and he was sure it was orders. Those few words, spoken almost casually but with the emphasis and inflection due an interesting piece of news, released all the thoughts and dreams I had been keeping rigidly under control since the news of my son's arrival in this world. Suddenly it was true that I would really get home, and soon, home to my beautiful young wife, to the son I had never seen, to my mother and dad and naval aviator brother, if he were still in the States, and to all the other people and the country I loved and missed.

I have to admit that I ran all the way to NOB and didn't even care that it took the yeoman there forever to find that dispatch, or even that it had been received three days before and probably would have gathered dust for another week if an interested friend had not spotted it. It was orders all right, orders for my relief by one "Lt.(jg) C. S. Coffey, Jr., D-V(G) USNR," orders for me to report to the nearest naval district (all in the United States) for further assignment.

Back aboard ship, Roughan, now yeoman first class and recommended for warrant officer, typed up further orders, using that dispatch as authority. They were a masterpiece—from me to me, giving me per diem expenses en route and authorizing air travel. Then to the airport in an official jeep with a driver to arrange the authorized air travel and back to the ship to pack. My flight would leave at 0900 the next morning and I was to be ready with my gear at 0830.

The packing did not take long, a suitcase and a seabag, and a promise by Charlie to crate up what was left and ship it off after my departure. Charlie and I quickly inventoried the registered publications—a much easier job this time since he and Roughan had been keeping the inventory current—and signed over custody.

That last evening for me in the 692, Charlie, Wash, and I finished up the little that was left of Commander Ritchie's White Horse and I tried to think without notable success of any words of wisdom that might help them in whatever they would have to face in the coming months. It was hard because we had all had the same experiences and had learned from them in the same way, and whatever value my example might have held they already had that too. It was also hard in a different way because I was so indescribably full of joy to be doing what I knew they wanted so badly to do and deserved as much but would have to wait for, perhaps for a long time. And under all the joy, I knew I would miss Charlie and would never share with him again, nor probably with any man, the good and bad, make-or-break kind of things we had shared from Miami to Palermo and Salerno.

Sleep was hard to find that night. I kept dreaming that the orders were not real but just another dream like the dozens I had dreamed before about going home, and I kept waking up to assure myself of reality.

The next morning was just as hard. Casey fixed a special breakfast but all I could force down was a bowl of oatmeal and some coffee. Quarters were at 0730 and I found myself for the last time standing in the open, pilothouse-end of that familiar box of the familiar faces of men I knew, from living and fighting in such close quarters and from the forced duty of censoring their mail, better than I knew many of my own relatives or people I had known from childhood.

Morton's engineers were on my left, with the chief himself at their head, black shoes shined, dungarees and chambray shirt immaculate as always, even the khaki cover of the cap covering his neatly combed dark hair spotless, as though he were standing captain's inspection rather than morning quarters for change of command. I had time to think again, as I had done so often, how fortunate I had been, as an inexperienced young CO, to be blessed with a man like Ham Morton to whom I could in effect delegate most of the responsibility for half the crew with perfect confidence. Although he was my senior by a number of years, I felt a sort of paternal pride that he had risen to chief petty officer and would one day be appointed warrant machinist, perhaps the only one in the navy to be also a qualified and experienced officer of the deck under way.

Lined up behind Morton inboard of the starboard 20-mm were big, steady, serious Curt Christman, always the man on the engine controls when a sure hand was needed; then stocky, affable, skilled, and multifarious Charlie Casey, long-time custodian and guardian of the starboard engine, now looking unaccustomedly serious; beside Casey his taller, darker buddy, electrician and Smoke King Bennie Braverman; then tall, quiet First Class Machinist's Mate Elvin Hoffner from somewhere around Raleigh; and Casey's opposite number in charge of the port engine, a clean-cut Georgia boy, fireman Ervin Posey, the unsuccessful evader of the shore patrol in Bermuda; skinny, rumpled-looking Frank Hagan, always and still the junior man in the engine room; and standing proudly with the engineers, doing the job of a fireman with skill and dedication even though the rating badge on his chambray shirt was that of a mess attendant second class, still the only black face at quarters, lookout extraordinaire and undefeated softball pitcher, Cleveland Ray.

Across from the "black gang," the engineers, on the port side, stood the deck force, with Arnold Kapfer, now that Boats and Nader were gone, the leading bosun's mate. I thought of that bad night off Bermuda when he had held on with both hands and I with one, but somehow we had managed to get his bleeding scalp put back together. Ranged on that same side were the well-known faces of Gunner Walter, so competent aboard and so unreliable ashore, who, I remembered, wanted whatever Lana Turner had; and beside him gunner's mate Tony Curato, who had nearly lost his life to a shark off North

Front row, left, Radioman Harold Earl Kidwell, the only man aboard to win the Purple Heart; right, Gunner's Mate Anthony Curato, whose family came from Palermo and who spoke the language like a native. Back row, left, Signalman Normand Archie LaFlamme, who came aboard as a striker and left as a first class for officer training; right, Sonarman Roland Charles Senecal, leading sonarman and mail clerk. (Anthony Curato)

Africa thanks to my lack of caution and whose talent as an interpreter had served the ship and me so well.

Ranged athwartship, facing the three officers, were the men not easily classified in either category; indispensable and totally reliable yeoman first John Roughan, like Morton, recommended for warrant rank but still the ship's best helmsman; leading radioman Earl Kidwell, now fully recovered from his illness and his wound; quartermaster Elmer André, his white hat as always jauntily cocked down over his left eye and now fully conversant with the navigational running fix obtained by doubling the angle on the bow; bright and handsome Archie LaFlamme, who had come aboard as striker and was now fully qualified as signalman second; young Myron Wells, whose devo-

Lieutenant E. P. Stafford, commanding officer of the SC 692 from January to October 1943, and the author. Photo taken after return to Miami and promotion, December 1943.

tion to his priceless SF radar had earned him his third class rate; and slender, personable, perennial leading sonarman and mailman Roland Senecal.

I tried to look each man in the eye as I read my orders and Charlie read his. Then, after all the things I had planned to say, when the moment came I could only tell these men how lucky I had been in my first command to have such a crew, what total confidence I had in Charlie and in their ability to continue to take on any task assigned and do it well. Then I could only wish my crew, which was now no longer my crew, the most heartfelt good luck possible, shake hands with Wash and wish him well, salute Charlie, say "Goodbye, Captain," salute the colors aft, and step ashore.

The USS SC 692 had a lot more war to fight, and so did her former captain, but she would remain for as long as he lived as solid a part of his life as the tough juniper strakes of her sides still scarred by the shrapnel of Empedocle and Salerno.

EPILOGUE

For the SC 692 there was a respite of about three months before she was once more in heavy action, and during that time she underwent dry-docking and overhaul at Palermo and escorted convoys of landing craft back and forth between that familiar port and Naples and Bizerte.

On the first of December, alongside the 978 at the French pier in Bizerte, quarters were held and the Purple Heart awarded to Radioman First Class Harold Earl Kidwell. Despite all the hostile fire at Gela, Empedocle, Salerno, and later at Anzio and southern France; despite the additional air raids at Bizerte, Palermo, and later at Naples, Kidwell was the only member of the SC's crew ever to be wounded in action. And he had been hit by shrapnel while walking to the movies in Bizerte.

In the same little ceremony, helmsman, sonar and radar operator, and champion lookout and softball pitcher Cleveland Hodge Ray, his request for a change of rate to fireman having been repeatedly turned down by the Bureau of Naval Personnel (presumably because of the color of his skin), despite the fact that he had not worked in that rate since Key West, was promoted to mess attendant first class, the only way left to recognize and reward his abilities as an all-around man-of-warsman.

At the same time Myron Wells, who had reported aboard in Norfolk with his beloved and invaluable radar as a seaman first striker, became radarman second class, and the next month John Roughan and Curtis Christman both donned the caps and coats of chief petty officers, and sonarman and mailman Roland Senecal and signalman Archie LaFlamme made first class.

The little ship spent Christmas with her many sisters at the French pier, and the next day the affable and multifarious Charlie Casey and his friend electrician, Smoke King Bennie Braverman, were transferred to the LST 387, permanently moored at Bizerte as a floating repair shop.

With the new year things began to heat up again and the familiar pattern of rehearse, invade, withdraw, rehearse, and invade again resumed. In midmonth the SC was back off the beaches of Salerno, practicing for landings farther north, and in the course of those rehearsals saved the lives of thirty-three soldiers and their colonel from the Seventh Infantry Division plus the five-man crew of a sinking LCVP from LST 379.

That rescue itself turned out to be a kind of rehearsal. Early in the morning of 21 January 1944 the 692 was under way for the invasion beaches of Anzio-Netuno, north of Rome, screening the starboard bow of a convoy of troop-laden landing craft, and halfway through the mid watch on the twenty-second she led the second assault wave of LCVPs to the line of departure six hundred yards offshore. There was no opposition, a most misleading indication of what was to come. Twice that morning Christman's expert 20-mm fire detonated mines cut loose by sweepers, but just after 1000 one of those sweepers herself was mined and sank in five minutes, leaving only fifteen feet of her bow protruding from the sea. She was the *Portent* (AM 107), and under Charlie Coffey's sure hand the 692 came alongside the sinking ship and took off a deck-load of survivors.

Three days later, on the twenty-fifth, the 692 was involved in another rescue operation, and yet again on the twenty-ninth, as the enemy responded with characteristic ferocity to the threat posed by the Anzio bridgehead.

The incident of the twenty-fifth was the worst. To shoreward of the SC's patrol line, the YMS 30 had completed a sweep and was sinking the resultant floaters with rifle and machine-gun fire when a mine detonated under the keel of the little wooden sweeper. What happened was what every man of the 692 had feared and dreaded and tried to drive from his mind on all the night passages through those narrow seas in which floating mines were seen and sunk each day. There was a thudding blast and a livid flash of flame, and when the smoke cleared, only a scattering of small pieces of floating debris remained. Half a dozen nearby ships converged on the spot, among them the YMSs 62 and 69, with which the 692 had been operating off and on since the passage from Miami to Norfolk ten months before. The SC pulled fifteen men and an officer out of the littered gulf, recovered the bodies of another officer and three more sailors, and raced at flank speed back to the anchorage for medical help. Ensign Nielson patched up a couple of men with open head wounds, but before they could be transferred, one of the rescued sailors and an officer died on the subchaser's deck.

The effort to transfer the wounded men and the bodies to the LST 348 was hindered and finally stopped by a sudden storm that kicked up vicious seas, parted lines, and splintered the SC's rub rails and deck edges until Charlie was forced to cast off with three bodies still aboard to prevent further damage to his ship. The storm continued into the next day, accompanied by nonstop air raids and the need to make smoke, and finally on the twenty-seventh, Charlie broke out his Bible, held a little service, and buried the two sweeper sailors and an officer, one of them unidentifiable, in those bitterly contested waters.

Exactly one hour after the YMS casualties had been committed to the sea, another raid came in and an Me 109 passed directly over the SC at one thousand feet. All three twenties, the forty and the .50-caliber aft got on and fired long and accurate bursts. The fighter broke off its attack, smoking, and turned away northward toward enemy-held territory. Charlie Coffey reported it "damaged and possibly destroyed."

January twenty-ninth was nearly as bad a day. A heavy raid came in toward evening and was met by spouting torrents of tracers and large caliber AA. But two of the new German guided bombs found their targets. One hit the British light cruiser *Spartan* only seventy-five yards from where the 692 was laying down her protective blanket of smoke. The force of the explosion knocked out the SC's port generator, tore the air compressor from its mountings, and split cooling water and fuel lines to the port engine. But Chief Christman and his men were able to make temporary repairs and when the stricken cruiser capsized just after 1900, the little ship was there to assist a fleet of LCVPs and small boats with rescue operations. The *Spartan*, with her sister ship the *Phoebe*, had been conducting shore bombardment

A nest of nine SCs in the harbor at Salerno shortly after the port was taken. The 692 is inboard at extreme left. Three ships outboard is Prent Horne's 535. Two ships outboard of her is the 530, which chased away the enemy cruisers, with John Hinkley's 691 moored to her port side. (Anthony Curato)

in support of the landing force. A year before, the 692 had escorted the *Phoebe,* en route to New York for repairs, from Key West to Jacksonville.

The second bomb struck the nearby Liberty ship *Samuel Huntington,* loaded with gasoline and ammunition, and set her afire. A salvage tug came alongside to help fight the fires but was herself gashed and torn by near misses when a final raid swept across the anchorage. The SC's men watched helplessly while the Liberty lighted the area with her flames until she finally exploded in a fountain of fire in the closing minutes of the mid watch.

After another week of raids by high level bombers and dive-bombers while alongside the dock in the harbor at Anzio, the 692 had her generator remounted and her broken lines replaced by a repair ship off Naples and spent the remainder of February on the thankfully peaceful patrol lines off Palermo. But in mid-March it was back to still-contested Anzio and another close call when a night raid hit a freighter four hundred yards away and sank the tug tied up along her side.

French navy patrouilleur M.713, formerly the USS SC 692, on patrol as usual, off Sfax, Tunisia, September 1956. (Enseigne de Vaisseau Philippe Raillard)

In April there were runs to places she had never been, in Corsica and Sardinia, but Anzio would not go away, and there she was near-missed yet again: once when a delayed-action bomb exploded 150 yards astern and again when four more bombs fell within 400 yards.

The spring was spent between well-known Bizerte, Palermo, Salerno, and Naples, and on 7 June 1944, the day after the Allied landings in Normandy, Charlie Coffey turned over the command of the veteran little ship to Roy Washer and went home at last.

Wash was skipper in July when there were more invasion rehearsals and in August when once more the SC led her waves of landing craft to their beaches, this time in the south of France, and again put down her smoke and fired at attacking planes. She spent most of September on antisub and anti–E-boat patrols in the Gulf of Fréjus, between Saint-Tropez and Cap d'Antibes, returned for a final time to Palermo in October, and from there in November sailed with the 695 and the 503 to Toulon, France.

In Toulon, on 17 November 1944, after weeks of tedious inventories and paperwork, Roy Washer signed the documents that brought the worn and faded little ensign with its stars and stripes down from her truck and raised the tricolor of France in their place. Within hours the "SC 692" on her bow had been painted out and replaced by her new designation, "M.713." The gallant little ship that had sailed and fought in her country's cause and faced the enemy in a score of actions, from Key West to southern France, that had performed with credit and dispatch every task and mission assigned without the death or even injury of any man aboard, had fittingly been reincarnated and begun a new career. Bonne chance and Godspeed.

A Final Note

A total of fifty subchasers were transferred to the French under lend-lease in 1944, most in the fall of the year. The scrappy little 530, which had turned back the two Italian cruisers off Ustica and driven off the Stukas at San Stefano, and the 771, which had shared the Palermo patrol, changed flags on the same day as the 692; and Prent Horne's 535 went the day before. Ben Partridge's 978 had already made the change on 26 October, and the 692's sister ship, John Hinkley's 693, a month before that. Chuck Highfield's 1030 was transferred on the second of October.

Charlie Coffey went back to an instructor's job in Boston and then out to Japan in an attack transport at the war's end.

Roy Washer was also assigned as an instructor of reserve midshipmen, first at Throgs Neck and then at Columbia University in New York, where he finished out the war.

Ben Partridge, who insisted firmly on remaining in command, became the temporary CO of another subchaser being fitted out at Daytona Beach for turnover to the Soviet Union, then commanded a new PC, which he took through the canal and across the Pacific late in the war.

Prent Horne got married, returned to SCTC to enter the destroyer escort program, and served as first lieutenant and executive officer on two successive DEs in the Pacific.

Both Morton and Roughan became warrant officers as they richly deserved. Archie LaFlamme went to midshipman's school and earned a commission. Charlie Casey and Bennie Braverman finished out the war on their LST repair ship in Bizerte, and Tony Curato got married and spent the remainder of the war in Norfolk, supervising the unloading and disposition of ammunition being returned in Liberty ships and other freighters for storage.

Lieutenant Commander Lowther's attack on a hostile submarine in the Strait of Sicily the night of 30 July 1943 was proved successful; his PC 624 sank the U-375.

The two Italian light cruisers frightened off unknowingly by the SC 530 on 5 August 1943 off Ustica were the *Raimondo Montecuccoli* and the *Eugenio di Savoia*. They had left their base in Sardinia with orders to bombard Palermo.

Captain Reed of the Porto Empedocle fiasco was awarded the Legion of Merit for his "efficiency in the handling of landing operations at Gela."

The 692's second CO, your author, made it home via Port Lyautey, Bathhurst, Dakar, Natal, Belém, Trinidad, Bermuda, and New York in time to see and hold my new son before he was three months old and to be an usher at Prent Horne's wedding in Orange, New Jersey, on the thirteenth of November, 1943. Then, like the groom, I went back to SCTC and several more training schools before reporting as first lieutenant to a destroyer escort under construction in Orange, Texas. For the story of the adventures of that DE in the Pacific, see *Little Ship, Big War,* New York: William Morrow, 1984, by the same author.

CHRONOLOGY OF
SIGNIFICANT EVENTS

1942

25 November	USS SC 692 commissioned at Calderwood Yacht Yard, Manchester, Massachusetts.
1 December	Under way to Boston.
2 December– 15 December	Fitting out, Boston Naval Shipyard.
16 December	Under way to Cape Cod Canal.
17 December	Under way to Northport, Long Island, New York.
18 December	Under way to Section Base, Staten Island, New York.
19 December– 23 December	Drills and shakedown, Gravesend Bay.
24 December	Under way with convoy to Delaware Bay.
25 December– 26 December	Under way to Naval Operating Base, Norfolk, Virginia.

233

27 December– 29 December	Under way to Section Base, Charleston, South Carolina.

1943

31 December– 1 January	Under way to Miami, Florida.
6 January	Ensign C. O. Newlin detached as executive officer.
6 January– 8 January	Drills and training at Submarine Chaser Training Center, Miami.
8 January	Lt. (jg) C. S. Coffey reported as executive officer. Ensign R. J. Washer reported as gunnery officer.
9 January	Change of command; Ensign P. V. Snyder re- lieved by Lt. (jg) E. P. Stafford.
9 January– 10 January	Under way from SCTC Miami to Convoy Center, Craig Docks, Key West.
11 January– 14 January	Under way as escort for HMS *Phoebe* to Jack- sonville, then return to Miami.
15 January– 16 January	Under way for drills and training, Miami.
16 January– 17 January	Under way, Miami to Key West.
19 January– 21 January	Out of water on marine railway, Key West.
22 January– 25 January	"Industrial availability," Naval Operating Base, Key West.
26 January– 2 February	Under way daily for antisubmarine training, Key West.
6 February– 8 February	Under way as escort for single Liberty ship to Nuevitas, Cuba.
9 February– 10 February	Under way, Key West to Miami.
11 February– 12 February	Under way, Miami to Key West.
1 March– 4 March	Under way with Task Unit 91.1.2, Key West to Guantánamo.
5 March– 8 March	Under way, Guantánamo to Key West.
9 March– 10 March	Under way, Key West to Miami.

10 March	SC 1470 rammed and seriously damaged by PC 1123 off Alligator Reef.
11 March– 14 March	Under way, Miami to Norfolk.
15 March– 27 March	Undergoing "maximum matériel improvement," Norfolk Naval Shipyard, Portsmouth, Virginia.
29 March– 30 March	Under way for gunnery and training, Chesapeake Bay.
1 April– 4 April	Under way with Task Group 68.2, Norfolk to Bermuda.
2 April	Port life raft lost and pram staved in by seas in heavy weather.
13 April– 30 April	Under way, Bermuda to Gibraltar.
28 April	Temporarily separated from convoy.
2 May–3 May	Under way, Gibraltar to Nemours, Algeria.
4 May	The liberation of the shoes.
8 May	Under way, Nemours to Beni Saf and return. Damage to starboard propeller.
8 May–10 May	Under way on submarine search.
12 May	Under way, Nemours to Beni Saf.
14 May–16 May	Under way, Beni Saf to Nemours and patrol.
17 May	Gunner's Mate Curato attacked by shark during man-overboard drill.
21 May–22 May	Under way, Nemours to Oran, Algeria.
23 May	Under way, Oran to Beni Saf.
27 May–29 May	Attempting to be hauled on marine railway, Beni Saf.
30 May	Under way, Beni Saf to Nemours.
4 June	Under way, Nemours to Oran. PC 496 mined and sunk off Bizerte.
4 June– 11 June	Dry-docked, Oran.
16 June– 17 June	Under way, Oran to Algiers.
22 June	LSTs 333 and 387 torpedoed off Algiers.
23 June– 24 June	Under way for invasion rehearsals, Algiers Bay.
27 June– 30 June	Under way with Convoy Arrow Six, Algiers to Tunis, Tunisia.

29 June	Repair ship *Redwing* mined and sunk off Bizerte.
30 June–7 July	Harbor patrols, Tunis.
8 July–10 July	Under way with Task Force 81, Gela Attack Force, for invasion of Sicily.
10 July	D-day, Landing craft control off Blue and Yellow beaches, Gela, Sicily. Fired on enemy aircraft. Destroyer *Maddox* and minesweeper *Sentinel* bombed and sunk off Gela. LST 313 bombed and burned on beach. PC 543 shoots down two enemy planes off Gela.
10 July–11 July	Under way, Gela to Tunis.
13 July–14 July	Under way, Tunis to Gela. Destroyed four floating mines by 20-mm fire. Salvaged motor whaleboat from *Seer* and rescued two-man crew.
14 July	SC 1030 rammed and heavily damaged by PC 591 off Scoglitti, Sicily.
15 July	Under fire from enemy shore batteries off Porto Empedocle.
16 July–18 July	Under way, Gela to Bizerte.
19 July–20 July	Under way, Bizerte to Licata, Sicily.
20 July–21 July	Patrols off Licata.
21 July–22 July	Under way, Licata to Bizerte.
25 July	Benito Mussolini resigns.
27 July–28 July	Under way, Bizerte to Palermo, Sicily.
30 July	PC 624 sinks U-375 off Pantelleria.
30 July–31 July	Under way, Palermo to Bizerte.
6 August	SC 530 frightens off two Italian light cruisers off Ustica.
7 August	Air raid, Bizerte.
8 August–9 August	Under way, Bizerte to Palermo.
10 August	Tug USS *Brant* shot up by destroyer USS *Benson* in case of mistaken identity in Strait of Sicily.
10 August–12 August	Under way, Palermo to Bizerte. Destroyed floating mine.
14 August–15 August	Under way, Bizerte to Palermo.

15 August– 16 August	CO participates in PT/E-boat engagement off the Lipari Islands.
18 August– 19 August	Under way, Palermo to Licata.
19 August– 21 August	Patrols off Licata.
21 August– 22 August	Under way, Licata to Palermo.
23 August	Air raid, Palermo. SCs 694 and 696 sunk with heavy casualties. Fired on enemy aircraft.
25 August– 5 September	Patrols and local escort, Palermo.
6 September	Dry-docked, Palermo.
8 September	Italy surrenders.
9 September	Allies land at Salerno.
10 September	Boarded Italian hospital ship *Toscana*.
11 September	Light cruiser *Savannah* heavily damaged by radio-controlled bomb.
7 September– 16 September	Patrols and local escort, Palermo.
16 September	Chief Boatswain's Mate Murphy transferred for further assignment.
17 September– 18 September	Under way, Palermo to Gulf of Salerno, Italy.
17 September	Fired full pattern of depth charges on sonar target.
18 September– 29 September	Patrols and smoke screen duties, Gulf of Salerno. Daily air raids and shore fire. Near-missed by bombs and howitzer fire.
28 September	Violent electrical storm off Salerno parts anchor rode, big Danforth lost.
29 September– 30 September	Under way, Salerno to Palermo.
1 October– 8 November	Patrols and local escort, Palermo.
13 October	Lt. (jg) E. P. Stafford relieved as CO. Lt. (jg) C. S. Coffey assumes command.
15 October	Ensign W. S. Nielson reported as gunnery officer.
9 November	Dry-docked for bottom work, Palermo.

17 November– 24 November	Industrial availability for repair and over-haul of generators.
1 December	Radioman First Kidwell awarded Purple Heart.
11 December– 13 December	Under way, Palermo to Naples.
15 December– 16 December	Under way, Naples to Palermo.
17 December– 18 December	Under way, Palermo to Bizerte.
29 December– 31 December	Under way, Bizerte to Nisida, Italy.

1944

1 January	Anchor rode parted in heavy weather, re-anchored with spare.
6 January– 7 January	Christman and Roughan promoted to chief petty officer.
10 January– 12 January	Under way, Bizerte to Naples area.
18 January	Under way for invasion rehearsal, Gulf of Salerno. Rescued thirty-eight men from sinking LCVP.
21 January	Under way for landings at Anzio.
22 January	Acting as control vessel for second wave of landing craft, Anzio. Destroyed two floating mines. Took aboard thirteen survivors from *Portent,* which had been mined and sunk. Many air attacks.
22 January– 9 February	Patrolling and making smoke off Anzio. Re-peated daily air attacks.
25 January	Took aboard twenty dead and wounded from YMS 30, which had been mined and sunk.
25 January– 26 January	Under way to ride out storm.
26 January	Heavy torpedo, level, and dive-bombing attacks.
27 January	Buried at sea three bodies from YMS 30. Position 41-30 N, 12-25 E. Fired on Me 109. Plane turned away smoking.

29 January	Took part in rescue operations after HMS *Spartan* bombed and sunk. Damage to engineering plant from proximity to bomb hit on *Spartan*.
29 January– 30 January	Liberty ship SS *Samuel Huntington* loaded with ammunition and gasoline, bombed, burned, and exploded nearby.
1 February– 8 February	Patrolling and making smoke. Numerous daily air raids.
9 February– 10 February	Under way, Anzio to Naples.
15 February– 16 February	Alongside repair ship for repairs to engineering plant.
17 February– 18 February	Under way, Naples to Palermo.
19 February– 2 March	Patrols, Palermo.
3 March– 4 March	Under way, Palermo to Naples.
6 March– 7 March	Under way, Naples to Anzio.
7 March– 11 March	Patrolling and making smoke off Anzio. Repeated daily air attacks.
12 March	Under way, Anzio to Naples.
15 March	Air raid, Naples. Many bomb hits close by. Freighter four hundred yards away hit, tug alongside her sunk.
16 March– 18 March	Under way, Naples to Bizerte.
16 March	Destroyed floating mine.
25 March– 26 March	Under way, Bizerte to Palermo.
26 March– 2 April	Patrols, Palermo.
2 April– 3 April	Under way, Palermo to Bizerte.
3 April– 8 April	Under way, Bizerte to Ajaccio, Corsica.
6 April	Fired mousetraps at sonar contact.
12 April– 14 April	Under way, Ajaccio to Naples via Maddalena, Sardinia.
15 April	Under way, Naples to Anzio.

15 April– 22 April	Patrolling and making smoke, Anzio. Repeated daily air attacks.
19 April	Smoke generator exploded, starting fire on fantail. Extinguished with CO_2.
21 April	Delayed-action bomb exploded 150 yards away. No damage or casualties.
23 April	Under way, Anzio to Naples.
24 April	Air raid, Naples. Four bomb hits within four hundred yards.
28 April	Under way, Naples to Anzio.
29 April–5 May	Patrolling and making smoke, Anzio. Daily air raids.
6 May	Under way, Anzio to Salerno for training exercises.
7 May	Under way on sub search.
10 May–11 May	Under way, Salerno to Palermo.
11 May–12 May	Under way, Palermo to Bizerte.
13 May–19 May	Patrols, Bizerte.
20 May–21 May	Under way, Bizerte to Palermo.
22 May–23 May	Patrols, Palermo.
28 May–29 May	Under way, Palermo to Naples.
30 May–31 May	Under way, Naples to Anzio.
1 June–6 June	Patrolling and making smoke, Anzio.
4 June	Ensign John L. Pineault reports as gunnery officer.
6 June–7 June	Under way, Anzio to Naples.
7 June	Change of command, Lt. (jg) R. J. Washer relieves Lt. (jg) C. S. Coffey as commanding officer.
7 June–10 June	Under way, Naples to Ajaccio, Corsica.
10 June	Under way, Ajaccio to Porto-Vecchio, Corsica.
11 June–12 June	Under way, Porto-Vecchio to Bizerte.
14 June–15 June	Under way, Bizerte to Palermo.
16 June–19 June	Patrols, Palermo.
20 June–21 June	Under way, Palermo to Naples.
23 June	Under way, Naples to Salerno.
24 June–25 June	Patrols, Salerno.
26 June–27 June	Under way, Salerno to Palermo.

30 June–10 July	Patrols and antisub and antiaircraft training, Palermo.
11 July–13 July	Under way, Palermo to Cagliari, Sardinia.
14 July–15 July	Under way, Cagliari to Palermo.
15 July–16 July	Under way, Palermo to Salerno.
17 July–22 July	Maneuvers and training, Salerno.
23 July	Under way, Salerno to Naples.
24 July– 2 August	Repairs and replenishment, Naples.
3 August– 4 August	Under way, Naples to Salerno.
6 August– 7 August	Invasion rehearsals, Gulf of Gaeta.
12 August– 15 August	Under way with Convoy SM-1 for the invasion of southern France.
15 August	Acting as reference vessel and making smoke, Gulf of Fréjus, France.
16 August– 31 August	Patrolling and making smoke, Gulf of Fréjus.
18 August	Fired on enemy aircraft.
1 September– 19 September	Antisub and anti–E-boat patrols, Gulf of Fréjus.
20 September	Under way, Gulf of Fréjus to Toulon, France.
22 September– 24 September	Under way, Toulon to Palermo.
25 September– 24 October	Patrols, Palermo.
25 October– 27 October	Under way, Palermo to Toulon.
31 October– 1 November	Under way, Toulon to Marseille.
4 November	Under way, Marseille to Toulon.
5 November– 16 November	Patrols and training, Toulon.
17 November	USS SC 692 decommissioned and transferred to French navy.

BIBLIOGRAPHICAL NOTES

The primary source for this story is the detailed personal day-to-day journal I kept during my tour as commanding officer of the SC 692, from her departure from Norfolk until relieved of command in Palermo (March–October 1943). Although admittedly illegal at the time, that document was classified "Confidential," marked for destruction with other classified publications in the event of the loss or abandonment of the ship, and kept with other such material in the ship's safe. The period covered by the journal is also that of the main body of the book, since the detail necessary for similar coverage of the life of the SC and her crew before April and after October 1943 does not exist.

To flesh out, confirm, and corroborate the story told in the journal, I have used the ship's log and her war diary and action reports. The same official sources were also used to describe actions and incidents in which other ships were involved.

A few of the incidents described come from my personal letters to my wife and family written at the time and fortunately preserved for more than forty years.

243

For the "big picture" of the war in the Mediterranean in 1943 and 1944, I have depended, as any chronicler of those events must do, on Samuel Eliot Morison's indispensable and definitive *History of United States Naval Operations in World War II,* Vol. 9, *Sicily-Salerno-Anzio, January 1943 – June 1944* (Boston: Little, Brown, 1954).

INDEX

245